Oneida Iroquois Folklore, Myth, and History

The Iroquois and Their Neighbors
Christopher Vecsey, *Series Editor*

ONEIDA IROQUOIS FOLKLORE, MYTH, AND HISTORY

*New York Oral Narrative from the
Notes of H. E. Allen and Others*

ANTHONY
WONDERLEY

SYRACUSE UNIVERSITY PRESS

Copyright© 2004 by Anthony Wonderley

Syracuse University Press
Syracuse, New York 13244-5290

First Paperback Edition 2024
24 25 26 27 28 29   6 5 4 3 2 1

For a listing of books published and distributed by Syracuse University Press,
visit https://press.syr.edu.

ISBN: 978-0-8156-0830-1 (hardcover)
      978-0-8156-0694-9 (paperback)
      978-0-8156-5728-6 (e-book)

Library of Congress Cataloging-in-Publication Data
Wonderley, Anthony Wayne, 1949-
  Oneida Iroquois folklore, myth, and history : New York oral narrative from the notes of
H. E. Allen and others/ Anthony Wonderley.- 1st ed.
      p. cm. - (Iroquois and their neighbors)
  Includes bibliographical references and index.
  ISBN 0-8156-0830-6 (hardcover (cloth): alk. paper)
  1. Oneida Indians-Folklore. 2. Oneida mythology. 3. Oneida Indians-History. 4.
Oral tradition-New York (State) I. Allen, Hope Emily. II. Title. III. Series.
E99.O45W75 2004
398.2'089'975543-dc22   2004021116

To the *Onyota'a:ka* and to my life partner—
siempre te estoy agradecido, querida Paulina.

Anthony Wonderley (PhD, Cornell) worked for the Oneida Indian Nation in its cultural management and preservation programs and for the Oneida Community Mansion House as Curator of Collections and Interpretation. A Fulbright post-doctoral fellow and a fellow of the New York State Archaeological Association, Wonderley publishes on New York history and Iroquois archaeology and oral narrative. His books include *At the Font of the Marvelous: Exploring Oral Narrative and Mythic Imagery of the Iroquois and Their Neighbors* (Syracuse University Press, 2009), *Oneida Utopia: A Community Searching for Human Happiness and Prosperity* (Cornell University Press, 2017), and (co-author) *Origins of the Iroquois League: Narratives, Symbols, and Archaeology* (Syracuse University Press, 2019).

Contents

Oneida Oral Narratives

Illustrations

Maps

Acknowledgments

Owing an immeasurable debt to my employer, the Oneida Indian Nation, I am very grateful to be working for them. However, the opinions expressed in this work are mine alone and are not official statements of the Oneida Indian Nation. In the workplace of the Oneida Nation, many colleagues have helped this book along the way. I especially thank Brian Patterson, Sheri Beglen, S. J. Capecelatro, Richard Franklin, Jim Heins, Rebecca Karst, Helen S. Schwartz, and Margaret Splain.

This book was greatly improved by suggestions and encouragement offered by Christopher Vecsey and an anonymous reviewer. It also is enhanced by quality artwork done by Daniyel Faulkner (ills. 2, 4, and 20), Julia Meyerson (ills. 15–16), and Philippa "Flip" Brown (ills. 22–23). Artists and reviewers: thank you very much.

What a pleasure it has been receiving repeated and substantive assistance in research matters from Clifford Abbott, William N. Fenton, Michael K. Foster, George R. Hamell, and Bruce L. Pearson. In this little corner of central New York, I gratefully acknowledge the help given me by Randall L. Ericson and Kelly Rose (Hamilton College Library) and Mrs. Henry G. (Dink) Allen (Oneida Community Mansion House). Thanks also to Benoît Thériault who opened to me the archives of the Canadian Museum of Civilization.

Introduction

The Oneida Indian Nation in New York numbers about eleven hundred enrolled members who still trace membership in Iroquois clans and nations (or tribes) through the mother's line and have done so since, as the legal phrase has it, time immemorial. Perhaps half of the nation's members reside in the core of the ancient residential zone in present upstate New York between the old Erie Canal cities of Utica and Syracuse. Through gaming and other enterprises, the Oneidas recently have begun to enjoy an unprecedented economic success.

It has been my great privilege to work as a historian for the Oneida Nation for nearly a decade. An important aspect of my duties is repatriation: trying to bring home what has disappeared through long years of poverty and dispossession within the larger American society. In early 2001, I came across a manuscript placed in the Hamilton College Library more than fifty years earlier by a nonnative woman named Hope Emily Allen.[1] The text consisted of a series of Oneida narratives that Allen had collected from Oneida informants about a quarter-century earlier. Finding these notes was, for me, a satisfying act of repatriation because they preserve much that otherwise would have been lost. The material has taught

---

1. Allen's manuscript is accessioned at the Hamilton College Library, Clinton, N.Y. (Allen 1948b). The file comprises seventy-seven typed sheets, mostly material recorded from 1918 to 1925. Another set of Allen's papers pertaining to the Oneidas is at the Syracuse University Library (Allen 1948a). This file comprises about eighty unnumbered pages, typed but often filled with Allen's handwritten revisions. This material includes at least two Oneida stories of 1925 ("Where the Earth Opens" and "The Misogamist" given in chapter 8) and an undated essay ("Cycles of Time"). About fifty-five pages seem to be an introduction—repeatedly rewritten, mostly in 1948—to the stories. Allen intended to get this text in shape for publication, probably in the *Journal of American Folklore*. I added the alphabetic letters to reference these sheaves and individual pages.

me a great deal about the Oneida people and spirit and encouraged me to look at what I thought I knew in new ways. This book has come of it.

By presenting a number of Oneida stories, this is a book *of* Oneida folklore. It is also a book *about* Oneida folklore because the stories are examined for the light they shed on the culture and outlook of this native Iroquois people. Generally, I aim to place the subject matter in a larger comparative context, hoping thereby to see what might be distinctively Iroquois and what has been received into Iroquois oral tradition from elsewhere. Most of all, this work is a historical study reflecting the direction of my interest and profession. I "use" the oral narratives—mostly folktales and myths—to inquire into how old they may be, how they change over time, how they may be employed to filter and interpret the past.

This book is innovative in some respects. It presents a substantial body of material for the first time. It is the first major study of Iroquois oral narrative in nearly a century and covers one of the longest historical spans of any study of its kind anywhere. In the eastern United States, it is the first work to grapple with strong continuity in oral tradition spanning four centuries or more.

"Firsts" give the appearance of being forward-looking, but I am not very original. Each of my interests—studying oral narrative to get at aspects of Oneida life otherwise undocumented, comparing it with oral literatures elsewhere, and researching its historical ramifications—led me back to a body of data and writings nearly a century old. So let me first try to situate this work within a larger anthropological picture.

Early in the twentieth century, the cultures of innumerable Native American groups were documented under the influence or tutelage of Franz Boas. American anthropologists of that era gave considerable priority to preserving the oral narrative, and recorded an astonishingly vast body of mythic data. Committed to understanding each culture or tribe on its own terms, anthropologists were drawn to myths and folktales as mirrors reflecting aspects of culture ranging from details of daily life to symbols and values. And because such content was, in effect, chosen by the people themselves, oral narrative appealed to anthropologists as a kind of tribal autobiography providing an insider's view of the culture (Boas 1916, 393). Insofar as myths and folktales preserve memories of activities no longer practiced, they also were important documents in cultural reconstruction.

Boas and his colleagues were interested in the group's past, but, in the absence of written documents, they examined spatial relationships among groups by studying distributions of traits—how certain things apparently had spread or diffused from one group to another. This method had implications for time depth and became a form of historical analysis through the age-area principle. If, Boas reasoned, a widely distributed phenomenon was of at least moderate complexity, it was far more likely to have spread from one point of origin than to have been independently invented repeatedly (1940, 425–45). Because a trait was likely to diffuse outward, its oldest occurrence logically would be sought in the center of the trait's distribution. And, in general, the age of the trait was proportionate to the size of its distribution (Sapir 1994, 57–60; Wissler 1938, 315). At about the same time, European folklore researchers were developing similar methodology of study based on similar premises: the Finnish historico-geographical school (Dundes 1999, 40; Krohn 1971). An American folklorist of this approach, Stith Thompson, compiled a reference tool for such comparative analysis—a classification of the motifs or incidents characteristic of North American native lore (1929).

Such assumptions seem absurd in contexts for which multiple independent inventions have been documented. Yet, as Munro Edmonson notes,

> It is otherwise in fields of cultural experience less intimately related to environment. Indeed, we may say that the broad range of the materials of folklore generally support the assumption that in this aspect of culture the recurrence of even very simple elements can never be satisfactorily traced to independent invention but is invariably a consequence of communicative contact on some historical level. Here the "diffusionists" seem justified in their assumption of limited human creativity. (1971, 45)

The fact is, it is easier to borrow a myth than to invent it.

These people were not flashy theorists by today's standards. But through study of oral narrative and application of age-area premises, they opened up an awe-inspiring vista of ancient native America in which a history of thoughts could be traced back into unimaginably distant times, and sometimes even linked to other continents. Their vision has scarcely been equaled and never, I believe, followed up. They compiled the material and began to invent tools to work it out. Then anthropology took a different turn. It was as if they spread their work out on the table, went to lunch, and never clocked back in.

By the end of the third decade of the twentieth century, many anthropologists and folklorists lost interest in oral narrative as a focus of research. For some, the change reflected impatience with an inductivist approach that seemed an inefficient way to employ limited resources. When young William Fenton went into the field in the 1930s, his mentor, a first-generation Boasian named Edward Sapir, told him to define a research problem and not to waste his time collecting stories (personal communication). Boas himself turned his back on distributional studies to emphasize myth as a key to unlocking the secrets of a single culture (Bierhorst 1985, 4). Indeed, Alan Dundes attributes a general cessation of comparative studies of American Indian oral narrative to the anthropologists' "deep intellectual commitment to cultural relativism, that is, to study one culture at a time in depth" (1967, 63).

In succeeding decades, the study of Native American oral narrative declined overall, and its interpretive focus progressively narrowed. Some memorable studies moved toward more psychologically informed demonstrations that myth can reflect the personality patterns, values, and worldviews of a group (see Barnouw 1977; Hallowell 1976; and Overholt and Callicott 1982). More recently, researchers have tended to emphasize the act and context of storytelling, maintaining that "oral tradition is better understood as a social activity than as reified text," and that "meanings do not inhere in a story but are created in the everyday situations in which they are told" (Cruikshank 1998, xv). Of course, if the primary meaning of oral narrative is to be found in how a story is used by several people at one time and place, then the story itself ceases to matter and any larger perspective requiring comparative and historical information becomes irrelevant.

A notable exception to geographical parochializing is the work of French anthropologist Claude Lévi-Strauss, intercontinental in scope and global in vision (see 1981, 1987, and 1988). Armed with encyclopedic knowledge and a wonderfully discursive style, Lévi-Strauss has interpreted perhaps a thousand folktales and myths (he does not distinguish between them), chiefly from South America. For Lévi-Strauss, the human mind takes the measure of the world through such metaphors of oppositional relationship as hot-cold, high-low, male-female, and culture-nature. Having phrased the matter discontinuously, the mind seeks deliverance from contradiction and paradox through symbolic operations that mediate opposites into something else. Oral narratives are one way the mind works through such symbolic problems. If, therefore, a story is really an associational arrangement the mind finds congenial at an unconscious level, its meaning should be sought in those deep structures unknown to the storyteller, not in such superficialities as plot.

Obviously, however, content matters. I do not deny that different levels and kinds of meanings may be discerned in oral narrative, or that multiple interpretive approaches may enrich our appreciation of it. My point is that a story's meaning includes the story's content: plot, incidents and motifs, actors, settings, objects, and so on. No story exists without content, and no story can be understood without reference to it. A tale "means what it says" (Thompson 1965, 177).

It is true, however, that the tales in this book are remote from their native tongue and distant from the social circumstances in which they were enjoyed. They are in the form of texts, almost all of which have been written in English. Yet their *content* survives, and, even though the material is divorced from its living Oneida setting, a study of content and plot is not dependent on the Oneida language.[2]

I consider oral narrative to be that sector of traditional expressive culture composing the verbal art or oral literature (also lore). For all people, the world is a place of abstraction and language—a shared symbolic world. "People learn the perception of the world as it comes to them in the talk of people around them and is encapsulated in the categorization of reality and the presumptions about time, space, and causation in that world. The rich complexity of the narrative about reality that each of us gets sets the tone and character of our lives" (Goldschmidt 2000, 802). Especially in a nonliterate setting, a culture's narratives are an important medium for conveying such premises of belief and perception, concepts often expressed in mythopoeic language favoring memorable comparison and evoking vivid imagery. Such stories serve as signposts for people navigating together through the richly symbolic landscape that is the human condition.

2. Scholars who have concluded that the study of folklore content is not language dependent include Boas (1914, 388), Colby (1973, 645), Dundes (1999, 43) and Fischer (1963, 268–69).

If oral narrative is a way in which we make cultural sense of the world to ourselves, its function (or at least one of its functions) is broadly explanatory. As a means of making sense, it can serve—as anthropologist Bronislaw Malinowski said of some myths—as a social charter: it legitimates the present order asserting its naturalness and rightness (1984). Other oral narratives explain in the sense that they comment on problematic aspects of social reality and, perhaps, provide the symbolic tools to resolve or think through dilemmas (Drummond 1981). Some stories of this sort may well supply a psychical palliative for problems that cannot be solved or even openly stated (Zipes 2002, 6–7).

Oral narrative's explanatory bent makes for a strong retrospectively oriented gaze—these stories "anchor the present generations in a meaningful, significant past, functioning as eternal and ideal models for human behavior and goals" (Vecsey 1988, 24; cf. Cruikshank 1994, 407). Trying to make sense of the past, some oral narratives not only talk about history, but also "attempt to reconcile a view of 'what really happened' with an understanding of 'what ought to have happened' " (Hill 1988, 10). Oral narrative can transform the experienced past (Ireland 1988) and guide one's experience of history (Bricker 1981; Erickson 2003).

A people's oral narratives are transmitted from one generation to the next through storytelling. A teller and an audience compose a performative setting that, to be effective, means that the story must be meaningful, contemporary expression (Zipes 2002, 60). In part, the story is only as old as the moment in time it is told. In part, a story is a transaction that is not *wholly* a product or end result (Oring 1986, 10). Paradoxically, perhaps, the conditions of being performed and negotiated imply fluidity, and, in fact, oral narrative changes over time. It responds to historical events and social reality (see Urton 1990).

Although I stress the broadly explanatory character of oral narrative, it surely does and is other things besides. It entertains. Some oral narrative provides aesthetic satisfaction. More or less formal creations polished in the retelling, stories please in the art of their figurative and poetic expression. And oral narrative educates the young. This role seems to have been the primary function recognized by native people throughout the continent. Aside, however, from specific lessons and morals, a culture's stories "teach more indirectly by means of a consistent and coherent set of underlying assumptions about the nature of reality which in one way or another is repeated in them again and again" (Overholt and Callicott 1982, 140). Oral narrative is an important agency of socialization.

Oral narrative in this book comprises three genres: myths, folktales, and legends. A tremendous amount of ink has been spilled defining these genres for a century and a half, and I am not aware that any consensus has been reached. Most of the early-twentieth-century material I draw on in this book reflects a Boasian distinction between myth as sacred and folktale as secular (with legends being of comparatively little interest). To cite the most appropriate example, the Iroquois were said to partition their oral tradition into three categories expressed in English as "things which truly happened," "it is as if an animal walked," and "they went to the woods to hunt for meat." Grounded in the Boasian dichotomy, William Fenton understood "things which truly happened" to mean "myth"—apparently the most important Iroquois narratives, and the ones used by some Iroquois to periodize their own history (creation story, league tradition, teachings of Handsome Lake). The other two categories evidently are animal tales and human adventures—both belonging to the genre of folktales, although some human stories might also qualify as myths (Fenton 1947, 390; 1978, 298, 319; Fenton and Moore 1974, 66).

I do not attempt to apply such categories to the Oneida material featured in this work because Allen's informants never acknowledged such distinctions. But, like many before me, I find it useful to recognize the genres of myth, legend, and folktale while cheerfully conceding they can be ambiguous and difficult to distinguish (Nabokov 2002, 65; cf. Dundes 1964, 27; and Lankford 1987, 50–51).

Myths are a people's important stories, the ones that explain how the world came to be ordered or how something significant came about. Among the Iroquois, a myth is a narrative that begins in primal time and usually includes cosmic activities. Supernaturals and culture heroes are prominent characters. Myths tend to be regarded as old, sacred, serious, and true, but those qualities are not necessary to my definition or (I hope) usage. I am certainly not using *myth* to mean something patently untrue, or believed only by ignorant, superstitious simpletons. Likewise, *folktale* should not be understood to mean "fiction," and *legendary* is not synonymous with "fictitious."

Folklore or tales are animal stories or human adventures. They may be humorous or sympathetic. They seem more secular and may have considerable entertainment value. Most stories presented here are of this sort, as the title indicates. Admittedly, however, this category is residual for everything not obviously myth or legend.

Legends involve human action "locally bound and historically rooted" (Grantham 2002, 3). Very likely, all three genres were regarded as true, but legends, especially, claim credibility by making reference to what is regarded as historically true (Fischer 1963, 236). Legends usually seem pointed to answer such questions as "What is it? Why is it so? What can be done about it?" (Dégh 1972, 74). Because legends illustrate interesting links with history, I discuss them in the context of history. These topics together open and close the book in chapters meant to take the exposition into and out of nontime or the timelessness of folklore and myth constituting the main body of the work.

⧓

In addition to connecting oral narrative with Oneida Nation history, I relate verbal art to material culture. Each chapter about oral narrative features a subsidiary section on some material aspect of Oneida life—craft works or archaeological artifacts. The things highlighted in this fashion are representations of obvious symbolic import or are otherwise invested with cultural meaning. What are some of the relationships between narrative and object?

For one thing, folklore can serve as a medium through which knowledge of old things can be retained and even explained. For example, a centrally located fireplace described in one folktale seems to be an archaic detail that the plot does not require (see sidebar, chapter 2). In other cases, physical and verbal modes of expression seem more like complementary voices uniting in the social context of their creation. Certainly, oral and material traditions were learned and practiced in the same setting, as evidenced by allusions to basket making in Oneida folklore (see sidebar, chapter 7).

Iroquois culture attaches a strong sense of physicality to the spoken language in the form of a token, some concrete substance, that acts to intensify and verify the words of a message. The kind of object most frequently linked to language is the shell-bead material known as wampum, and wampum undoubtedly is the most symbolically charged substance known to Iroquois people today. This deep emotional resonance finds expression in folklore and myth (see sidebar, chapter 5).

Wampum, unfortunately, is not a representational medium, and the words to which it is welded leave no physical trace. Far more interesting to a historically minded folklorist is the object depicting something else, for when "an artifact is a representation, an illustration, it carries anecdotes just as narratives do" (Glassie 1988, 85). On the other hand, myth has its own pictorial quality. Some people remember narrative as a series of images (Fischer 1963, 269), a phenomenon that imparts a potential physicality to any good story. Artistic communication in either words or objects leads us into the creation of meaning. And meaning, whether expressed in word or physical material, must be coming out of the same reservoir of the culture's metaphoric and symbolic codes.

A popular theme depicted in diverse media of ancient Oneida art was a pair of people (see sidebar, chapter 3). The allusion here may be to twins who played a prominent role in the Oneida creation myth, which, in turn, would suggest Oneidas liked to be reminded of a key narrative in the course of daily life.

An iconographically complex design, far more complicated than twins, is found on several old Oneida and other Iroquoian pipes (see sidebar, chapter 6). Like narrative, the imagery featured in this composition requires a certain sequential order of presentation to make sense. Here it looks as though there may have been an accompanying myth. One wonders whether parts of such a hypothetical narrative might survive among the traditions of horned serpents and Thunders discussed elsewhere in this work.

Oneida pottery is well known among archaeologists for its naturalistic depictions of humanlike figures. These effigies may have been fashioned in the image of cornhusk people, mythical beings personifying domesticated plant foods (see sidebar, chapter 4). In any event, this representational art was probably invested with corn-related meaning. Here, therefore, a distinctive form of decoration implies that the theme of maize was more significant in the past than it is in the present.

Admittedly speculative, these sections explore possible links between material culture and narrative art. "Cultural objects and preserved traditions," as Robert Hall knows, "can tell stories beyond count when they are approached like respected elders and their mysteries sought out" (1997, 171). Hoping to recover something of what is otherwise lost or mute, I believe an important way to grant voice to Oneidas in the past is to "put tongues in inanimate objects" (Glassie 1988, 86).

△

The main current of the book flows in the following fashion. The first chapter will survey about five centuries of the Oneidas' historical experience, including their situation on the eve of European encounter, the transformation of their lives during the era of European colonization, the heroic role they played fighting on the patriot side in the Revolutionary War, and the impoverishment they suffered immediately after. In 1850, the Oneidas were seemingly ruined, and their national emblem, the Oneida Stone, was carried off to the growing city of Utica to consecrate a new cemetery.

What happened to the Oneida Stone frames the historical content of this chapter and highlights the nature of the mythmaking process. As a prominent feature of the nonnative graveyard, the Oneida Stone connected Utica to a local past infinitely older and more colorful than the Erie Canal. Stories about the tribal emblem were elaborated and so fundamentally altered that they became a new myth—in effect, the white man's legend of the Oneida Stone. Asserting the Indians were doomed to fall under civilization's advance, the recently invented tradition conformed with popular thinking justifying expansion at Indian expense and appropriation of the stone.

All people recast historical events in figurative and metaphoric terms to make sense of the present. Though not an Indian myth but a myth about Indians fashioned through literary means, the story of the Oneida Stone is a vivid introduction to the origin and uses of oral narrative.

Chapter 2 brings the Oneida story into the early twentieth century and into the realm of verbal literature. By about 1900, the Oneidas were regarded as Indians who had lost their traditions because they looked much like the nonnative people around them. Trying to take a closer look, non-Indian scholar Hope Emily Allen found that Oneidas opened up only after a series of life crises drew her and two Oneida women, Anna Johnson and Lydia Doxtater, closely together. With their help, Allen recorded oral narratives normally hidden from white eyes. Secretly, the Oneidas shared an expressive culture of storytelling that bound the two Oneida settlements in common experience and linked them to Indians elsewhere.

This chapter highlights the last story Allen documented, a hero tale about a small boy who magically overcomes a wealthy cannibal to revivify his people. Considered comparatively, the story seems quintessentially and traditionally Iroquois in its actors, incidents, and plot. Probably the central fact of life to Oneidas early in the twentieth century was continued loss of land resulting from allotment. Considered within this local context, the story surely expressed contemporaneous Oneida concerns in a traditional format.

Like the white owners of the Oneida Stone, Oneidas gave voice to their outlook through figurative expression linking past to present. The difference was that, for whites, the history to be rendered familiar and right through a mythopoeic lens dealt with the experience of appropriation and expansion. Oneidas, in contrast, struggled to make symbolic sense of dispossession and reduction.

Chapter 3 addresses the Iroquois story of creation, possibly the most thoroughly documented view of world origin anywhere in North America and certainly among the earliest cosmogonies recorded there. These characteristics make it an ideal subject for historical inquiry, the theme of the first part of this chapter. Did the origin myth change? If so, can one get at how, when, or why?

Much of the myth was recorded early in the seventeenth century among the Hurons, Iroquoian speakers of Ontario. A woman, falling from the sky and landing on Turtle's back, delivered a daughter who, in turn, bore male twins. One named Flint perished in a fight with his brother. The surviving twin was a benevolent deity responsible for crops and game. In contrast, his grandmother (the woman from the sky) was considered a malefic god. Although this creation story can be projected back into pre-European time, some features, such as the earth-diver motif, must be very much older to judge by their wide geographical distributions.

Little is known of this story among the Iroquois of New York until the late 1700s. At that time and place, the story evidently focused on the sibling rivalry of the twins—one bad and still named Flint, the other good and called Sky Holder. The latter is a culture hero responsible for giving corn to humans. He seems to embody a horticultural way of life in competition with hunting personified by Flint. This fraternal contest did not, however, bring people into existence, nor did it result in a world ordered for human benefit. The late-eighteenth-century accounts do not agree on a principal duality conceived as ethical opposites. If such a thing existed, it probably was good grandson-evil grandmother as the Hurons knew it and not good twin-evil twin as the Iroquois would know it later.

When the myth changed rapidly early in the nineteenth century, the brothers assumed greater importance as the new central duality, and their rivalry was redefined as a struggle over creation. Sky Holder, recast as the Good Spirit, ordained the world for human benefit and created human beings out of earth. Objecting to such easy living, the Evil Spirit (Flint) attempted to counter or negate each of his brother's acts. What took place between these two explains the world, offers moral guidance, and warns of postmortal consequences.

This diachronic (over time) study suggests, therefore, that the Iroquoian tale of beginnings was pretty stable across a large area for about 150 years. When change occurred, however, the myth was transformed virtually overnight around 1820. These changes are congruent with the innovations introduced about that time by Handsome Lake.

Hope Allen took down two new and previously unknown versions. Although they contain much that is ancient and pre-European, these narratives present the twins as personifications of good and evil struggling over creation and, thus, relate to the form of the story fashionable since the 1820s. They expand the corpus of the modern era and constitute the focus for the remainder of the chapter.

Examined synchronically (at one point in time), both Oneida accounts share peculiarities of plot and treatment that may indicate a local style. Both take care to ground the story in the local setting. To a greater extent than is usually possible, one can identify sources accounting for differences between the two. The Johnson version, more traditional in feel, evinces Canadian Iroquois influence. The more cosmopolitan account by Doxtater incorporates different native sources and exemplifies innovation introduced by the storyteller.

Oneidas enjoyed stories about Little People, Flying Heads, Stone Giants, and Vampire Corpses—all supernatural beings of the woods familiar to Iroquois throughout New York and Ontario. Among the most popular topics in every Iroquois community, they make up much of what is distinctive in Iroquois folklore, the topic of chapter 4. Even though none was documented earlier than the nineteenth century, this suite of forest races may be very old, to judge by close and consistent similarities found in Wyandot lore. Such resemblances are probably cognate beliefs derived from a stock of oral traditions held in common by seventeenth-century ancestors of Iroquois and Wyandots. In the absence of documentary evidence, this consideration is important in assessing the age of Iroquois folklore.

Oneidas believed in Thunders, humanlike beings responsible for rain and for protecting people from such monsters as horned water serpents who escaped their subterranean confinement to move about on the earth. Thunders were in the sky above, but, living behind waterfalls, they also inhabited the terrestrial world, and their battle with snakes took place across the local landscape.

As benevolent and familiar figures in the Oneida world, Thunders were favorite topics of stories given in chapter 5. Telling how a child, half-human and half-Thunder in parentage, became a Thunder himself, Oneidas emphasized the close family ties between the races. They also related tales of young people taken in marriage by serpents and how important human aid could be to the Thunders struggling ceaselessly against evil, gigantic enemies. These stories place Oneidas squarely in the mainstream of lore shared by Iroquois everywhere at the turn of the twentieth century.

The Oneidas, however, were not communicants in the Handsome Lake religion in which Thunders were high-ranking beings in a well-defined pantheon. Longhouse worshipers of the Handsome Lake sect honored Thunders in ceremonies, regarding them as renewers and purifiers of nature, though not as gods specifically dedicated to agriculture. Although Thunders were acknowledged as guardians of humans, the notion of huge bloodsuckers and snakes writhing menacingly just beneath the ground was not emphasized in formal religious events.

The near identity of Iroquois with Wyandot Thunder lore suggests sky beings were regarded as more human- than birdlike as early as the seventeenth century. Sky Holder may have been performing thunder duties during the late 1600s, but, by the late 1700s, his storm-making responsibilities had been delegated to a humanlike associate—that is, Thunder. The conceptual shift from the good twin in charge of thunder to Thunder as the Creator's appointee apparently occurred between 1827 and 1851.

Oneida beliefs in Thunders probably had ancient roots in a widely distributed myth of enmity between sky creatures and underwater beings, especially birds and snakes. My comparative survey reveals a specific link with the Southeast, a region in which Thunder gods included a pair of brothers who freed game animals impounded underground. A similar Iroquois incident, of course, is connected with the twin brothers of the Iroquois creation narrative. Because Sky Holder historically had thunder attributes, Iroquoia and the Southeast had in common a mythic perspective relating thunder to a pair of brothers and to the emancipation of the game.

Oneida folklore absorbed some Euro-American material such as "The Magic Bull," the story opening chapter 6. The closest relatives of this narrative are other native-told stories that collectively imply the adoption of certain Old World wonder tales throughout the greater Northeast by the early 1800s.

Yet this apparently foreign story contains Native American themes of great antiquity. The first is an "obstacle flight," an incident common in Iroquois storytelling but also present across much of Europe and Asia. The age-area principle (vast and continuous distribution of a theme indicates great antiquity) suggests the obstacle flight is thousands of years old. Further, this motif may attest to the entry of people into the Americas by way of Siberia and Alaska.

The second is an allusion to red willow or red osier dogwood, a plant of remarkable importance in Iroquois folklore. Evidently, red willow was used as an emetic internally and as a whip externally to purify the body following an encounter with the supernatural. Not only was its smoke considered a powerful substance, but its branches were also employed to slay ferocious, otherworldly enemies. Narratives describing the plant used as medicine or a weapon against supernatural foes can be dated, through documentary means, to the late 1700s. The Iroquois, however, considered the subject to be as old as the beginning of our world.

Oddly, the package of beliefs pertaining to red osier dogwood seems confined to Iroquois country. This fact is suggestive of a relatively recent date in a comparative sense. On the other hand, the ideas linked by the Iroquois to osier are widely distributed and presumably of proportionate antiquity. It is just that elsewhere, such themes occur separately and mostly independently of one another. For example, a mythic justification for red willow as a smoking substance is found in the Midwest, whereas a belief in emetically purging the body as spiritual preparation is strong in the Southeast. Viewed in this light, Iroquois beliefs about the plant are most clearly affiliated with those two regions.

In chapter 7, some fifteen texts given by half a dozen informants illustrate the scope and vitality of Oneida folklore at the turn of the twentieth century. Most are typical of Iroquois folklore, although there are also European tales customized to an Oneida setting. This material includes mythic fragments whose roots reach deep into the autochthonous past, and it contains certain motifs linked to unexpectedly distant regions in native North America.

There is variation in the form and length of Oneida oral literature and considerable variety in motif and theme. This world is one in which hungry children are transformed into birds, corn and beans intertwine as married partners, and married partners are told how to behave. A boastful bird might be the chickadee who inspired a figure of speech common in eighteenth-century diplomacy. Fox is always one trick ahead of (usually) good-natured Bear. And a hero returning home must stick his hands through the door to establish his identity because the foxes played too many tricks on his waiting relative. Often humorous and sometimes scary, these stories entertained. They also taught lessons and offered advice about the ways of the world.

Chapter 8 returns the Oneida story to calendric time, bringing history up to the present and updating an Oneida mythic perspective. In the present time, no less than in the past, social reality and oral narrative prove to be related. Something in one is likely to find echo or reflection in the other.

A few matriarchal families in the eastern Oneida community managed to weather the 1800s retaining a little land in the Orchard. However, the larger western community suffered more severely from land loss, and, in the opening years of the twentieth century, the last of its residents on communally owned land were thrown into the road as the result of a mortgage foreclosure. This chapter traces the complex legal proceedings, known collectively as *Boylan v. George et al.* (1905–1909), which culminated in the Oneida eviction. Its byzantine plot illustrates how state allotment policy worked to the benefit of nonnatives looking to acquire Indian land.

In this instance, however, the land was contested in another series of legal proceedings, *United States v. Boylan et al.* (1916–1919). Begun as a suit brought by the United States on behalf of the Oneidas, this epic court struggle was waged at every level of the federal justice system until the Oneidas' acres were won back. These *Boylan* cases established a principle crucial to subsequent land claims: New York had no jurisdiction in disposing of Oneida property because the Oneida Nation still existed and had never ceased being a federally recognized tribe.

It was a landmark victory for the Oneidas, but one that was not achieved for Oneida reasons or explained in Oneida terms. Lost in the extremely legalistic language of the *Boylan* decisions was the Oneida view that the federal government helped because of its unique relationship with the Oneida Nation. Because the Oneidas had rendered crucial aid to the Americans during the Revolutionary War, it was simple justice that the United States should acknowledge its gratitude to Oneida allies and recognize its continuing ties to them.

Soon after Hope Allen heard folklore from one community of Oneidas, local newspaper readers learned of an old and mythically resonant Oneida tradition of the Revolution, dusted off and placed in the public domain by Oneidas of the other community. The legend of Polly Cooper told how Oneidas brought corn to the American army at Valley Forge, and how one native woman, Polly Cooper, helped Americans there throughout the balance of the winter. She refused payment for her aid but did accept the gift of a shawl from the grateful Americans. Still extant, that shawl testifies to the truth of the covenant linking the American and Oneida governments.

After 1960, the thirty-two-acre parcel took center stage for further Oneida renaissance. Not surprisingly, this event of historic fact resonated with mythic significance: the Oneida Stone was returned from Utica to the Oneida Nation.

The foundation for further revival was laid in a second set of legal proceedings: the Oneida land claims. These successfully established that New York's acquisitions within the 1788 reservation were illegal without federal approval. Out of such victories, the Oneidas fashioned their own success story. Thus, the twentieth century was a legalistic time, a mythic time, and a time when a resurgent Oneida Nation arose from the ashes.

An epilogue offers summary observations on the content and nature of Oneida and Iroquois folklore. It closes with remarks on evaluating the age and connections of native oral narrative.

Above all, I hope this book conveys something of the experience, life, and spirit of the People of the Standing Stone. Their story is an extraordinary one of endurance and adaptability, an American tragedy and an American success. Working through the voices of Oneida oral narrative is, as Boas, discerned, an approach more likely to convey an Oneida perspective than almost any other.

Oneida Iroquois Folklore, Myth, and History

1

A People Undone

Co-opting the Stone

The social event of central New York in 1850 was a massive gathering to dedicate Forest Hill, a cemetery just outside Utica. A bustling center on the Erie Canal, that city had grown in a quarter century from five thousand to seventeen thousand inhabitants, and the new graveyard was an important civic statement for a young place becoming conscious of itself. "The burial place of a people always furnishes an unmistakable [*sic*] index to their condition, sentiments and affections," remarked one Utican at the time (P. Jones 1851, 603).

The townsfolk situated their cemetery on a high bluff affording a good view of Utica and the canal. Requiring that the setting be made suitable for eternal repose and for contemplation of life's transitoriness, they had the "primitive forest" landscaped into "the luxurious richness of an ancient park" ("Consecration of Forest Hill Cemetery," *Utica Daily Gazette,* June 15, 1850). So now, as a community, thousands of Uticans paused to consider who they were and what they would become.

The centerpiece of their celebration was the "Oneida Stone," said to be the emblem of the indigenous occupants and owners of the land on which Utica and its graveyard stood. The object had been called to the attention of the cemetery trustees through the writings of Henry Schoolcraft, a pioneer in recording native folklore and mythology. Schoolcraft's work would soon inspire Henry Wadsworth Longfellow to recast a story of Great Lakes Indian mythology under an Iroquois name *(Hiawatha,* published 1855) into one of the literary masterpieces of the young American republic.

By 1845, Schoolcraft had fallen in love with the stone as a romantic symbol of the Oneidas and their (to him) past greatness. When he visited

1

1. From Primes Hill looking northwest toward Oneida Lake. Henry Schoolcraft visited the Oneida Stone at this location in 1845. "No person," he recalled, "can stand on this height, and survey the wide prospect of cultivation and the elements of high agricultural and moral civilization . . . without calling to mind that once proud and indomitable race of hunters and warriors, whose name the country bears" (1851, 138).

the Oneida Stone, an unworked rock on the summit of Primes Hill some six miles south of Oneida, Schoolcraft's first reaction "was one of disappointment at its size, but this feeling soon subsided in light of its antiquity and national associations" (1975, 47). The Oneida Stone, he wrote, "is indissolubly associated with [the Oneidas'] early history and origin, and is spoken of, in their traditions, as if it were the Palladium of their liberties, and the symbolical record of their very nationality" (1851–57, 134).

The trustees of the Utica cemetery may have read those sentiments or they may have seen a later notice describing a lecture Schoolcraft gave on the subject ("Aboriginal Palladium," *Utica Daily Gazette*, July 18, 1849). In either event, cemetery officials moved to acquire the stone, believing its

2. *The Oneida Stone after a drawing by Schoolcraft (Schoolcraft 1851, Plate 45); photo courtesy of Hamilton College Library.*

new Utica home would "tend to diffuse more widely the interest attached to it" ("The Oneida Stone—An Interesting Relic Preserved," *Utica Daily Gazette*, November 13, 1849). That fall they took a wagon to Primes Hill, secured permission from the nonnative farmer, then hauled it back to Utica. Crowds attending Forest Hill's opening the following June encountered the Oneida Stone as a prominent monument greeting visitors near the entrance.

The dedicatory address was delivered by banker William Tracy, the most historically minded of the cemetery trustees. About 150 Oneida and Onondaga Indians were present in the audience, and at one point, in a florid oration peppered with allusions to the classical world, Tracy turned to them to deliver himself of these sentiments:

> I see before me some of the sons of an ancient race who once chased the deer over the beautiful land we now occupy. We have invited them here

to join hands with us in dedicating the spot to the dead. . . . The altar around which they . . . assembled to celebrate the rites of their religion before the Gospel of a purer faith had reached their ears, has been brought here in the hope that it may remain to future generations a lasting memorial of the people to whom it gave its name, and who from the day the first pale face visited their wigwam were known as the white man's friends. We welcome you brothers—Children of the Stone, to a participation with us in the ceremonies of this day. We have prepared a resting place around the stone whose beautiful legend has been the theme of song and story, where you may deposit your children and friends when the angel of death shall pierce their hearts with his arrows. The stone of your fathers unwrought by human hands shall be their monument—prouder and richer in its associations than the sculptured marble which the hand of wealth may rear to tell the story of its splendor and magnificence. The breeze which fans our and our children's dust shall at the same time breathe gently over yours. ("Consecration of Forest Hill Cemetery," *Utica Daily Gazette,* June 15, 1850)

Tracy's words indicate that the cultural appropriation of the Oneida Stone was not regarded as an ignoble or hypocritical act. Indeed, the newcomers extended what must have seemed a generous offer to a people they saw as defeated by the advance of civilization. Just as Uticans insisted rich and poor would repose together in Forest Hill, so they also made room for white and red to share, in death, the same earth.

It was not a small sentiment. In the year 1850, the fortunes of the Oneidas had sunk very low, too low, perhaps, ever to rise again.

The Oneidas at the Time of European Encounter

The Iroquois tribes or nations encountered by Europeans in present upstate New York were (east to west) the Mohawks, Oneidas, Onondagas, Cayugas, and Senecas (map 1). These five historically known groups developed directly out of an archaeological culture called Owasco in existence by about A.D. 1000. But who was ancestral to Owasco? Were Owasco people descended from local populations occupying the same country for some four thousand years, as linguist Floyd Lounsbury (1978) suspected? Or were they more recent invaders who displaced indigenous people of a different tongue in about A.D. 900 (Snow 1995a) or A.D. 600

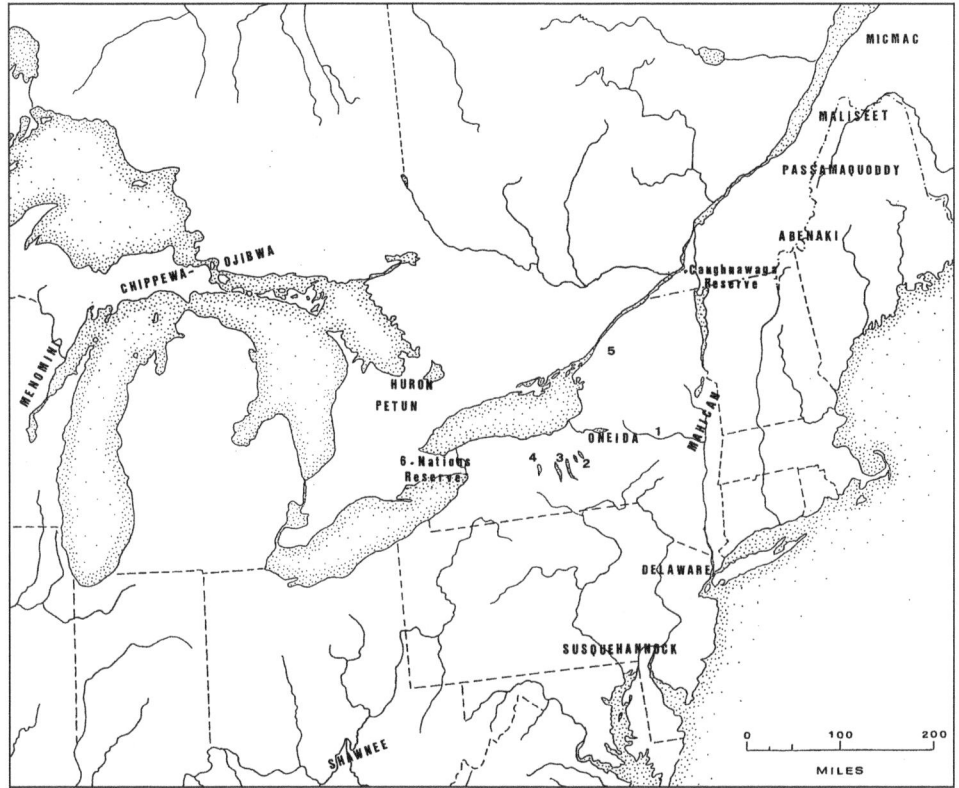

Map 1. The Northeast. Locations of native groups mentioned in text are indicated. Within the present state of New York, 1 represents the location of the Mohawks; 2, the Onondagas; 3, the Cayugas; 4, the Senecas; and 5, the Jefferson County province of the St. Lawrence Iroquoians.

(Snow 1996)? Scholars continue to debate the merits of these scenarios and others (see Clermont 1996).

Because no Owasco villages are known within the Oneida residential heartland, the origin of the Oneida Nation presents a more specific puzzle. In 1845, an Oneida told Schoolcraft that the Oneidas considered themselves descended from a pair of Onondaga brothers. This tradition (if such it is) agrees with one aspect of the archaeological record: the earliest Oneida villages apparently are the ones closest to Onondaga territory. On the other hand, the ceramics of Nichols Pond, the oldest Oneida site known in any detail (ca. A.D. 1450), "are nearly identical with Mohawk ceramics of this period. . . . This supports the view that the Mohawks and Oneidas were essentially a single culture in this period. Upstream people gravitated towards the Onondagas farther west, eventually becoming the Oneidas, while the downstream people drew themselves into the middle Mohawk Valley" (Snow 1995b, 91). This situation is consistent with the linguistic evidence: the Oneida language is very close to Mohawk, not Onondaga. The Oneidas themselves, according to a person more knowledgeable than Schoolcraft (as discussed in chapter 3), said they were autochthonous, having come out of the ground in their own homeland (Dean 1915).

Each of these sources may be partially correct if the Oneida Nation coalesced out of several previously distinct bands, as may have occurred elsewhere in the Iroquois world at about the same time. At any rate, sometime about 1350 to 1450, we pick up the archaeological record of people who were the ancestors of the historically known Oneidas living, in classically Iroquois fashion, in permanent villages of bark-covered houses. The settlement was often surrounded by a palisaded wall beyond which lay fields containing the domesticated crops corn, beans, and squash.

The Oneidas generally had a single principal village that moved over time in response to increasing scarcity of firewood, progressive deterioration of the homes, and decreasing fertility of the soil. Changing its location every ten to fifty years, the Oneida village can be traced continuously over perhaps four centuries in present Madison County from just south of Canastota (Nichols Pond) to south of the present city of Oneida (Primes Hill). Very likely, the village retained the same name over the centuries: Oneida. The first extant account of a European visiting the Oneidas in 1634–35 names the village as *Onneyuttehage* (Gehring and Starna 1988, 14, 44), a fair rendering of *Oneida* in the Oneida language: *Onyota'a:ka* (pronounced O-ni-yo-da-ah-ga). Used as a village name, the term meant, as Schoolcraft reported two centuries later, the People of the Standing Stone—the Oneida tribe or nation.

The European visitor Harmen Meyndertsz van den Bogaert stated the Oneida village was "on a very high hill and was surrounded with two rows of palisades, 767 steps in circumference, in which there are 66 houses" (Gehring and Starna 1988, 13). Van den Bogaert may have visited what archaeologists know as the four-acre Thurston site, near Munnsville, about eight miles south of present Oneida (Bennett 1988, 1991; Pratt 1976, 134; Whitney 1964). He did not record the population of the town, although, eighty years later, the principal Oneida settlement was said to have a log wall twelve feet high in which eleven hundred to twelve hundred Oneidas lived (Andrews 1714, 125). That village, Primes Hill, occupied at least two acres (Bennett 1983, 1988).

The defensive walls were composed of upright stakes among which bark and branches were interwoven. They and the generally high locations of the villages testify to the threat of violence. Above the main entrance of the village van den Bogaert entered "stood three large wooden images, carved as men, by which three locks fluttered that they had cut from the heads of slain Indians as a token of truth, that is to say, victory" (Gehring and Starna 1988, 12). These scalps probably were trophies from feuds with distant villages. The goal of such fighting was to incorporate into the home group an enemy for each individual lost from one's own community. An enemy's scalp counted as such a tally, but it was preferable to bring home the living enemy. Ideally, the prisoner was adopted into a family and thereby replaced a deceased family member by assuming that person's name, rights, and responsibilities. Extreme grief or hatred, however, could lead to a different ending. Adopted only figuratively, the unlucky prisoner looked forward to torture and execution in a public rite in which the community absorbed the captive's spirit by ceremonially ingesting his flesh.

"Built much better and higher than all the others," Oneida houses were constructed of elm-bark shingles set on a framework of saplings and logs (Gehring and Starna 1988, 13). About twenty feet high and wide, such a residence might be sixty to two hundred feet long depending on how many families lived within. The greater part of the building was divided into apartments twelve to twenty-five feet long. On one side, the living area was open to the central aisle running the length of the house. On the other, it was furnished with a bench or sleeping platform attached to an exterior wall. Each apartment was occupied by a nuclear family sharing a hearth or cooking fire with a similar family across the central corridor (see sidebar, chapter 2).

A gender-based allocation of labor requiring reciprocal duties of spouses found expression in Iroquois thought: the village and clearing were the realm of women, the forest and foreign lands the domain of men.

Women were responsible for collecting firewood and gathering such wild foods as berries and nuts. Women tended the maize fields and cooked the meals consisting primarily of corn gruel.

Men were warriors and diplomats, but, above all, they hunted. Whatever contribution maize made to the diet, hunting was the more culturally prestigious subsistence pursuit (Fenton 1978, 298). Jacques Bruyas, a French missionary among the Oneidas in 1668, put it this way:

> It is a savage's supreme good to have fresh meat; he then considers himself the happiest person in the world; and the women do hardly anything else, all the winter, but go and get the flesh of the deer or of the moose that the men have killed, sometimes fifty leagues away from the village. I am often asked if they eat the meat of the moose, bear, etc. in paradise; and I answer them that, if they desire to eat it, their desires will be satisfied. (Thwaites 1896–1901, 51:129)

Since this way of life necessitated the absence of males for long periods of time, it appears that the fundamental social unit was not the nuclear unit but the extended family reckoned through the mother's line. Such a matrilineage typically comprised a grandmother and her daughters and grandchildren along with various spouses. Most bark houses probably were home to such a family and under the supervision of the senior matron.

These female-centered families belonged, in turn, to a matrilineal clan, a grouping of families presumed related through the female line. Van den Bogaert noticed the gable ends of the longhouses "were painted with all sorts of animals" (Gehring and Starna 1988, 13). These pictures may have been of the three Oneida clans: bear, turtle, and wolf.

Clan groupings were important in ceremonial and social life and fundamental to the Oneida government. Each clan had a deliberative body composed of counselors or senior men, most of whom haled from certain prestigious families looked up to as a kind of aristocracy. Owning most of the available wampum beads, these families collected and disbursed whatever wampum was needed for national business.

To the Oneidas and other Iroquois, the truth of a statement was established by an accompanying object. Although any gift might serve as physical testimony to the spoken word, the preferred substance was wampum beads made from ocean shells found off the New England coast.

Handled in the form of individual strings of beads or as several strings fashioned together as a belt, the amount of wampum was regarded as proportional to the importance of the statement (see sidebar, chapter 5) (Fenton 1998, 224–39; Fenton and Moore 1974, 310).

Probably composed of the clan councils, the ruling committee of the Oneida village served simultaneously as the national council. That it was a government capable of functioning without state-level means of coercion was something that amazed the European visitor Bruyas. "There is among them neither prison nor gibbet; each one lives according to his fancy; and I am surprised that, in so great impunity, they are not daily cutting each other's throats" (Thwaites 1896–1901, 51:125). Order in this society was kept by force of public opinion and the leaders' ability to inspire confidence. Avoiding contentious issues whenever possible, the effective leader cultivated a climate of tolerance, consensus, and good-mindedness. An example of this spirit emerges from the first recorded meeting of Europeans with the Oneidas. The discourteous Dutch visitors (van den Bogaert and two companions) had failed to present gifts acknowledging the hospitality of their hosts. The breach of etiquette created a volatile situation that an Oneida sought to correct.

> An Indian once again called us scoundrels . . . and he was very malicious so that Willem Tomassen became so angry that the tears ran from his eyes. The Indian seeing that we were upset, asked us why we looked at him with such anger. We were sitting during this time with their 46 persons around and near us. Had they had any malicious intentions, they could have easily grabbed us with their hands and killed us without much trouble. However, when I heard his screaming long enough, I told him that he was the scoundrel. He began to laugh and said that he was not angry and said "You must not be angry. We are happy that you have come here." (Gehring and Starna 1988, 14)

A good leader depended on his power of persuasion, and formal oratory was a highly developed art form with its own language and style of delivery. A very distant sense of how Oneidas experienced oral expression can be gleaned from a French missionary's account of a chance encounter with an Oneida party in October 1655. In reply to French speeches, the Oneida leader Atondatochan began the song of response; and all commenced to sing, in wondrous harmony, in a manner somewhat resembling our plain-chant. The first song said that it would take all the rest of the day to thank the Father for so good a speech as he had made them. The second was to congratulate him upon his journey and his arrival. They sang a third time to light him a fire, that he might take possession of it. The fourth song made us all relatives and brothers; the fifth hurled the hatchet into the deepest abyss, in order that peace might reign in all these countries; and the sixth was designed to make the French masters of the [Salmon River, in present Oswego County, some forty-five miles north of Oneida]. At this point the Captain invited the salmon, brill, and other fish, to leap into our [the Frenchmen's] nets, and to fill that river for our service only. He told them they should consider themselves fortunate to end their lives so honorably; named all the fishes of that river, down to the smallest, making a humorous address to each kind; and added a thousand things besides, which excited laughter in all those present. The seventh song pleased us still more, its purpose being to open their hearts, and let us read their joy at our coming. At the close of their songs, they made us a present of two thousand porcelain [wampum] beads. (Thwaites 1896–1901, 42:79)

The earliest documented reference to the Iroquois Confederacy dates to van den Bogaert's Oneida visit (Gehring and Starna 1988, 16–17, 46). The most famous native government in North America, the Confederacy or League of the Iroquois would exercise a profound influence on the course of American colonial history for nearly two centuries. Opinions about the date of league formation range from about fifteen hundred to four hundred years ago (Beauchamp 1892, 16; Kuhn and Sempowski 2001).

Iroquois tradition speaks of a violent age in which the five nations developed a union to prevent bloodshed among themselves. The best-known versions, committed to paper around the turn of the twentieth century, describe the league as resulting from the efforts of a prophet, Deganawidah, in partnership with grief-stricken Chief Hiawatha (he whose name Longfellow appropriated), to enlist the nations and win over the evil sorcerer Thadodaho (Fenton 1998, 19–103; Hale 1969, 18–38; Hewitt 1892; Parker 1916; Scott 1912; Woodbury, Henry, and Webster 1992). The Iroquois visualized their league as a giant longhouse extending across upstate New York in which the confederated nations dwelt together as relatives.

The continuance of the Iroquois Confederacy rested on an elaborate ritual performance called the Condolence Ceremony that comforted the family of a deceased chief and consecrated a successor to the chiefly office (Tooker 1978a). Because the newly designated chief assumed the name and duties of his predecessor, the deceased was, in a sense, brought back to life.

In part, the Condolence Ceremony was a specialized application of the adoption custom prevalent in Iroquois culture and history. Additionally, however, the Condolence Ceremony provided a model for alliance making. Europeans quickly found that they had to learn the protocols of condolence in order to conduct treaties with the Iroquois (Fenton 1985). In a larger sense, a package combining adoption, mourning, and alliance-making behaviors may have ancient roots in the eastern woodlands (Hall 1997).

The contemporary Condolence Ceremony is composed of a series of ritual performances, including the Greeting at the Wood's Edge, an address by the mourners welcoming the condolers to a fire outside the mourners' settlement; the Roll Call of the Chiefs, a chant performed by the visiting condolers naming the original founders of the Iroquois League; and the Three Bare (or Rare) Words in which each party metaphorically clears the organs of communication (today the eyes, ears, and throat) of the other (Fenton 1998, 135–202). These aspects of the Condolence Ceremony were long-established features of Oneida diplomacy by the year 1674:

[When a foreign embassy has] arrived within a musket-shot from the palisade, a fire is lighted, as a sign of peace, at the spot where the elders of the village are going to wait for them; and, after smoking for some time and receiving the savage compliments that they pay one another, they are led to the cabin set apart for them. They all march gravely and in file. One of the most notable men walks at the head, and pronounces a long string of words which have been handed down to them by tradition, and which are repeated by the others after him. The ambassador who is to be the spokesman comes last of all, singing in a rather agreeable tone; he continues his song until he has entered his cabin, around which he also walks five or six times, still singing; then he sits down, last of all. There the pledges of friendship are renewed, and presents are given to dispel fatigue; to wipe away tears; to remove scales from their eyes, so that they may more easily see one another; and, finally, to open their throats and give freer passage to their voices. (Thwaites 1896–1901, 58:187–89)

The earliest European observers documented two aspects of Oneida religious beliefs. In one instance, a medicine society or curing group of about a dozen men danced about a patient as a woman chanted and shook a turtle rattle. Their faces painted red, the dancers wore curious headbands decorated with white crosses. Evidently, they were engaged in a classic form of shamanistic cure in which a foreign substance (possibly a grub or a feather) was sucked out of a patient's body. They also "threw fire, ate fire, and threw around hot ashes and embers in such a way that I ran out of the house" (Gehring and Starna 1988, 18).

In the second case, the Oneidas are known to have celebrated the *Onnonhouaroia* (Midwinter) ceremony, probably in early 1658 (Thwaites 1896–1901, 44:31). This occasion was sacred to Taronhiaouagon or Holder-Up-of-the-Sky (hereafter, Sky Holder), the most important god of all the Iroquois nations, and the principal deity to express his will through dreams (51:61). Believing that unfulfilled dreams could lead to evil consequences for the community, the Iroquois honored dreams and devoted this dream-guessing festival to satisfying their inner wishes (Tooker 1970, 83–103). As psychological therapy, this ceremony doubtlessly was as effective as anything then known in Europe (Wallace 1972, 59–75). However, the early missionaries regarded the dream as particularly threatening to Christian belief. "As it is the oldest [evil], it is very hard to cure," Bruyas remarked of the Oneidas. "It is the divinity of the savages, for which they have no less respect than we have for the most holy things. All that they dream must be carried out; otherwise, one draws upon himself the hatred of all the dreamer's relatives and exposes himself to feel the effects of their anger" (Thwaites 1896–1901, 51:125).

Bruyas, one of the first Europeans to live among the Oneidas, called his hosts "the least populous, the proudest, and the most insolent of all" the Iroquois nations (Thwaites 1896–1901, 51:221). "God will perhaps humiliate our Onneiouts [Oneidas]," the unsympathetic Frenchman mused hopefully, "who, up to the present, have always lived in prosperity and abundance" (131).

European Colonization, ca. 1620–1775

The first permanent European settlements in the Northeast were made early in the 1600s with the hope of turning a quick profit. Although Europeans discovered no gold, silver, spices, or sugar, they did find the pelt of the beaver. At precisely that moment in Europe, felted hats, made from the soft inner fur of that animal, were becoming fashionable, and the Old World supply of beaver was running out (Wolf 1982, 159–60).

The Iroquois welcomed trade with the newcomers and quickly adopted foreign goods as improved versions of familiar materials. In exchange for beaver skins and other furs at Albany (founded 1624), they took home brass kettles, spun cloth, and iron tools. In many ways lighter, sharper, and more durable than native pottery vessels, animal-skin clothing, and stone tools, these foreign-made goods caused a technological revolution in the archaeological record. By about 1675, for example, native-made pottery had disappeared. Yet the new objects apparently did not transform Oneida life or outlook aside from the loss of several manufacturing techniques (Richter 1992, 79).

At least one European item, however, was introduced into Oneida life with terrible consequences. When Iroquois people first acquired a taste for Dutch wine, French brandy, or English rum, they probably considered it as similar to dreams or tobacco—a path to the spirit world (Richter 1992, 86). But as the Oneidas endured interminable disease and war during the 1600s, alcohol became a "socially sanctioned time-out," a justifiable way to release aggression (Axtell 1985, 64). Thus, visiting French priests who described drunkenness also (unwittingly) identified its purpose. "Although they often become intoxicated with the intention of killing those to whom they bear ill will," Bruyas observed at Oneida in 1668, "yet all is then forgiven, and you have no other satisfaction than this: 'What wouldst thou have me do? I had no sense; I was drunk' " (Thwaites 1896–1901, 51:125).

The European presence also contributed to an escalation of warfare in native America. Ethnocentric Europeans of the time viewed the Iroquois as cruel savages attacking tribes everywhere and even destroying whole nations. The Oneidas, for example, took part in the destruction of the Huron Confederacy in Ontario (1648–49), the Erie Nation in northern Ohio (1657), and the Susquehannock Nation in Pennsylvania (1670s). In addition to these campaigns, Oneida warriors ranged from the St. Lawrence to Virginia and from the Great Lakes to New England. Why did they fight so much?

Historians have reasoned that the introduction of European firearms led to an uncontrollable spiral of violence during the seventeenth century. Obtaining guns in trade required beaver pelts, which, for Iroquois living far from the best beaver habitats, meant encroaching on the hunting territories or trade routes of others. This competition, in turn, required more guns (to defend and to attack), which further fueled rivalry for beaver pelts. The so-called Beaver Wars, therefore, were caused by native people motivated by European imperatives and economic incentives.

More recent scholarship focuses on native reasons for fighting, and particularly on the native response to microbiological killers arriving on American shores from Europe. Native Americans had no defenses against infectious diseases of the Old World, including smallpox, influenza, and chicken pox. When these afflictions hit Americans, 55 percent to 95 percent of the population died. Such massive epidemics struck repeatedly from at least the 1630s through the 1690s. Prior to Europeans, there may have been three thousand to four thousand Oneidas (Starna 1988, 16). During most of the 1600s and 1700s, however, the Oneidas (always the smallest nation of the Iroquois Confederacy) numbered in the neighborhood of one thousand to fifteen hundred people.

The sense of hopelessness experienced by those Oneidas who survived epidemics is beyond imagining. One response was to intensify the traditional practice of adoption, thereby increasing the chances for the nation's survival. Large-scale assimilation of foreign people, often through war, was the result (see Brandão 1997; Dennis 1993; and Jennings 1984, 92–96). In 1668, Bruyas claimed that two-thirds of the Oneida people had been born Algonquins and Hurons but had become Iroquois in "temper and inclination" (Thwaites 1896–1901, 51:123).

Gaining numbers through war is a strategy with a high cost in human suffering. Being vulnerable to reprisal raids, for example, must have created an atmosphere of pervasive anxiety in the Oneida village. Bruyas reported an instance of what may have been fear-inspired hysteria in 1670. An Oneida woman announced that Sky Holder, "the great god of the Iroquois," warned her of an impending Susquehannock *(Andastogué)* raid in which the Oneidas would capture one of their most feared enemies. "It is asserted that the voice of that Andastogué was heard; from the bottom of a kettle he uttered wailing cries, like the cries of those who are being burned. This woman—mad or possessed—is believed in all that she says. Every day there is a gathering at her house, where there is nothing but dancing, singing, and feasting" (Thwaites 1896–1901, 53:253).

Oneida war parties often suffered losses and sometimes defeat. In 1691, for example, a party of Mohawks and Oneidas sustained heavy casualties fighting Canadian Indians in the French interest (Brandão 1997, 265–66; O'Callaghan 1853–87, 3:815). Whereas all Iroquois populations dwindled from war in the 1690s, the Oneidas were hardest hit. A contemporary Englishman estimated the number of Oneida warriors fell from 180 to 70 during the closing years of the century (O'Callaghan 1849–51, 1:690).

Oneida society was attacked from within by another foe: French missionaries belonging to the Society of Jesus (Jesuits). Jacques Bruyas, living in the Oneida village from 1667 to 1671, was succeeded by Pierre Millet up to about 1684, then again at Oneida from 1689 to 1694. The Oneidas probably found something to admire in the deportment of these men. The visitors shared in daily life and participated in the Oneida language. Their sense of moral correctness resembled Oneida values, and their vows of poverty prevented any suggestion of obvious self-enrichment. Believing, however, that fundamental institutions of Oneida life and religion were incompatible with Christianity, the Jesuits aimed to destroy the fabric of customary behavior. They labored to discredit non-Christian belief, to attach influential leaders to their cause, and to exploit internal cleavages caused by the assimilation of foreigners (Axtell 1985, 71–127).

Zealous and highly disciplined, these missionaries were fairly successful. Once converted, the native Christians were urged to remove themselves from pagan relatives by emigrating to Jesuit-supervised reserves in Canada where they were lost to the home population forever. How many Oneidas trekked north during these years is unknown, but the number must have been substantial (Richter 1992, 105–28).

The European century reckoned as the 1600s was a calamitous time for the Oneidas, but they did not suffer actual invasion until the final years. In 1687, the French seized Iroquois peace emissaries (Oneidas among them) and sent them to end their days as galley slaves in the Mediterranean (O'Callaghan 1849–51, 3:532, 557–61; Preston 1958, 47–48, 172–73). In retaliation, Oneidas joined in the Iroquois attack on Lachine, a French settlement near Montreal. These hostilities enmeshed the Iroquois in a European war (War of the League of Augsburg) extended to American soil (King William's War, 1689–97). In theory, the English and Iroquois were allies, although English help proved to be nonexistent when Iroquois settlements were threatened. In 1696, a French army arrived on the hill overlooking present Vernon to destroy the Oneidas. After submitting to the French conditions for peace, a number of Oneidas remained in their village to make the French welcome. But "the only favor they obtained was to be made prisoners and carried to Montreal" (Colden 1964, 171) as their village went up in flames (Thwaites 1896–1901, 65:25–27).

Long after the Europeans stopped fighting each other, the Iroquois achieved their own peace at both Montreal and Albany in 1701 (Fenton 1998, 330–60). Apparently, they overhauled their foreign policy after absorbing hard lessons of the recent past (Aquila 1997). Iroquois leaders of the 1700s played off the interests of competing European colonies (French and English, as well as individual British colonies) to Iroquois advantage.

The Iroquois were never entirely neutral during the Anglo-French struggle because they were linked to the English as brothers in the "Covenant Chain," a series of contracts attaching diverse native peoples to the Iroquois and the Iroquois to the English at Albany. From the late 1660s on, the Iroquois used the Covenant Chain to promote the interests of the Iroquois League and allied tribes and to reduce conflict between English and Indians. Through mediation, the Iroquois won status and room to maneuver by becoming indispensable to all parties (Jennings 1984; Richter 1992).

That the Iroquois could maintain some semblance of neutrality between English and French while fulfilling treaty obligations to the English was no mean feat. Franco-British competition flared into fighting during Queen Ann's War (1702–13) and King George's War (1744–48). Pressed by the English for aid, Oneidas and other Iroquois joined English forces massing to invade Canada in 1709, 1711, and 1746 (Richter 1992, 226–28). Although nothing came of these campaigns, it could not be said the Oneidas reneged on their pledges.

Oneidas gave limited support to both European powers during the French and Indian War (1754–63) until the conflict turned decisively against the French. With the French driven from America, the diplomatic options available to the Iroquois vanished. In about 1758, the Oneidas permitted the British to build a fort at the Oneida Carrying Place in the heart of Oneida country (Fort Stanwix, present Rome). Thereafter, English guns loomed over the most important portage for traffic between the Atlantic and the Great Lakes.

Oneida war parties continued to go out during the early 1700s, but they almost always headed south to raid the Catawbas and other native people of South Carolina and Virginia (Merrell 1987). Rather small in scale, this style of warfare revived the older pattern of feuding with distant villages (Aquila 1997, 205–32).

At the same time, however, the Oneidas and other Iroquois renounced war as a means of gathering large numbers of new citizens, and, again, they were able to achieve the same result through diplomacy. Since the formation of the Iroquois Confederacy, the Mohawks and Senecas had been known as keepers of the eastern and western doors of the league's metaphorical longhouse. During the eighteenth century, the Oneidas and Cayugas began acting as keepers of a southern door opening to the Susquehanna River as it passed through Pennsylvania and Maryland. The Oneida Nation usually became responsible in those reaches for adopting native groups fleeing wars and English settlement in Great Britain's southern colonies.

Oneidas assigned such groups to a particular tract that the guests could use, but not sell, for as long as they wished. Refugee people were expected to support their Oneida hosts in time of war but were otherwise free to speak their own languages and retain their own customs. On these terms, the Oneidas adopted such southern groups as the Tuscaroras and Nanticokes. Later, in the 1770s and 1780s, the Oneidas also took in two amalgamated groups of Christian Indians from the East: the Stockbridges (mostly Mahicans from Stockbridge, Massachusetts) and the Brothertons (Narragansetts, Pequots, Montauketts, Mohegans, and others from southern New England and Long Island). The latter were fixed in the vicinity of Deansboro, twelve miles southwest of present Utica (Wonderley 2000a).

By the 1770s, Oneidas were hard-pressed by the expanding English population. In the Mohawk Valley to the east, what was left of the once proud Mohawk Nation was confined to two tiny islands in a sea of perhaps ten thousand colonial people. Land had replaced furs as the most desired form of wealth, and Euro-Americans had arrived at the borders of Oneida country.

Responding peacefully and practically, the Oneidas adopted features of foreign life to better preserve their customs and sovereignty. The principal Oneida village, present Oneida Castle, probably looked similar to non-Indian towns in the Mohawk Valley. There were orchards of fruit trees and herds of grazing stock, including cattle and sheep. The Oneidas owned numerous horses (along with harnesses, saddles, and sleighs) for traveling and hauling firewood. There were at least sixty houses, nearly half of which were built of logs or framed with lumber. More than seven hundred village residents, dressed in European-derived cloth, used metal tools of foreign origin (Wonderley 1998).

The influence of Presbyterian missionary Samuel Kirkland, in Oneida Castle since 1766, was reflected in an impressive framed church with a steeple sixty feet high. Its tolling bell (probably one Oneidas helped to capture from the French in 1759) proclaimed that many Oneidas considered themselves Christians. Curious about religion, Oneidas sought out non-Indian ministers to baptize their children with such Christian names as Thomas or John, Sara or Hannah. This arrangement was not done to the exclusion of their traditions, however, and few Oneidas renounced older beliefs as Kirkland demanded.

On the eve of the Revolutionary War, Oneidas remained traditional in lifestyle and outlook. Even in homes reflecting foreign construction styles, the hearth was placed in the center of the room and people slept on benches against the wall—both as had been done anciently in the longhouses. Around the central fire, families still told the old stories in the old ways. Furniture was available, but Oneidas did not like to clutter up their interiors with it. Men and women continued to fulfill their traditional duties, and it made no difference to them that a woman now cooked in a copper kettle or that a man now hunted with a flintlock rifle.

Revolution and Dispossession, 1775–1850

Tradition holds that, during the American Revolution, the League of the Iroquois covered its council fire, meaning that it was left to individual nations to make their own choices. Correctly judging that the British could supply more needed goods than the impoverished Americans, most Iroquois ended up fighting for the English. Most Oneidas, in contrast and against their own material interests, pledged their lives to the American cause. "Brothers, it is well known that the defection of part of our Confederacy is owing to the frequent presents made them by the King," Oneida leader Good Peter explained to his American allies, "but we are determined to adhere to you" (Penrose 1981, 160).

Many Iroquois also chose to support the British side because of the Crown's promise to protect Indian land from acquisitive pioneers. Oneidas had reason to be skeptical of this claim, however, because it came from Sir William Johnson, the royal superintendent of Indian affairs and the biggest landowner in the colony of New York. Most Oneida land had been lost not as small farms to individual settlers but in enormous tracts to Sir William and his land-speculating friends (Billington 1944; Guzzardo 1976; D. V. Jones 1982).

In 1777, the British believed they could win the war by launching several invasions intended to converge on Albany. The largest army would proceed south from Canada across Lakes George and Champlain. A second was assigned to capture American-held Fort Stanwix, then proceed down the Mohawk Valley. A third force, quartered in New York City, would (it was hoped) move up the Hudson Valley to join the other two.

The Oneidas entered the war when they learned a hostile army was crossing their territory at the Oneida Carrying Place. As the British force approached Fort Stanwix, an extraordinary meeting occurred between an Oneida boy named Powless and pro-British Iroquois leader Joseph Brant. The substance of their conversation was long remembered in Oneida tradition:

> Brant insinuatingly offered him a large reward, and aplenty as long as he should live, if he would only join the King's side, and induce other Oneidas to do so, and help the British to take Fort Stanwix. Powless firmly rejected any such blandishments, saying he and his brother Oneidas had

joined their fortunes with those of the Americans, and should share with them whatever good or ill might come. Brant portrayed the great and re-sistless power of the King, and profess[ed] to deplore the ruin of the Oneidas if they should foolishly and recklessly persist in their determina-tion. Powless replied that he and the Oneidas would persevere, if need be, till all were annihilated; and that was all he had to say, when each re-tired his own way. (Draper n.d., 203–4)

Several days later, Oneidas joined a body of American militia advanc-ing to relieve the besieged fort. Following a bloody ambush prepared by the British near Oriskany, the militia and Oneidas fought royal troops and their Indian allies to a standstill. Other Oneidas assisted in the defense of the fort. When the British retreated from Fort Stanwix in late August, Oneidas rushed east to Saratoga where they served with distinction in a second campaign ending in British defeat.

Events of 1777 in which Oneidas played such a signal role proved de-cisive to the outcome of the war. These American triumphs prompted France to enter the war, and it was French aid that secured the final victory at Yorktown in 1781. Hence, in a year of destiny, the Oneida Nation con-tributed more to the birth of the United States than any other community of comparable size in the colonies.

According to oral tradition, Oneidas offered corn and other assistance to the Continental army bivouacked at Valley Forge, Pennsylvania, during the winter of 1777–78, a subject to which I return in chapter 8. About fifty Oneidas reinforced Washington's army at Valley Forge the following spring and joined an expedition to probe British defenses near Philadel-phia. Against orders, the American troops took up a fixed position, which the English promptly surrounded. The alarm raised by Oneida pickets en-gaging the enemy enabled some twenty-two hundred Americans to scam-per to safety at the last possible moment.

When the Tory Iroquois destroyed Oneida Castle in the summer of 1780, the Oneidas withdrew into the Mohawk Valley. There, as refugees lacking shelter, food, and adequate clothing, they suffered profoundly for three years. They continued to fight, however, participating in battles in the Mohawk Valley against large raiding parties in 1780 and 1781.

The Oneidas had effectively served the cause of American liberty at terrible cost to themselves. However, when they returned to Oneida Castle about 1783, their future seemed bright as the only Iroquois nation blessed with the good wishes of the new United States. Both the United States and the state of New York thanked them and promised to respect Oneida sovereignty (Campisi 1988).

But New York coveted all Iroquois land to the west for economic and military reasons. In the aftermath of war, the state's treasury was empty, and its plan for economic recovery required the benefits anticipated from owning Iroquois territory. Income would materialize, of course, from selling the land. Indirectly, possession of the vast country served as collateral backing loans and currency. Paying veterans in land rather than money helped to reduce the state's debt. Finally, there was a general prospect that land inhabited by a population of nonnative farmers would render the state more militarily secure while providing a productive tax base.

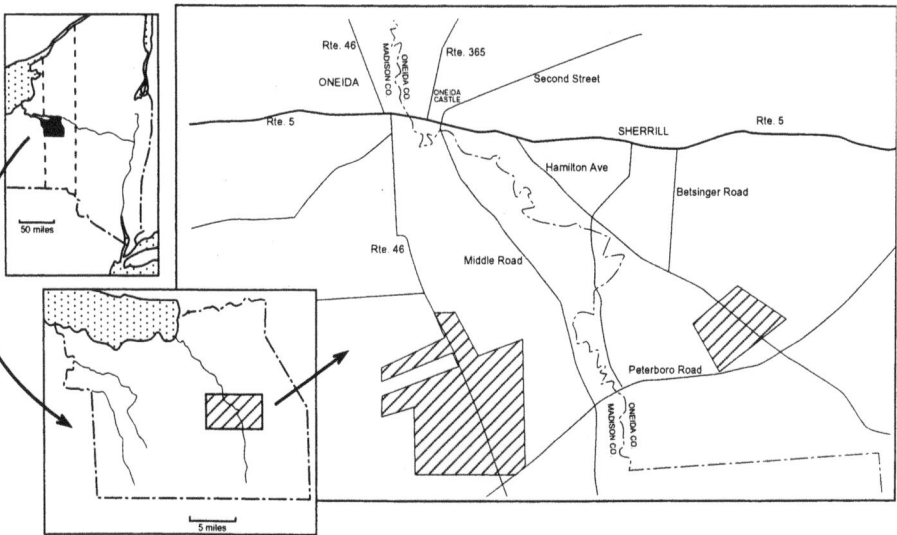

Map 2. Oneida Land Loss. The country aboriginally owned by the Oneidas (area bounded by dashed lines) is shown, very approximately, on the inset at upper left. Oneida land was reduced in the New York Treaty of 1788 to an area of some three hundred thousand acres (darkened in upper left inset, enlarged in the lower left view). New York continued to acquire land within this "Oneida Reservation" until 1842, when only two small tracts remained to the Oneidas (cross-hatched zones on the principal map). The western parcel in Madison County became known as the Windfall. Originally called the Orchard, the eastern parcel in Oneida County survived as the Marble Hill community.

New York would have to move quickly to establish its ownership before competitors could stake claims. State officials particularly feared Massachusetts, which could argue for title based on royal charter, a rationale superior to New York's pretensions. A bigger rival was the federal government, the only party empowered to negotiate for Indian land under the Articles of Confederation (1781) and the Constitution (1789). The federal government, however, did not intervene during the crucial years New York was moving aggressively to acquire Indian holdings (Graymont 1976).

Almost immediately, New York turned on its Oneida allies. The vast majority of Oneida land (some five million acres) went to the state in a 1788 treaty regarded as a purchase by New York but as a lease by the Oneidas (see map 2) (Geier 1980, 93–115; Lehman 1990). "After this," Good Peter recollected, "the Governor of New York said to us: You have now leased to me all your territory, exclusive of the reservation as long as the grass shall grow and rivers run. He did not say 'I buy your country;' nor did we say 'We sell it to you' " (Pickering n.d., 60:127A–28).

Suddenly the Oneida Nation was engulfed by thousands of nonnatives who leveled the forests in every direction and regarded the original inhabitants with contempt or pity. Robbed of the land base supporting the old ways, Oneidas experienced hunger and disillusion, leading many to wonder whether their nation had been cursed. One Oneida chief, according to Samuel Kirkland,

> would frequently have turns of dejection and depression of spirits, and break out with a heavy sigh, in these words, or similar expressions: "Oh! The vast difference between the white people and my Nation! What can make this difference? The God of the white people must be the God of the Indians also! Has he decreed, has he fixed in his counsels that there should be this difference? Oh! Poor Indians! O my Nation! My Nation!" (Pilkington 1980, 227–28)

Iroquois leaders everywhere struggled to discern a future for their people in these hard times. Among the Oneidas, Chief Skenandoa advocated accommodation—taking up Christianity and the American style of plow farming—as the most likely path of survival. Because his leadership extended as far back as the 1750s, he provided essential continuity for the

Oneida Nation. With his passing in 1816, there was no one of comparable stature to inspire unity.

Although the Oneidas lost most of their country in 1788, they did apparently reserve to themselves forever their residential heartland measuring close to three hundred thousand acres. During the 1790s, the federal government pledged, through law and treaty, to protect this so-called Oneida Reservation. Embracing most of Madison County and a western part of Oneida County, it is today's land-claim area.

Nevertheless, New York continued to eat away at Oneida holdings in a series of treaties from 1795 to 1842. Ostensibly purchases, these transactions often were forced cessions involving threats and bribes that divided the Oneidas. Suffering internal disruption and erosion of their land base, the Oneidas experienced increasing pressure to vacate New York. A broad spectrum of nonnative interests—including land speculators, missionaries, settlers, boosters of Erie Canal development, sometimes even federal officials—wanted the Indians gone (Hauptman 1999).

Nearly half the Oneidas were induced to move to the Midwest by the early 1830s (Horsman 1999). Their descendants, still residing near Green Bay, are known as the Oneida Tribe of Wisconsin. Another large contingent left for Canada in the 1840s (Campisi 1974, 262–67). Their descendants constitute the Oneida of the Thames Band in Ontario.

By that decade, New York was evidently committed to terminating government-to-government dealings with the Oneidas. In 1839, the state absolved itself of the obligation to make annual payments as stipulated in earlier Oneida treaties. The same law transferred responsibility for Indian land dealings from the governor to a lower-level commission authorized to buy the remaining Oneida land. These unilateral actions all but eliminated conditions under which New York would have to recognize an Oneida government within the state and deal with Oneidas on anything other than an individual basis.

New York conducted the last of its Oneida treaties in 1842 with what, by then, were two groups of Oneidas living about two miles apart. Under the terms of these instruments of cession, Oneidas wishing to move to Canada sold their share of the commonly owned land to New York in order to finance their emigration from New York. Earlier treaties acknowledged that the remaining land was owned collectively by those Oneidas who stayed, and so did the 1842 agreements. However, a schedule appended to the treaty with the western group stated that each tract was now owned in severalty by an Oneida family.[1] The following year, the state declared the action legal under its own laws through legislation authorizing Oneidas to own land in severalty. To many, it seemed New York had thus established the private ownership of Oneida land (see chapter 8).

As of 1850, two groups of Oneidas totaling about 160 people stubbornly maintained themselves in the ancient homeland (Schoolcraft 1975, 191). The eastern community, called the Orchard (and later Marble Hill), contained some 65 acres in Oneida County. Soon to be known as the Windfall, the western community in Madison County comprised about 750 acres.

Their plight moved one visitor to remark that the Oneidas "are as aliens in the land of their fathers" (Strong 1857, 506). As a people, another observed, they feel "they are wasting away . . . being broken, scattered and dispirited" (P. Jones 1851, 864).

Romancing the Stone

The Oneida Stone at the center of Utica's festivities in 1850 was an important Oneida symbol, though we know little about beliefs connected with it. The few sources conveying something of what may be an authentic Oneida viewpoint are as follows.

As noted earlier, the first European account of the Oneidas in 1634–35 indicates that the name of the tribe (People of the Standing Stone) also designated the Oneidas' settlement (Gehring and Starna 1988, 14, 44). In about 1668, Jacques Bruyas, the Jesuit missionary residing in the Oneida village, gave his address as the village of Oneida, "Nation of the Stone" (Thwaites 1896–1901, 52:145). On a document recording an agreement with France in 1700, the signature of the Oneida Nation is represented by a drawing of a stone (Fenton 1998, 345).

An anonymous French document of 1736 states the Oneida village has "for a device a stone in a fork of a tree" (O'Callaghan 1849–51, 1:22).

---

1. In contrast, New York's treaty of June 25, 1842, with the eastern Oneida (Orchard) group contained no provisions mentioning private ownership. However, de facto allotment was achieved by confining the Oneidas there to a single lot (Treaties 1842).

Such a symbol seemingly combines the sacred stone with an allusion to the title by which Oneidas were traditionally addressed in league council: They of the Great Log or Big Tree (Fenton 1998, 62; Woodbury, Henry, and Webster 1992, 555). And when Oneidas on a war expedition in 1746 were asked to display their national symbol, they actually placed a red-painted rock in a tree (O'Callaghan 1849–51, 4:432).

Somewhere south of Oneida Castle in 1796, travelers Jeremy Belknap and Jedidiah Morse encountered an Oneida stone in front of the home of "an old man named Silversmith, aged about eighty" (Belknap 1882, 21). Silversmith's ideas about the rock were said to be these sentiments:

> Some of them address their devotions to the wind—others to the clouds and thunder—he to the rocks and mountains, which he believed to have an invisible, as well as visible existence, and an agency over human actions. To this kind of superintending power he had always trusted for his success in hunting and in war, and generally obtained his desire. He had either killed or taken captive his enemy, and had been fortunate in the chase.
>
> He regarded the ONEIDA STONE as a proper emblem or representation of the divinity which he worshiped. . . . The tradition is, that it follows the nation in their removals. From it the name of the nation is derived, for Oneida signifies "the upright stone." When it was set up in the crotch of a tree the nation was supposed invincible. (Belknap and Morse 1955, 9–10)

Several years later, Timothy Dwight observed a stone east of Oneida "which some of these people regard with religious reverence, and speak of it as their god. They say it has slowly followed their nation in their various removals" (1822, 215).

Evidently, then, the Oneidas regarded the stone from which they took their name as sacred. Emblematic of national existence, the stone was believed to affect the outcome of their wars and to follow them in their village removals. Each principal village may have had a stone because more than one was described (Beauchamp 1922, 157). The stone examined by Belknap and Morse in 1796, for example, was not on the summit of Primes Hill and could not have been the one removed to Utica in 1849.

Far more information about the Oneida Stone is inauthentic or, at least, derives from perspectives that are obviously non-Indian. By the time

Schoolcraft visited Primes Hill in 1845, that locale had already become a lodestone for white folklore about the Indians. The hilltop was said to be an ancient burial ground for metal-using giants and the scene of a monumental battle with invading Hurons in which all the Indians, thousands of them, perished (Hammond 1872, 102–3, 736–37).

A local newspaper account a few years later repeated this anecdote but added new details about the stone's associations with warfare. The Indians supposedly prepared their tomahawks and war paint at the Oneida Stone; then, as they went off to battle, the rock floated through the air above them. Having been offended, however, the stone refused to fly and the tribe withered away *(Oneida Free Press,* June 12, 1880).

The version of William Tracy—the trustee who had declaimed so eloquently at the opening of the Utica cemetery—was published in 1872. According to Tracy, when the Oneidas moved to Primes Hill, the stone

> followed in the train of its children, and seeking one of the most commanding and beautiful points of vision upon the hill, deposited itself in a beautiful butternut grove, from beneath whose branches the eye could look out upon the whole distant landscape, the most lovely portion of the national domain. Here it remained to witness the remainder of its people's history. It saw the Five Nations increase in power and importance until their name struck terror from the St. Lawrence to the Gulf of Mexico, and from the Hudson to the Father of Waters. Around this unhewn altar within its leafy temple, was gathered all the wisdom of the nation, when measures affecting its welfare were to be considered. There, eloquence as effective and beautiful as ever fell from Greek or Roman lip, was poured forth in the ear of its sons and daughters. . . . [T]here the sacred rites were celebrated at the return of each harvest moon and each new year, when every son and daughter of the Stone came up like the Jewish tribes of old, to join in the national festivities. This was the resting place of the Stone when the first news came that the pale face, wiser than the red children of the Great Spirit, had come from beyond the great water. It remained to see him, after the lapse of many years, penetrate the forest and come among its children a stranger; to see him welcomed by them to a home; to see them shrink and wither before his breath until the white man's sons and daughters occupied their abodes and ploughed the fields beneath whose forest covering, the bones of their fathers were laid. At length the council-fire of the Oneidas was extinguished. The Stone no

longer reeked with the blood of a sacrificial victim; its people were scattered, and there was no new resting place for them, to which it might betake itself and again become their altar. It was a stranger in the ancient home of its children, an exile upon its own soil. (1872, 38–39)

Evoking the image of Athenian statesmen in flowing togas, the history of the stone was thus classicized and sensationalized with the stench of sacrificial blood. Although most of Tracy's description is apparently fanciful, this version of the Oneida Stone was widely quoted and quickly became the definitive account (Canfield 1902, 195–98; Hueguenin 1956). It takes us so far from what we know of the Oneidas' tradition that it is really a new story. In effect, it is the white man's legend of the Oneida Stone.

An important point of the new legend is that the arrival of whites initiated inevitable decline. When the Indians faded away, the stone no longer served its original people and so no longer belonged in its old home.

These sentiments reflected the intellectual climate of about 1850 when it was widely believed the Indians were doomed to extinction in the face of approaching American civilization (Berkhofer 1978, 88–93; Ekirch 1951, 38–71; Horsman 1981, 189–207). President Andrew Jackson enunciated the view in 1830 to justify the forceful removal of Indian tribes out of the way of white Americans.

Humanity has often wept over the fate of the aborigines of this country, and Philanthropy has been long busily employed in devising means to avert it, but its progress has never for a moment been arrested, and one by one have many powerful tribes disappeared from the earth. To follow to the tomb the last of his race and to tread on the graves of extinct nations excite melancholy reflections. But true philanthropy reconciles the mind to these vicissitudes as it does to the extinction of one generation to make room for another. (Pearce 1965, 57)

And current events seemed to testify to the inexorability of American expansion. Under the banner of Manifest Destiny, Americans annexed Texas and acquired Oregon. After defeating Mexico in war, Americans obtained an even vaster new territory, then instantly peopled the far Pacific shore with a horde of gold prospectors.

The idea that Indians had to give way to American progress was a conviction Schoolcraft himself expressed as he surveyed the view from the Oneida Stone atop Primes Hill (see ill. 1):

> No person can stand on this height, and survey the wide prospect of cultivation and the elements of high agricultural and moral civilization, which it now presents . . . without calling to mind that once proud and indomitable race of hunters and warriors, whose name the country bears. . . . [But] the aboriginal state of the Oneida prosperity and power has passed away. Their independence, their pride, their warfare, the objects of their highest ambition and fondest hope, were mistaken, and were destined to fall before the footsteps of civilization. (1851–57, 138)

Schoolcraft's sad nostalgia echoed the literature of the day in which Indians were often depicted by means of the "Last of the Mohicans" motif, "in which no white person is present to witness the tragic but inevitable demise of a doomed people" (Kammen 1991, 87). The convention derived its name, of course, from Cooper's book of that title (published 1826), set in upstate New York near Utica.

This literary trend crested in 1855 with the publication of Longfellow's *Hiawatha*, based, as noted, on Indian folklore collected by Schoolcraft. *Hiawatha* spoke to a fundamental psychological dilemma—what to do about the doomed Indians? Longfellow's work

> salvaged the memories of a race fated to vanish from this land. Consequently, reading the epic and regarding it as part of American tradition seemed the next best thing to saving the Indian. Knowing and loving *Hiawatha* meant knowing the noble savage and perpetuating his traditions. Embarrassment (even shame) could be supplanted by vicarious pride via epic enchantment set in a remote and unknown place. (Kammen 1991, 85)

So just as white Americans appropriated Indian tradition to their own sense of heritage, Uticans, in 1850, employed the Oneida Stone toward the same end. Prominently displayed in the city's necropolis, the stone played a role in defining the newcomers' sense of community with a past substantially older and more interesting than the Erie Canal. The Oneida Stone provided a bridge connecting the natives' long-ago and far-away to

3. *The Oneida Stone in the Utica cemetery as imagined by Schoolcraft's lithographer (Schoolcraft 1855, Plate 24); photo courtesy of Hamilton College Library.*

the Uticans' here-and-now. Through the legend developed by Tracy and others, the stone could be appreciated as Kammen argued of *Hiawatha* (see ill. 3).

Yet this perspective could never be altogether satisfying as long as Oneidas still lived here, their very presence rebutting the idea they were gone and raising potentially awkward issues about possession. How could Uticans regard themselves as rightful owners of the Indian emblem if they had simply taken it from the Oneidas? Pearce has argued that American literature of these years attempted to expiate the sin of Indian destruction by making sense of Indians' deaths through symbolic means (1965). Considered from this vantage, the white man's myth fell short of symbolically mastering the Oneida Stone without embarrassment or guilt.

Mythic shortcomings, however, can be resolved through mythic means. As it happened, the same pamphlet that offered Tracy's fully developed stone legend also stated that the Indians consented to having the stone removed to Utica (Forest Hill 1872, 19–20). With further tweaking, Indian permission became part of the basic Oneida Stone story: Indians in Wisconsin had implored the city of Utica to take care of their stone for them (Canfield 1902, 198–99).

In sum, the Oneida tribal symbol, placed prominently within a new nonnative cemetery, visibly connected Utica to a local native past. What was known of the stone was elaborated and romanticized to the extent that it became a new Oneida Stone legend. Asserting the Indians had had their day but were now gone, the myth conformed with popular thinking justifying expansion at Indian expense and appropriation of the stone. Because surviving but distant Indians had requested it, people of Utica were the appropriate custodians of the stone and the stone's past.

The stone seemed to inspire figurative embellishment, expressing the national mood in a locally resonant manner. I do not think Tracy and originators of the legend were lying. More likely, they thought they were conveying authentic Oneida tradition cast into the appropriate literary wrapping of the period. And even though the new narrative of the stone came out of a literate, nonnative setting, it fired the mythic imagination of Uticans and was enthusiastically, perhaps subconsciously, accepted as expressing things as they should be.

This explanation, it seems to me, is a vivid example of how a genre of oral narrative can work to interpret the past. Originating in specific acts of individuals, a legend of this sort expresses common sentiment. Figuratively and mythopoetically, it makes the present feel comfortable as the fitting outcome of history's story. It helps us define ourselves and to make sense of our time and place.

Conversely, when Oneidas were separated from the Oneida Stone, *their* stories about the national emblem became diverse and discrepant. Franz Boas, for example, recorded a Wisconsin Oneida text explaining how the stone was created from a woman who, like Lot's wife, looked behind and became petrified (1909, 459–60).[2] According to a Canadian Oneida in 1912, the stone would appear only when the Oneidas were united, obedient to tradition, and amenable to the teachings of Seneca prophet Handsome Lake (see p. 72). On such occasions, the rock issued

---

2. Boas does not credit the source of this story. Floyd Lounsbury thought Boas obtained it in Wisconsin (personal communication).

instructions in the form of carvings visible on its surface (Waugh n.d., J. Schuyler 200 f 17:13).[3] And in New York, Oneida William Rockwell claimed:

> Yoo noo yood dae, Immovable Rock. Symbol of the Unchangeable Principles of Nature's Providence to the Human Being. . . . [It] means a large single boulder setting deep into the solid earth. A portion of it projecting conspicuously out of the supporting soil, [out] of which grows all of the necessary food for every human life and all of the life in the animal kingdom. This great outstanding constitution boulder is a symbol of faithfulness of my people to all of our Creator's plans to be the only solution to be followed for the salvation of all humanity, if their faith is continued as unchangeable as the great boulder's position, the faith of such people shall be rewarded with a life that shall last forever. (n.d., bI c2 f 3, bII c3 f 11)

Oneidas yearned for the stone but seemed to remember little of earlier traditions. Without the symbol, Oneida oral narrative about the object became garbled, as though the Oneidas had lost the national right to relate to their emblem.

---

3. Citing Waugh's unpublished papers (n.d.), I reference the informant (J. Schuyler), the box (200), the folder (f 17), and, when appropriate, the page (13). When the informant's name is unknown to me, I provide the story title ("Ooksayik" in chapter 6).

2

Where the Earth Opened

"This story was told me by Anna," wrote Hope Emily Allen, "a day or so before December 19, 1925, when I wrote it down as nearly as possible in her words (some of them I can still hear her say)" (1948a, A). Allen, a non-Indian person collecting Oneida folklore, had just recorded one of the longest and most important works she was able to document. Unfortunately, it was also the last story she ever obtained.[1]

"DA-DO-GA-LÁ-SAS: WHERE THE EARTH OPENS"

Once there was a little boy who lived alone with his grandmother in a little house. He was very, very little. In fact, he never grew. He was what the Oneida Indians call a Gig-no-[(H1F)]dá-le (Lydia says Go-ne-gwa-no-da-le) and, because of him, Indians often give very small people this name. Every day his grandmother had to go out and leave the little boy alone in the house all day and, when she left, she always told him that he must never go out while she was gone. He must always stay in and play with a wonderful bow and arrow that he had.

Every day the little boy tried to play with his bow and arrow,

---

1. *Da-do-ga-lá-sas* is the first of three Oneida words given in the text. All are unknown to the Oneida speakers and linguists I consulted. Possibly *Da-do-ga-lá-sas* (Place where the earth opens) is related to the name of the cannibal villain in a similar hero tale collected by Jeremiah Curtin among the Senecas during the 1880s. J. N. B. Hewitt gives the name as *Deadoeñdjadases,* "the Earth-Girdler" (1918, 135). Curtin has the name (for the same character in the same story) as *Dadyoeⁿdzadáses,* "one name for Wolf, he who travels around the world" (2001, 160). *Gig-no-dá-le* or *Go-ne-gwa-no-da-le* (tiny person) is unfamiliar to me anywhere in Iroquois folklore. *Gwa-gwa* (the name of the bird whose feathers were used to fletch the boy's magic arrow) might be *gwe'gwe',* the pileated woodpecker referenced in the text.

and once he had a great time shooting bedbugs. Finally his precious arrow stuck in a bedbug without killing it, and the bedbug crawled through a knothole and got outdoors. The little boy was very upset, he couldn't bear to lose his arrow, and after a while he worried over it so much that he simply had to crawl out after it through the knothole. He was so very tiny that he could do this.

He loved it when he got outdoors. He had never been out-of-doors before and, strange to say, when he went back in, he had grown. When his grandmother came back home that night, she knew at once that he had been out, and she was very upset, and spoke to him about it very seriously. "You must never go out again," she said but she didn't tell him why. He tried to deny what he had done, but it was no use. She knew that he had been out because he had grown.

He liked it outside so well that he didn't pay any attention to what his grandmother said. And again, the next day he went out, and again he grew, and again his grandmother came home and knew where he had been, because he had grown, so that she didn't believe him when he tried to deceive her. And on that third day before she went out herself in the morning, she told him the whole story.

There was a rich man who used to come from another village and kill all the people, and that was why it wasn't safe for the little boy to go out. There were a few houses left in the village where the little boy and his grandmother lived, but mostly they were all empty except the one where they lived and one other. So every day when the old grandmother went out, she told the little boy that he mustn't stir out of doors, for it wasn't safe, on account of the rich man who had killed all their neighbors except one.

"You see if you go out the rich man will eat you," the grandmother said. "It isn't safe for you at all."

"I want to go outdoors again and I'll find the rich man and kill him," said the boy.

"You?" said the grandmother. "What could you do? Why, he would finish you in one bite you are so little."

This day when the grandmother had gone, the boy went out for the third time through the knothole. And now he knew more and so he thought he would explore a little, for the other times he had only kept around his own house. Now he looked further and he found several houses left standing but they were all empty, for the rich man had killed all the people who had lived in them. But he went in another house and there he found a woman, but she had been half eaten by the rich man and her limbs were all torn. When she saw him she told him to run home at once, for the rich man was coming that day and it was almost time for him to come.

"Hurry," she said, "I can hear his wings now."

But the boy said he wouldn't go. He wanted to see the rich man and he would kill him.

"You kill him?" said the woman. "Why, you wouldn't make more than a bite for him you're so little."

"No matter," said the boy, "I am going to kill him."

"Then hide," said the woman, "for he is almost here. I can hear his wings."

Then the little boy hid in the fireplace in the center of the house, and when the rich man came he didn't come in but sat up on the roof, and called down the hole where the smoke came out. "I know you are there," he called down, "and I'm coming down to eat you."

But the boy answered not a word and kept as still as he could, but he got his bow and arrow ready and aimed. And when the rich man-eater started down the hole the boy shot his arrow, and it struck in the chest and stuck there. Then it commenced to sing, just like the bird whose feathers it was feathered with. This bird doesn't live around here, and the Indian name is Gwa-gwa and Anna says that if she could hear Mrs. Allen's washing machine go she could think of the sound it makes.

When the rich man was struck, he gave no sound, but he started right up and away from there. The boy went out to see in what direction he flew, and he marked it. Then he went back in the house and he spit on his hands (it sounds nasty) and rubbed on the woman, and it healed her, and she got right up as whole as she ever was.

Then the boy went home, but now he had been out so long that he had grown so much that he couldn't get in through the knothole, and he had to wait until his grandmother came home to let him in by the door.

When she came home she asked him where he had been, and he told her and he said he would have to go after his arrow, for it was the only one he had. And the next morning he started out after it, in the direction where he had seen the rich man flying off with the arrow in his chest.

He went on for three days, and then he came in sight of another village, and as he came in he met a boy as little as he had been, and he found that this boy too lived with a grandmother alone in a little house, and she was also away half the time, but in this case it was the night, and when she went she always told the boy never to go out. This boy asked the other to go home with him, and he did so, and stayed some days. And after a time, the two boys talked together, and the one who had come asked the other one where his grandmother went, but that boy didn't know.

"Find out where she goes," said the first boy, "but don't let her know who asked you."

Soon the other asked his grandmother one morning when she came in and she said she went every night to a rich man among them who was dying because he had an arrow in his chest, and all their witches were there, but none could get it out.

The boy who was visiting heard this, and he spoke up and said that he was a witch and could help. The grandmother said they would try him, for none of them could get the arrow out. The boy said that, if they did, they must do it just as he said in every way. The grandmother promised this and they went at once over to where the rich man lay sick.

Now the boy who owned the arrow was the only one who could pull it out. He told the grandmother that if he was to do this they must make the place as dark as possible and everyone must make all the noise they could, and she must be at the door to let him in. And she promised that it should be so.

So when they reached the rich man's house, there was such a noise that no one heard that, as soon as the boy appeared who owned the arrow, the arrow began to sing like the bird with whose feathers it had been feathered. When the grandmother let the boy in, everything was in total darkness, and there was a terrible noise, and the boy went straight up to the rich man and took hold of the singing arrow, but he did not pull it out. He thrust it in, and the noise was so great, no one heard the dying scream of the rich man, and he ran out before anyone knew what had happened.

Still the noise went on in the darkness, and the boy had gone a long way, before the people began to wonder whether the arrow had been taken out, and when they looked, it had been thrust in and the rich man was dead. Then they were very angry, and they called up to the woman who sat on the roof of the house. Now this woman had only one eye, but with it she could see farther than any other person could with two. She had wonderful eyesight.

They asked her if she had seen anyone leave the house and she said, "No." And then they asked her if she could see anyone going away from there far off and she said, "Yes." She could just see a black object moving and, if they wanted to catch it, they'd have to hurry. And so they all started.

They all followed, and they gained on him, but he knew he had one chance. Now there is in this world of ours a place where the earth opens and closes back, and if you can get there when it is closed, you can just step across, but in a few minutes it begins to open again, and then there is a great hole. (Lydia says this place is called Do-do-ga-lá-sas.) And the boy got there just as it was closing and he just got across, and before it began to open. And when the people from the other reservation got there it was open and they couldn't cross. So the boy got home.

When he got there, he went to the woman he had healed and asked her where the other people all were. She asked him if he didn't see bones lying around under the trees and outside the empty houses. And then he said to her, "Come out quick and help pick them up before the night catches us." And they picked up all the bones and heaped them under a tree.

Then he commenced kicking the tree. "Match yourselves up and jump up quick!" he cried to the bones. "The tree's going to fall on you." And they matched themselves and the tree fell and they all jumped up as well persons.

Hope Allen and the Secret Life of Oneidas

I described, in the previous chapter, the low state to which the Oneidas had been reduced by 1850. Two Oneida groups totaling about 160 people hung on precariously in the ancient homeland. The western community, known as the Windfall during the second half of the nineteenth century, started out with about 750 acres situated two and one-half miles south of the city of Oneida. The eastern community, the Orchard, consisted of some 65 acres just east of what would become the city of Sherrill later in the century (see ills. 4 and 5)

4. *Oneidas outside the Orchard church, 1892; photo courtesy of Madison County Historical Society, Oneida, N.Y.*

After Henry Schoolcraft expressed regret for the Oneidas' inevitable doom in the face of advancing civilization (see p. 28), he added: "Even they themselves [the Oneidas] have submitted to the truths of a higher and better ambition. . . . The remnant who linger in their beloved valley, have almost entirely conformed to the high state of industry and morals around them. Their only ambition now is the school, the church, the farm, and the workshop" (1851–57, 138).

Schoolcraft's faith in the assimilated state of the Oneidas was echoed repeatedly in subsequent years. Seeing how these Indians resembled their neighbors in dress and hous-ing, most observers concluded the Oneidas had lost their traditions and constituted no meaningful community (see "The Last of the Oneidas," *Utica Weekly Herald,* May 8, 1875; and Whipple et al. 1889, 1:46, 76).

That opinion was shared by Hope Emily Allen (1883–1960), who grew up in the community of Kenwood, just south of Sherrill (see ill. 6). A

5. *The Orchard church.*

6. *Hope Emily Allen,*
circa 1940s; photo courtesy
of Dink Allen.

distinguished medievalist, Allen's scholarly research centered on Middle English religious manuscripts, especially the works of such mystics as Margery Kempe and Richard Rolle (Hirsh 1988). She was the child of a couple who had belonged to the Oneida Community, a utopian and non-native fellowship of Christian communists active in Kenwood from 1848 to 1881 (Klaw 1993; Robertson 1970). Having grown up in the Oneida Community's "Mansion House," an enormous brick building complex located between the two Oneida settlements (see ill. 7), Hope Allen's face-to-face contacts with Oneidas were frequent, but of a sort peculiar to this time and place.

A number of Oneida women, especially from the Orchard, worked as domestics in the homes of Kenwood and Sherrill. Thus, Allen's primary informants, Anna Johnson and Lydia Doxtater, also were her cleaning ladies. Allen had known these women and their families all her life. Anna Johnson's mother built a wheeled basket to serve as infant Hope Allen's

7. *The Oneida Community Mansion House.*

baby carriage, and Lydia Doxtater's mother worked as the household maid during Hope's childhood (Allen 1948a, E, G).

Now an independent scholar in her forties, Allen again found herself living in the Mansion House. Cut off from European archives by World War I, she began to interest herself in local Indian lore. Allen's biographer suggests she felt an affinity for the Oneidas as people—like herself—who stood outside the American mainstream. In this view, Allen shared with Oneidas "a concern with values that humanize and do not dominate, that inform rather than rule" (Hirsh 1989, 52).

Allen said she began her Oneida folklore studies in 1916. If so, she made little progress until several life crises dramatically altered the chemistry between her and her Oneida informants.

Anna Johnson (1885–1966) was born in the western Oneida neighborhood, the Windfall. At the death of her father in about 1898, her mother "was obliged to send her six girls to the Thomas Indian School [a

8. *Anna Johnson at the Thomas Indian School, 1905; photo courtesy of Irma Altman.*

state institution, originally an orphanage] at Gowanda, New York on the Seneca Reservation where they stayed until the older ones were able to work and care for the younger. They forgot how to speak their own language" (see ill. 8) (Allen 1948b, 11). When Anna was able to return to Oneida, she stayed with her father's half sister, Lydia Doxtater, at the Orchard. There she met and married Josiah "Si" Johnson about 1908. The Johnson couple took up residence in a house of the Orchard very close to Lydia Doxtater's place (Allen 1948a, E).

In 1918, Anna Johnson (in her early thirties) nearly died from a severe illness that left her lame for the rest of her life (see ill. 9). Allen frequently visited Anna's home to help her. Only then did Anna begin to tell Indian stories she got from Si. Si, who would not speak directly to Allen about folklore, said he had heard the stories from his father, Baptist Johnson—an ardent Methodist lay preacher (G).

About the same time, sixty-year-old Lydia Doxtater was devastated by

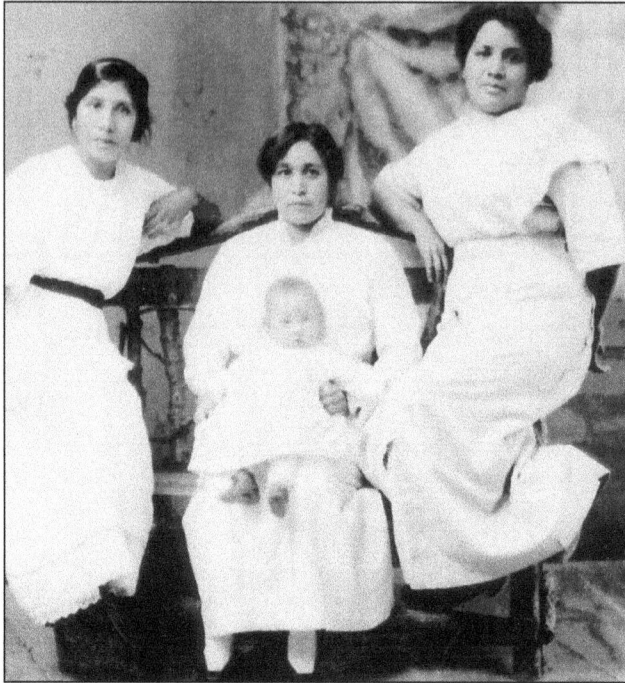

9. Anna Johnson (right) and her sisters, circa 1913; photo courtesy of Irma Altman.

the loss of her mother (see ill. 10). Allen thought the tragedy left Lydia feeling "very lonely and thinking back to old stories helped to interest her" (H). Certainly, that passing freed Lydia from a restraint imposed by her mother—never tell Indian stories to white people (G, H). When Allen herself contracted a serious illness (measles with sore eyes), it was Lydia, then Allen's domestic help, who came to her aid. That period was when Lydia began to tell Oneida stories (see ill. 11).

Suddenly, for Allen, the earth opened as she was introduced to a world of Oneida folklore she never suspected existed. Glimpsing a side of the Oneidas normally hidden from white eyes, Allen wrote of it with wonderment:

I had known Oneida Indians intimately from my earliest recollection but until this time did not dream they remembered anything of their old sto-

10. *Lydia Doxtater, possibly early 1920s; photo courtesy of Irma Altman.*

ries. . . . Nothing could have been more cordial than our relations with the Indians or more generous and courteous than their relations with us their white friends. But to this day friends whose families like mine had special Indian connections are astonished to hear that "our Indians" knew any stories. This was one thing the Oneidas who had lived so closely with white people . . . did not share. . . . In looking back I wonder if I could not have collected more stories if I had had faith that the stories were there. I begin to think that all my old friends remembered more than their shyness and dignity allowed them to venture to admit. (H)

Allen repeatedly emphasized that she had been accorded a privilege never previously extended to a local non-Indian person. "In spite of many most friendly relations between Oneidas and white neighbors," she wrote, "I doubt if stories were ever given by the Indians to those to whom they were so generous with material things" (I).

Over the next several years, Allen would take a text obtained from one

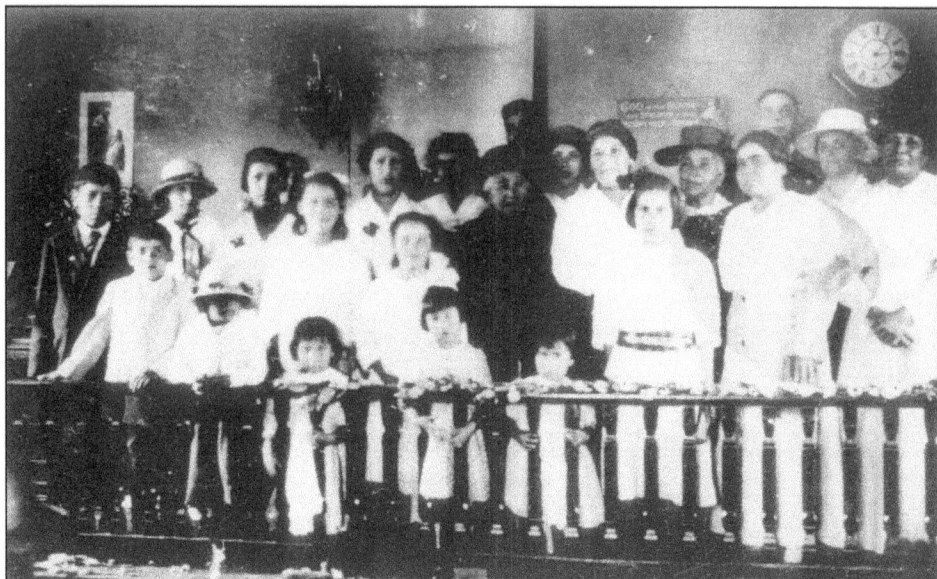

11. Oneidas inside the Orchard church, probably early 1920s; photo courtesy of Oneida Community Mansion House, Oneida, N.Y. According to a penciled notation, this photograph shows Hope Allen (probably wearing a white hat beneath the clock on the right) and Lydia Doxtater (presumably center right, her head covering the bottom left corner of a religious sign).

informant to review with another. Accordingly, after hearing "Where the Earth Opens" in December, Allen carried the story to Lydia Doxtater's on New Year's Day, 1926 (see map 3). With Lydia was "another very old-fashioned Oneida woman," Luisa Day Johns, who "never before had admitted to me that she knew anything of such things. . . . Lydia and Luisa approved the story as I read it to them" (A).

Lydia was in bed that day feeling out of sorts—the beginning of a terminal illness that would kill her within several weeks. Soon after (also 1926), Si Johnson passed away. The death of these two Oneidas effectively ended Hope Allen's folklore project.

Iroquois Folklore

Allen had discovered that folklore, like the Oneida language, was invisible to the Oneidas' neighbors. "My people were great story tellers," William

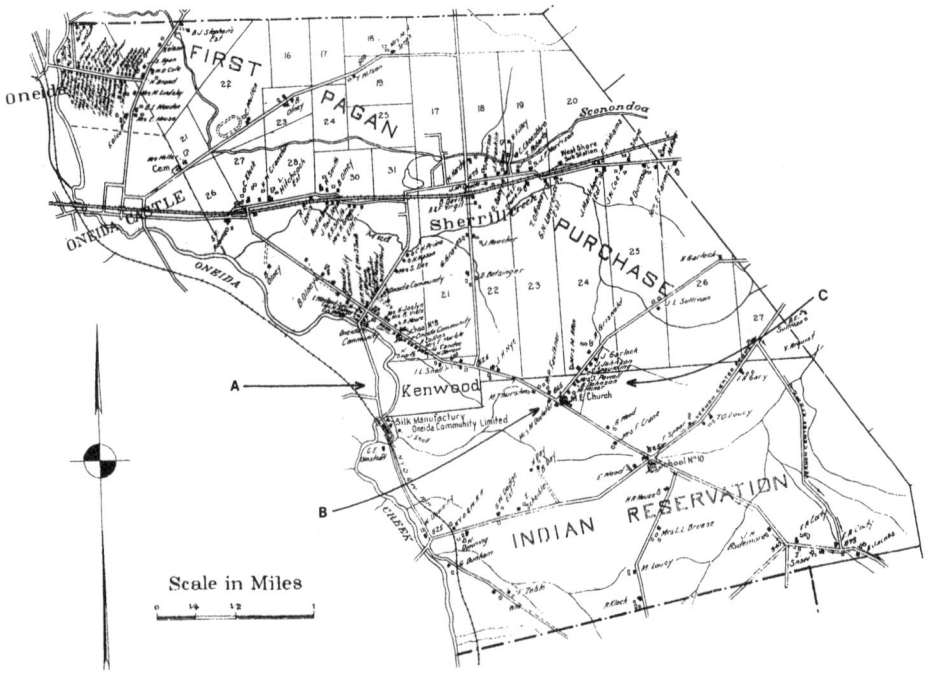

Map 3. Kenwood and the Orchard, 1907 (Century 1907, 77). (a) Location of Hope Allen's residence, the Oneida Community Mansion House; (b) Lydia Doxtater's house; (c) Anna Johnson's house.

Rockwell observed (n.d., bI c2 f1). Si Johnson, it turned out, was an electrifying storyteller capable of scaring the pants off his listeners (Allen 1948a, G). Anna Johnson suddenly remembered that her grandmother had been

> a great story-teller in her remote childhood. . . . The grandmother used to come over to call winter evenings carrying a lantern which had a patch of flour sacking that fell off as the glass became hot. Anna would "earn" stories by finding this patch, or filling her grandmother's pipe. Similarly, Mrs. Powlis told me . . . when she was young her first husband's mother used to tell a great many stories in the evening when she and her husband used to bind the old lady's baskets, for the sake of her stories. (B)

Lydia Doxtater (1859–1926) admitted she used to swap stories with Canadian Indians while selling baskets at Saratoga in the summer, then "compared notes with cousins 'up at Onondaga' " (Allen 1944, 280). And except when whites were in attendance, Lydia indicated the Oneidas were always telling stories. "The men used to spend the evenings story-telling and smoking and laughing in the winter—they specially were the story tellers. . . . When they went calling they told them. If a new person came into a neighborhood everyone was interested in his stories" (280–81).

> Hop-pickers then used to come down from Onondaga every year and while here used to tell stories tremendously with the local Oneidas. Some stories . . . concerned incidents which they said happened only a few years ago. . . . In general of course, the summer was not the season for Indian stories. . . . Oneidas did not tell stories "when the leaves were on the trees, for fear the snakes would hear them." Yet . . . modern Indians may disregard this tradition when opportunity offers a good audience for stories. (Allen 1948a, J)

Among themselves, then, the Oneidas were avid storytellers. Clearly, their folklore was a vigorous cultural expression binding the two Oneida settlements in common experience and linking them to Indians elsewhere. But one has to wonder about the content. Could there have been anything culturally Iroquois or even native in stories told by people who had been missionized for 250 years and colonized for 130?

The question is answerable with reference to a substantial body of folklore recorded throughout Iroquoia at approximately the same time. The years between about 1880 and 1925 were a sort of golden age for documenting such stories. William Beauchamp (1922), Elias Johnson (1881), Arthur Parker (1989), and Erminnie Smith (1983) published reasonably serious compilations of folktales. More substantial collections, taken at least partly in the native languages, were assembled by Jeremiah Curtin (2001), J. N. B. Hewitt (1918), and Frederick Waugh (n.d.; Randle 1953).[2] Very similar (and presumably closely related) Huron and Wyandot folklore was made available at the same time by other researchers

2. Material collected by Curtin is published both in Hewitt (1918, 75–492) and in the book posthumously attributed to Curtin (2001). Overlap in the two works is considerable and confusing. About two-thirds of the Curtin pieces in Hewitt also occur in the Curtin book. Conversely, about four-fifths of the stories in Curtin can be identified in some form within the pages of Hewitt.

(see Barbeau 1915; Connelley 1899; and Hale 1888, 1889). Hence, determining what was culturally Iroquois requires evaluating the Oneida story against this larger backdrop.

Viewed in this comparative context, Anna Johnson's story contains hardly anything not present in contemporaneous Iroquois material. The only anomaly I can identify is the one-eyed woman on the roof. Although she performs a traditionally Iroquois role as sentinel, her cyclopean aspect is an innovation possibly borrowed from the native folklore of New England (Simmons 1986, 209–10) or the Old World (see Zipes 2001, 461).

There are, to be sure, features of the story that occur infrequently in Iroquois folklore of the time. For example, the arrow emitting the noise of the bird whose feathers are attached is a somewhat unusual detail but one that is mentioned elsewhere (Curtin 2001, 309; Parker 1989, 101). The bird most frequently linked to arrow fletching is the pileated woodpecker, called *gwe' gwe'* by the Iroquois of the Six Nations Reserve in Canada (Waugh n.d., D. Jack 201 f24, T. Smoke 201 f27).

Or again, restoring to health a half-eaten person awaiting a cannibal's return seems an odd touch. Yet this incident can also be found elsewhere (ibid., P. John 201 f6), and it illustrates an important belief: a magician's saliva is a potent regenerating substance (Parker 1989, 30). The chasm where the earth opens is an uncommon example of the Iroquois "revolving door" or symplegades motif (Thompson 1929, 275–76, motif D931.3), but it, too, is present in the Iroquois lore of the age (see Curtin 2001, 373; and Parker 1989, 129–31).

The story's most strikingly original feature resides in its vision of twin villages—in effect, a suggestion of parallel, double, or perhaps inverted worlds. Whereas Iroquois tales frequently duplicate the hero as a double personality, a soul self, an alter ego, or an identical twin (Randle 1952, 21; 1953, 616), they rarely posit doppelgänger worlds.[3] The exceptions are

---

Canfield (1902), Converse (1908), and Powers (1923) also published books purporting to be on Iroquois folklore. Their narratives seem to me fanciful or so thoroughly reworked as to be worthless for comparative purposes. Similarly, Parker's *Skunny Wundy* (1994), a children's book of "Seneca Indian tales," is very much a consciously crafted literary work requiring caution as a source for oral narrative.

3. If one looks beyond the context of folklore, of course, the sky land described in the myth of creation would be another type of world parallel to our own.

interesting. In one instance reminiscent of the Book of Revelation, villagers whose town disappears in a world-ending cataclysm are whisked into the sky to inhabit a town identical to the one destroyed (Curtin 2001, 286–87). In a second, involving identical lodges and people on two planes, Parker was moved to remark that the concept seemed unique (1989, 170). These two examples aside, "Where the Earth Opens" develops the notion of a second world with greater clarity than almost any other Iroquois tale of the era.

Otherwise, "Where the Earth Opens" is typically Iroquois in its actors, in its incidents or motifs, and in the way those elements were assembled. Its plot is an example of a classic Iroquois story type in which a hero's magic power is pitted against the strength of wizards or witches (Randle 1953, 615).

"The most typical and frequent hero is a little boy, possessed of miraculous power" (1952, 13). He lives alone with an older (usually elderly) relative. The undersized boy is his generation's sole survivor, everyone else having been done away with by the villain. He is confined indoors for fear that he too will fall victim, but, in the end, the boy overcomes the enemy and restores his relatives to life.

This boy is adept with bow and arrow, having practiced on insect targets. His magic arrow is of the sort beloved by Iroquois storytellers—it never misses, and only its owner can extract it from the target. Commonly, the youth finds an alter ego. Generally, he must contend with the villain's early warning system, a sentinel (typically a flayed skin or an owl) placed on a high vantage point. In the end, the boy finds a pile of bones belonging to his deceased relatives and restores the skeletons to life by shouting, "Rise up, a tree is falling on you!" (Parker 1989, 27; Randle 1953, 615–16).

I cannot be certain the story is particularly old, although some details and incidents certainly are. The description of the central fire under the hole in the roof, for example, is suggestive of age (see sidebar, pp. 53–54). The incident in which the villain, wounded by an arrow, is approached for the kill by someone posing as a healer was present in Iroquois lore two centuries earlier (Fenton and Moore 1974, 248).[4]

---

4. I have not found the incident of the posturing healer in contemporaneous Iroquois folklore. However, it is common in Western Algonquian stories of the Great Lakes region where it possesses "remarkable stability of detail" (Fisher 1946, 231; cf. Chamberlain 1891,

Whatever its age, this distinctively Iroquois hero tale is said by Randle to dominate the Waugh Collection. I find it to be common among the Hewitt materials (1918, stories 21, 73, 75, 109–11, 116–17) and present in the compilations by William Beauchamp (1922, 19–30), Arthur Parker (1989, 200–204), and Erminnie Smith (1983, 13–16, 64–69).[5] In 1925, therefore, Oneidas were telling a story as culturally Iroquois as anything then being told anywhere.

A Need for Secrecy

Why did Oneidas feel they had to hide their folklore? Recall that by 1850, New York had induced them to accept private ownership of small tracts surrounded by non-Indian neighbors, an action anticipating a similar federal policy (one that had no effect on New York) by some forty years. The U.S. government's General Allotment, or Dawes, Act of 1887 aimed to compel assimilation by transforming Indians into private landowners.

Theodore Roosevelt called the Dawes Act "a mighty pulverizing engine for breaking up the tribal mass"—and it was (Prucha 1984, 671). Typically, individual Indians needing cash were encouraged to sign land-related documents for sale or, more commonly, for something more complicated—a lease or mortgage. Often the transactions were improperly supervised and the Indians received inadequate legal protection. As a result, native communities were devastated as their land melted away. In 1887, 138 million acres of the country were reckoned as Indian property. By 1934, Indian holdings had shrunk to 48 million acres (Prucha 1990, 225). Surveying these figures, Commissioner of Indian Affairs John Collier concluded, "It is difficult to imagine any other system which with equal effectiveness would pauperize the Indian while impoverishing him, and sicken and kill his soul while pauperizing him, and cast him in so ruined a condition" (Locklear 1988a, 85).

198, 202, 212; and Skinner 1919, 286). It is motif K1955, the sham doctor (Thompson 1929, 352–53).

5. Although Rand documented a similar story among the Micmac (Canadian Algonquian people bordering the Gulf of St. Lawrence), this tale surely is not characteristic of the Eastern Algonquian region as a whole, and I have not yet found it among other Native American folk (1894, 83–88).

The Dawes Act demonstrated on a national stage that allotment is the cheapest and easiest way to separate Indians from their land. Hence, when the state directed Oneidas into private landownership—and, moreover, into a checkerboard situation in which Oneida-owned tracts alternated with tracts owned by whites—the result was, at least in hindsight, predictable. By 1890, the 750 acres remaining to the Oneidas after the 1842 treaties had shrunk to about 350 acres (Carrington 1892, 25). In the course of a mortgage foreclosure twenty years later, the last Oneidas retaining a communally owned parcel in the western community were turned out of their homes. As Oneida William Rockwell, born on the Windfall in 1870, remembered:

> In 1909, my poor old helpless aunt Mary Schenandoah—on the day following after Thanksgiving she was carried out and dropped in the highway which is now Route 46. Mary Schenandoah was carried to the road five times because she managed to return to the house each time. She was picked up bodily and dropped so heavily into the roadway, she was not able to walk back to the house again that was her home. My uncle William Honyoust was treated in the same way. He kept returning to the house that was his home also. Seven burly sheriffs kept putting these two defenseless Indians out in the road until they were completely exhausted so they could not return to their home. The horse William Honyoust owned was turned out of the barn. Our furniture was thrown out to the road. Finally it was carted away into a lot by the woods by a white person. (n.d., bII c3 f11, bI c2 f4)

Land loss also occurred in the eastern settlement. Lydia Doxtater, it will be recalled, was terminally ill when Hope Allen consulted her about the story "Where the Earth Opens" on January 1, 1926. A week later, Lydia's will was rewritten by a local non-Indian minister and then, apparently, witnessed solely by that man and his wife. The minister's church was named as the beneficiary of Lydia's estate (Doxtater 1926).[6] Oneidas con-

6. Evidently, Doxtater's will was not contested directly or immediately. Obtaining legal representation the following year, Oneidas argued that, as Indian property, Doxtater's house could not be alienated out of tribal possession without consent of the federal government.

tested the property transfer but, in the end, had to accept the loss of Lydia's house to non-Indian owners.

One Oneida woman remembers living briefly in the Doxtater house when she was a child. When the court decision went against the Oneidas, this (today) elderly lady came home to find the house broken into and their furniture removed by the new owners. The young Oneida girl saw her toys—she still remembers a wicker doll carriage she loved—at a distance in the whites' possession. She was forbidden by her mother to say anything about it (Schwartz 1999).

These people felt they had to keep their heads down. Being inconspicuous, after all, is a time-tested survival strategy for the weak, one that goes far to explain why Oneidas were reticent to share their culture with whites.

Meanings

In her last conversation with Allen, Lydia Doxtater expressed an unusual concern. She insisted Allen understand the Indian significance of "Where the Earth Opens." As Allen put it:

> That day Lydia was slightly ailing (passing off her discomforts with her usual half-sarcastic laugh at herself, expressed in her softly grating pleasant Indian voice). In six weeks word came that she was dead and I am all the more glad for her general comment on Si's story, which I feel to be her deepest expression of faith in her Indian inheritance, something dignified and intelligent, which had inspired her desire to tell me to record for posterity, all of her people's stories and beliefs she could recall. "This story," she said, "shows how Nature and men and animals understood each other in the old days, according to the Indian idea—the earth opened, just to help the boy." (1948a, B)

"Where the Earth Opens" haunted Allen. More than twenty years later, she was still interviewing Oneidas about the meaning of the story. In 1946, she recorded:

> Last night I at last was able to read to Homer Johns the story of the boy shooting bedbugs etc. which I had from Si and Anna Johnson in Dec. 1925, [and] had verified by Lydia Doxtater and Luisa Day Johns New Years Day 1926. . . . Homer said that the story was as he remembered it.

. . . Then he gave some valuable information. He said "This is a story with a moral. It was told to children to teach them to stay at home and not run into dangers" (I had been thinking it was a tale primarily for grown-ups). . . . A valuable indication of the social use to which the Indians put story-telling is thus indicated. (C)

Oneidas, then, were inclined to stress the pedagogical uses of the narrative. Martha Champion Randle, on the other hand, believed this kind of story to be a psychological reflection of the storytellers. In the young hero who overcomes all enemies, she discerned "a typical wish-fulfillment fantasy, indicating a society where age brought power" (1952, 21).

I imagine the story reflects a different kind of wish. Consider how William Rockwell recalled his Oneida childhood:

Many of my people died with a broken heart. Pains of sorrow and grief took them to their graves. I was old enough to remember the kindly old men and women, how gently they would lay their hands on our heads, because they loved us so. And when they would turn away, their eyes were filled with tears. Some would cry with sympathy for us and future generations who were to lose the human freedom god gave the red-skinned children. The men also with a look of great concern would talk of the changes taking place. As they would look out over a great stretch, not a tree left standing. . . . Not only that, the land, as far as they could [see], was no longer theirs and ours. (n.d., bI c2 f 3)

The tiny boy-hero prevailing over all and restoring his diminished people must have been an appealing image to powerless folk yearning for a life in which Oneidas counted for something. We do not need to explain this story with reference to a bygone or speculative social structure.

A clue to the contemporaneous setting of "Where the Earth Opens" is given in the story's odd suggestion of twin villages or worlds. In the second, we learn for the first time where the boy's grandmother goes when she leaves the house. Knowing that the second grandmother has to attend the rich man at night, we now realize that the hero-boy's grandmother has to attend the rich man (or an inverted image of the rich man) during the day. Presumably, she is a domestic working in a Kenwood home. The story reflected, in other words, a very contemporary set of Oneida circumstances and longings expressed in a very traditional format. Oneida folklore preserved voices of the past, but it was the living who had the final word (Simmons 1986, 247).

▗▲▖

Embarking on a study of native lore, Hope Allen could draw on professional research skills and personal friendships of long duration. Even so, Oneidas opened up only after a series of life crises drew Allen and two Oneida women closer together. Allen documented Oneida traditions otherwise lost forever in what turned out to be a brief window of opportunity between 1918 and 1926.

The Oneidas lived a life through folklore kept hidden from white eyes. Uniting the two Oneida groups in common experience, folklore evidently was an important medium for expressing and maintaining ethnicity. Folklore also connected the Oneidas to Indians elsewhere, as demonstrated by the fact that "Where the Earth Opens" was typical of a pan-Iroquois repertoire distinctive to reservations of New York and Canada.

As collective and presumably unconscious projection, the story also provides up-to-date commentary on Oneida life, grounded in a specific time and place but phrased in the language of timeless tradition (Dundes 1980; Bascom 1965). It offers a kind of psychologically elegant solution to painful dilemmas.

The tale of the small boy revivifying his people indicates one way Oneidas grappled with understanding the social order through oral narrative. Like the white owners of the Oneida Stone, therefore, Oneidas gave voice to their outlook through figurative expression. In contrast to the whites, however, Oneidas struggled to make symbolic sense of dispossession and reduction. Deprivation moves people to look for signs of fulfillment and renewal, and tales of wonder can speak to that need (Zipes 2001, 849).

THE ONEIDA LONGHOUSE

The rich cannibal in "Where the Earth Opens" calls down through a hole in the roof "where the smoke comes out" to where the boy is hiding "in the fireplace in the center of the house." This passage seems to describe

12. *Oneida longhouses were "built much better and higher than all the others" (Gehring and Starna 1988, 13).*

features characteristic of a longhouse, the typically Iroquois bark home no person in 1925 had seen for more than a century (see ill. 12).

Down the middle of such a building ran a row of cooking hearths, each shared by two families facing each other across the central aisle. The smoke of each fire was vented through a hole in the roof directly above. Visitors found the arrangement notable, as when Richard Smith observed an Oneida house in 1769: "The fire is made in the middle of the entry and a hole is left in the roof for the smoke to escape for there is neither chimney nor window" (1989, 132). In 1796, another visitor to an Oneida bark house containing two hearths (therefore, two residential units comprising four families) noted: "There were four bunks, or raised platforms, on which they sleep; and two places in the middle where they make the fire, over which were two holes in the roof for the smoke to go out" (Belknap 1882, 21).

The greater part of a longhouse was composed of such residential units, or modules, with living areas facing one another across the central aisle. At each end of the structure, however, was a different kind of room:

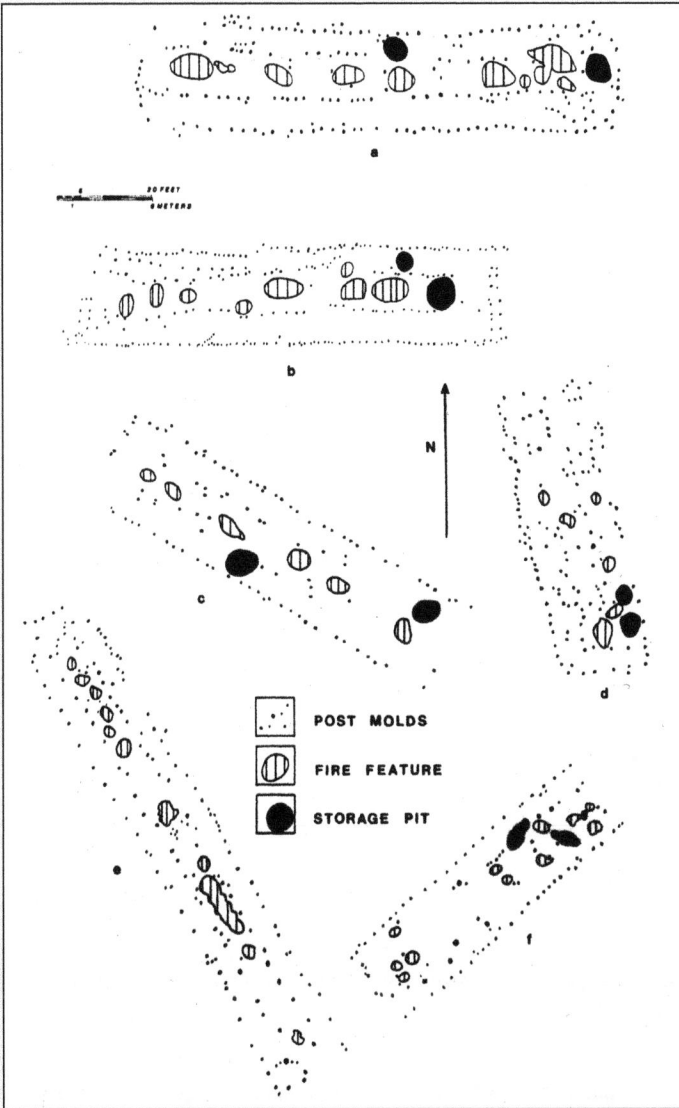

13. *Plans of excavated Oneida longhouses. Fire features show evidence of burning (hearths, roasting pits, and platforms). Post molds are discolorations in the soil marking the locations of vertically implanted wooden poles. (a) Cameron site, ca. 1590–1610 (after Bennett 1981, pl. 3); (b) Wilson, ca. 1610–1625 (after Hosbach and Gibson 1980, fig. 3); (c) Blowers, ca. 1610–1625 (after Bennett 1979, pl. 4); (d) Cameron (after Bennett and Hatton 1988, pl. B); (e) Buyea, ca. 1475? (after Whitney 1970, pl. 1); (f) Thurston, ca. 1625–1637 (after Bennett 1999, fig. 9).*

a lobby or vestibule usually said to be for storage (Fenton and Moore 1977, 21; Snow 1997, 65, 70). The visitors to Oneida bark houses quoted above said that when they entered such homes, they looked to the back and saw a storage room. "You first enter an enclosed shed or portus which serves as a wood house or kitchen and then the body of the edifice," Smith observed. "Almost every house has a room at the end opposite to the kitchen serving as a larder for provision" (1989, 131–32). And according to Jeremy Belknap, "At each end of the house was a separate apartment; one of which served as an entry, the other as a store-room" (1882, 21).

Both stated, in other words, that the nonresidential rooms at opposite ends of late-eighteenth-century Oneida bark houses were devoted to different uses. One was used primarily for storing food; the other was not. Excavated Oneida longhouses usually evince this characteristic. Whenever apparent storage pits have been present (five of the six examples in ill. 13), at least one occurs near one end of the structure. In three instances (ill. 13c, d, f), the storage features occurred exclusively at one end.

A functional difference between the end rooms is not reported in history or archaeology elsewhere as far as I know.[S1] That such a clear-cut difference should exist solely in Oneida homes is, admittedly, hard to believe. Yet, in an otherwise enigmatic statement, van den Bogaert implied an architectural distinctiveness about Oneida longhouses "built much better and higher than all the others" (Gehring and Starna 1988, 13).

That Oneidas in 1925 could recollect a central fire with a smoke hole is testimony to the importance of longhouses in Iroquois thinking. Emotionally resonant, longhouses were synonymous with domestic life and with such values as generosity and hospitality inculcated in the home. Symbolically important, *longhouse* also connoted social identity to the Iroquois, who called themselves the "People of the Longhouse."

S1. At Onondaga in 1743, however, Bartram described a special purpose "town house" as possessing a wood shed at one end but not, apparently, at the other (Snow 1997, 71).

3

⊶⟁⊷

The Creation

Two conversations shape the native folklore of New England, according to William Simmons (1986, vii). One dialogue occurs between the living and the changing world, the other between the living and the dead. In the preceding chapter, I emphasized folklore meaning as bound up with the dilemmas of the living. At the same time, I noted how those contemporaneous circumstances are expressed in language invoking the past and evoking the authority of the dead. Whether the traditional format itself is ancient, however, is unknown. In other words, the story "Where the Earth Opens" could well be very old, but that theory cannot be demonstrated from documentary evidence.

Hope Allen recorded two versions of the Iroquois narrative of beginning—an oral literature classic that is "one of the greatest mythological systems in North America" (Lévi-Strauss 1988, 129). It was among the earliest cosmogonies noted in North America, and it was recorded in writings spanning nearly four hundred years. I suspect it is probably the most completely documented view of world origin anywhere in North America. This circumstance offers an exceptional opportunity to examine changes in myth over time. I turn first, then, to these questions: How old is the Iroquois creation story? If it has changed over time, how has it changed?

The Hurons' Creation

The earliest evidence derives from the Hurons of Ontario on the eastern shore of Georgian Bay in Lake Huron. Speakers of an Iroquoian language related to the Iroquois tongues of New York, the Hurons also possessed a culture and mythology apparently very close to those of the Iroquois. French Jesuit missionary Jean de Brébeuf provided the most complete account of Huron creation in 1636 (Thwaites 1896–1901, 10:125–39).

Up in the sky, "there was and still is a land like ours, with woods, lakes, rivers and fields, and peoples who inhabit them" (127). Although the Hurons offered discrepant reasons for it, a pregnant woman named Aataentsic one day fell out of the sky land. Below, in our world, aquatic animals met in council to discuss what would be done for the human. They decided "they should all promptly set to work, dive to the bottom of the water, bring up soil to her [Turtle], and put it on her back" (129).

Here Brébeuf described what folklorists call the earth-diver motif—the incident of an animal obtaining material for dry land from the bottom of a primal sea (Thompson 1929, 279, motif A810–11). This theme has long impressed researchers with its nearly worldwide presence, from Finland east through much of Asia including Siberia and in most of native America north of Mexico (Köngäs 1960). Such a vast distribution might be the result of many independent inventions if the concept of earth diver satisfied psychological needs felt by humans everywhere (Dundes 1962). Regarding that conjecture as unlikely, most scholars interpretively incline in the direction of the age-area principle—the more widespread the trait, the older it is likely to be. Because a cultural feature once originated would spread outward from the point of origination, the resulting widespread distribution implies a considerable antiquity and an Old World origin (Count 1952; Hall 1997, 19; Rooth 1957, 498–500). In all probability, it was brought "eastward to America when people settled the New World" (Fenton 1962, 289).

In an apparent digression, Brébeuf pauses in his story of Aataentsic to provide an alternate Huron account of creation: a man on a tiny spot of land induced a martenlike animal to dive to the ocean bottom for mud, which, in turn, resulted in our island continent (Thwaites 1896–1901, 10:131–33). This tale simply repeats the earth-diver episode in a fashion resembling how the Hurons' Algonquian neighbors to the west handled the motif (Chamberlain 1891). Such evidence suggested to Gladys Reichard that the earth-diver theme diffused outward from a Central Woodland origin (1921).

At any rate, Brébeuf goes on to say the woman landed safely on the soil platform and delivered a daughter. The daughter, in turn, somehow became pregnant and delivered twin boys: Iouskeha—which, according to later sources, may mean "the good one" (Barbeau 1914, 292; Hale 1888, 181)—and Tawiskaron, meaning "flint" (and hereafter called Flint). Turtle, a female, taught Iouskeha the art of making fire. The brothers battled, Flint ineffectually armed with "some fruits of the wild rosebush," while Iouskeha was equipped with the properly lethal "horns of a stag." Iouskeha killed Flint, whose blood turned into flint stones.

Clearly, there were twin brothers who fought in this earliest account of world beginning, yet the role of Flint remains enigmatic because he is not mentioned elsewhere. Iouskeha, in contrast, was very important in the Huron scheme of how things came about.

> Moreover, they esteem themselves greatly obliged to [Iouskeha]. . . . [W]ithout him we would not have so many fine rivers and so many beautiful lakes. In the beginning of the world, they say, the earth was dry and arid; all the waters were collected under the armpit of a large frog, so that Iouskeha could not have a drop except through its agency. One day, he resolved to deliver himself and all his posterity from this servitude; and, in order to attain this, he made an incision under the armpit, whence the waters came forth in such abundance that they spread throughout the whole earth, and hence the origin of rivers, lakes, and seas . . . They hold also that without Iouskeha their kettles would not boil. . . . Were it not for him, they would not have such good hunting . . . [f]or they believe that animals were not at liberty from the beginning of the world, but that they were shut up in a great cavern, where Iouskeha guarded them. . . . However, one day he determined to give them liberty in order that they might multiply and fill the forests. . . . [I]t is Iouskeha who gives them the [maize] they eat, it is he who makes it grow and brings it to maturity. If they see their fields verdant in the spring, if they reap good and abundant harvests, and if their cabins are crammed with ears of corn, they owe it to Iouskeha. (Thwaites 1896–1901, 10:135–39)

Evidently, then, the Huron world began with Iouskeha performing a series of acts disposing the landscape to yield fish, meat, and domesticated crops. Regarded as a keeper of the game and a patron of agricultural produce, the Huron good twin, Iouskeha, was thanked for providing food.

Brébeuf went on to say that Aataentsic and her grandson Iouskeha lived in a distant place but maintained contact with the Hurons. Whereas Iouskeha's involvement in human affairs was beneficent, Aataentsic was regarded as dangerous and wicked. All of the French chroniclers familiar with Huron belief in the 1610s through the 1630s emphasized the existence of dual gods comprising a grandmother and grandson of opposite disposition. In 1623, Recollect missionary Gabriel Sagard reported:

> The general belief of our Hurons (although they understand it themselves very imperfectly and speak of it in very different ways) is that the Creator who made the whole world is called Yoscaha . . . and he has also a grandmother named Ataensiq. . . . They say that they live far away . . . and that his house or lodge is made like theirs, with plenty of corn in it and everything else necessary to maintain human life. He sows corn, works, drinks, eats, and sleeps like others. All the animals on earth belong to him and are like servants of his. By nature he is very kind, and makes everything grow, and all he does is done well, and he gives us fine weather and everything else good and advantageous. But on the contrary his grandmother is spiteful, and she often spoils all the good her grandson has done. (Wrong 1939, 169–70)

The concepts of malicious grandmother and kindly disposed grandson (the good twin) must date to pre-European times because they are documented before Christianity could have had much impact on Huron thinking.

The Early Iroquois Creation

Little is known about New York Iroquois views of creation until the nearly simultaneous appearance of a trio of mythological narratives written in English by John Norton, the adopted Mohawk chief, and James Dean, a fluent speaker of Oneida (Dean 1915; Klinck and Talman 1970, 88–97; Wonderley 2000b, 2001). First documented in 1815–1816, these three versions reflect memories extending well into the 1700s. The Dean and Norton accounts provide the first reasonably complete picture of important cosmogonic episodes known to Iroquois people.

As in the Huron account, the Iroquois story begins in a world of abundance and happiness above ours inhabited by humanlike beings. The longer of Norton's two accounts (Klinck and Talman 1970, 91–97; hereafter, Norton 2) is a lengthy text, more than half of which describes events taking place in that celestial realm prior to the creation of our world.

Norton 2 opens with a couple whose son dies and is placed on a scaffold outside the house. The deceased's widow continues to live with her parents-in-law, occupying a bunk across the fire from theirs. That elderly couple, however, is rather shocked to discover that the widow engages in nightly conversations with an unknown visitor. The young widow says it is her husband she receives at night. The widow bears a daughter. The grandparents realize the deceased was the child's father when they see the child in possession of wampum belts originally interred with the corpse.

A marriage for the daughter, now grown, is arranged to a chief in a distant village. The girl receives careful instructions about what she is to do from her grandfather. She must ignore a suitor who will importune her, cross a stream while disregarding the threat posed by a swinging tree, identify which house in the village belongs to the chief by the great tree at its door, present the chief with bread she has brought him, and then cook mush for him while enduring painful burns and licking by his white dog. Successfully completing these tasks, the daughter and the chief are now married. They sleep on opposite sides of the fire, however, never sexually consummating their union.

The wife becomes pregnant. Supposing she has "had connection with some other man," the chief becomes ill with depression. Asked to explain his melancholy, the chief requests a great tree be uprooted, then pushes his wife into the resulting chasm.

All three accounts take up the story from the time a pregnant woman is expelled from the heavens, and all three relate incidents leading up to the death of an evil brother. The three stories are not identical. Only the Norton accounts, to give one example, include an incident in which the good twin frees animals imprisoned by his brother. Known to the Hurons a century and a half earlier, this mythic theme enjoyed a wide distribution beyond Iroquois country and may be of substantial age. "The story of two boys obtaining or releasing game animals from a cave within a mountain," Robert Hall argues, "is so widespread in the eastern United States that it surely must date back three thousand years or more and to the Archaic period or earlier" (1997, 139).

Undoubtedly, there was considerable variation in the creation story as it was told across Iroquoia in the late 1700s. Yet the similarity of these three versions is impressive. Both Dean and Norton insisted there was widespread agreement on the major points (Dwight 1822, 197; Klinck and Talman 1970, 97). Just how similar they seem is illustrated by the close fit between the two longer accounts. If the jealous chief with the great tree in Norton 2 is identified with the melancholic young man concerned with a white pine in Dean (see below), the two story segments fit together seamlessly. The sky-world portion of Norton 2 could literally be pasted to the beginning of Dean—with no adjustment of detail, character, or personality—in a longer telling of the same narrative. Combining the two, in fact, enhances each because otherwise enigmatic motives become clarified in both. Now it is a little clearer why Norton's chief pushed his wife away (he thought this act would recover his health) and why Dean's young man felt betrayed (he knew he was not the one who impregnated his wife). Dean's Oneida account (1915) is given below as the most detailed creation recorded prior to the late nineteenth century:

THE CREATION

An unlimited expanse of water once filled the space now occupied by the world we inhabit. Here was the abode of total darkness which no ray of light ever penetrates. At this time, the human family dwelt in a country situated in the upper regions of the air, abounding in every thing conducive to the comfort and convenience of life. The forests were full of game; the lakes and streams swarmed with fish and fowl, while the earth and fields spontaneously produced a profusion of vegetables for the use of men. An unclouded sun enlivened their days, and storms and tempests were unknown in that happy region. The inhabitants were strangers to death, and its harbingers pain and disease, while their minds were free from the corroding passions of jealousy, hatred, malice, and revenge, so that their state was perfectly happy.

At length, however, an event occurred which interrupted their tranquility and introduced care and anxiety, till then unknown. A certain youth was noticed to withdraw himself from the circle of their social amusements. The solitary recesses of the grove became his favorite walks. Care and chagrin were depicted in his countenance, and his body from long abstinence presented to the view of his friends the mere skeleton of a man. Anxious solicitude again and again explored the cause of his grief, until at length debilitated both in body and mind, he yielded to the importunities of his associates and promised to disclose the cause of his troubles on condition that they would dig up the roots of a certain white pine tree, lay him on his blanket by the side of the hole, and seat his wife by his side. In a moment all hands were ready, the fatal tree was taken up by the roots in doing which the earth was perforated, and a passage opened to the abyss below. The blanket was placed by the side of the hole, the youth laid thereon, and his wife took her seat by his side. The multitude eager to learn the cause of such strange and unusual conduct pressed around, when, on a sudden, to their horror and astonishment, he seized upon the woman—she enceinte—and precipitated her headlong into the darkness below; then arising from the ground, he informed the assembly that he had for some time suspected the chastity of his wife, and, that now, having disposed of the cause of his trouble he should soon recover his usual health and vivacity.

All those amphibious animals which now inhabit the earth, then roamed through the watery waste to which the woman in her fall was hastening. The loon first discovered her coming, and called a council in haste, to prepare for her reception. Observing that the animal which approached was a human being, they knew that earth was indispensably necessary for her accommodation. The first subject of deliberation was, who should support the burden. The sea bear first presented himself for a trial of his strength. Instantly the other animals gathered around and scrambled upon his back, while the bear, unable to support the weight, sank beneath the surface of the water and was judged by the whole assembly unequal to the task of supporting the earth. Several others in succession presented themselves as candidates for the honor, and with similar success. Last of all the turtle modestly advanced, tendering his broad shell as the basis of the earth now about to be formed. The beasts then made trial of his strength to bear, and finding their united pressure unable to sink him below the surface, adjudged to him the honor of supporting the world. A foundation being thus provided, the next subject of deliberation was, how to procure earth. It was concluded that it must be obtained from the bottom of the sea. Several of the most expert divers went in quest of it, and uniformly floated up dead to the surface of the water. The mink at length took the dangerous plunge, and after a long absence arose dead. By a critical examination, a small quantity of earth was discovered in one of his claws, which he had scratched from the bottom. This being carefully preserved was placed on the back of the turtle. In the meantime, the woman continued falling, and at length alighted on the back of the turtle. The earth had already grown to the size of a man's foot, when she stood covering one foot with the other. Shortly after she had room for both feet and was soon able to sit down. The earth continued to expand and soon formed a small island, skirted with willow and other aquatic shrubbery, and at length stretched out into a widely extended plain, interspersed with views and smaller streams which with gentle current moved forward their tributary waters to the ocean.

She repaired to the seashore, erected a habitation, and settled in her new abode. Not long after, she became the mother of a daughter and was supported by the spontaneous productions of the earth until the child arrived at adult years. She was then solicited in marriage by several animals changed into the form of young men. The loon first presented himself as a solicitor, in the form of a tall, well-dressed, fine-looking young man. After due consultation with the mother, his suit was rejected. Several others presented themselves and were rejected by the mother, until at length the turtle, with his short neck, short bandy legs, and humped back offered himself as a suitor and was received.

After she had lain herself down to sleep, the turtle placed upon her abdomen two arrows in the form of a cross, one headed with flint, the other with the rough bark of a tree, and took his leave. She in due time became a mother of two sons, but died in giving them birth. When the time arrived that the children should be born, they consulted together about the best mode of egress from their place of confinement. The younger determined to make his exit by the natural passage, whilst the other resolved to take the shortest route, by breaking through the walls of his prison, in effecting which he consequently destroyed his mother, thus giving the first evidence of his malignant disposition. The grandmother, enraged at her daughter's death, resolved to destroy the children, and taking them in her arms, threw them into the sea. Scarcely had she reached her wigwam when the children overtook her at the door. The experiment was several times repeated but in vain. Discouraged by her ill success, she determined to let them live. Then dividing the corpse of her daughter into two parts, she threw them upwards towards the heavens, when the upper part became the sun, and the lower part the moon, which is the reason she has always presented the form of the human face.

Then began the succession of day and night in our world. The children speedily became men and expert archers. The elder, whose name was Than-wisk-a-law (a term expressive of the greatest degree of malignity and cruelty) had the arrow of the turtle pointed with flint, and killed with it the largest beasts of the forest. The younger whose name was Tan-lon-ghy-au-wan-goon (a name denoting unbounded goodness and benevolence) had the arrow headed with bark. The former was by his malignant disposition and his skill and success in hunting, a favorite with his grandmother. They lived in the midst of plenty, but would not permit the younger brother, whose arrow was insufficient to destroy anything but birds, to share in their abundance.

As this young man was one day wandering along the shore, he saw a bird perched upon a bough projecting over the water. He attempted to kill it, but his arrow, until that time unswerving, flew wide of the mark and sank into the sea. He determined to recover it, and swimming to the place where it fell, plunged to the bottom. Here he was astonished to find himself in a small cottage.

A venerable old man who was sitting in it received him with a smile of fraternal complacency, and thus addressed him. "My son, I welcome you to the habitation of your father. To obtain this interview I have directed all the circumstances which have conspired to bring you hither. Here is your arrow, and here is an ear of corn, which you will find pleasant and wholesome food. I have watched the unkindness both of your grandmother and brother. While he lives the earth can never be peopled. You must therefore take his life. When you return home, you must traverse the whole earth, collect all the flint stones into heaps which you find, and hang up all the buckhorns. These are the only things of which your brother is afraid, or which can make any impression upon his body, which is made of flint. They will furnish you with weapons, always at hand, wherever he may direct his course."

Having received these and other instructions from his father and returning to the world, he began immediately to obey his father's instructions. This being done, the elder at length resolved on a hunting excursion. On their way to the hunting grounds he inquired of the younger what were the objects of his greatest aversion. He informed him (falsely) that there was nothing so terrific to him as beech boughs and bulrushes, and inquired in turn of Than-wisk-a-law what he most dreaded. He answered, nothing so much as flintstones and buckhorns, and that nothing else could injure him, and that lately he had been much annoyed by them, wherever he went. Having arrived at their place of destination, the elder went in quest of game, leaving the younger to attend to the menial occupation of erecting his hut, and preparing such other accommodation as he required.

After an absence of some time, he returned, exhausted with fatigue and hunger. Having taken a hearty repast prepared by his brother, he retired to his hut to sleep. When he had fallen into a profound slumber, the younger kindled a large fire at its entrance. After a time, he found himself extremely incommoded by the heat, and the flinty materials of his body, expanded by its intensity, were exploding in large scales from his carcass. In a great rage and burning with a desire for revenge, he broke through the fire from the hut, hastened to a neighboring beech, armed himself with a large bough and returned to chastise and destroy his brother. Finding that his repeated and violent blows had no effect upon his brother, who pelted him with flint stones and belaboured him with bucks horns, by which the flinty scales fell from his body in large showers, he betook himself to a neighboring marsh, where he supplied himself with a bundle of bull rushes and returned to the contest, but with the same want of success.

Finding himself deceived, and failing of his purpose, he sought safety in flight. As he fled the earth trembled. A verdant plain bounded by the distant ocean lay before him; behind him the earth sank in deep valleys and frightful chasms, or rose with lofty mountains or stupendous precipices. The streams ceased to roll in silence, and bursting their barriers, poured down from the cliffs in cataracts, or foamed through their rocky channels to the ocean. The younger brother followed the fugitive with vigorous steps, and wounded him continually with his weapons. At length, in a far distant region, beyond the savannahs of the west, he breathed his last and loaded the earth with his flinty form (supposed by the Indians to make the Rocky Mountains).

The great enemy of the race of the turtle being destroyed, they came up out of the ground in human form, and for some time multiplied in peace and spread extensively over the surface. The Oneidas so long as they were in a pagan state, used to show the precise spot of ground, a small hollow, where they said their ancestors came up.

The grandmother roused to furious resentment for the loss of her darling son, resolved to be avenged. For many days successively she caused the rain to descend in torrents from the clouds until the whole surface of the earth and even the highest mountains were covered. The inhabitants fled to their canoes and escaped impending destruction.

The disappointed grandmother then caused the rain to cease, and the waters to subside. The inhabitants returned to their former places of abode. She then determined to effect her purpose in another manner and covered the earth with a deluge of snow. To escape this new evil, they betook themselves to their snowshoes and thus eluded her vengeance. Chagrined at length by these disappointments, she gave up the hope of destroying the whole human race at once, and determined to wreak her vengeance upon them in a manner which although less violent, would be more efficacious. She has ever since been employed in gratifying her malignant disposition by inflicting upon mankind all those evils which are suffered in the present world. Tau-lon-ghy-au-wau-goon, on the other hand, displays the infinite benevolence of his nature by bestowing on the human race the blessings they enjoy, all of which flow from his bountiful providence. The name literally translated is "the holder or supporter of the heavens."[1]

Taulonghyauwaugoon was introduced in chapter 1 as the Iroquois god called Taronhiaouagon by the Jesuits. This word for Sky Holder is documented as the Iroquois name for the good twin as early as 1644 (Jameson 1909, 178). We have also met the brother of evil disposition, Thanwiskalaw (also meaning "flint" in Oneida), among the Hurons some 150 years earlier. The same name for the same character is good evidence for the presence of the same narrative in both areas.

And, indeed, the basic identity of the Huron and Iroquois creation story has long been recognized and widely accepted (Tooker 1991, 151). From Sagard's earliest Huron version of 1623 through recent Iroquois accounts, we seem to be dealing with "one continuous mythological tradition," or, more simply, one and the same myth (Fenton 1998, 34). And because it seems basically the same, we can infer that Iroquois portions of the myth probably date to the period they are documented among the Hurons (Fenton 1947, 391).

Around 1900, Wyandot descendants of the Hurons still knew the names of both twins as given in Huronia nearly three hundred years earlier. Though we know little of the twins in their Huron context, the Wyandots remembered a tale of sibling rivalry similar to the one known among the Iroquois in the late 1700s (Barbeau 1915, 37–51; Connelley 1899, 120–23; Hale 1888). Like their Iroquois counterparts, the Wyandot twins usually debate how they will leave the womb, the evil one declaring his intention to exit in a manner that will kill his mother (Thompson 1929, 279, motif T575, called "Twins Quarrel Before Birth").

---

1. A typed transcription of Dean's manuscript is on file in the New York State Library (Dean 1915). The account has been published twice (Dwight 1822, 190–95; Lounsbury and Gick 2000, 155–62).

Very likely, the Algonquian-speaking Delawares south of the Iroquois also knew this story of rival twins. Their evil brother may have been named Flint, but far clearer was the Delaware name for the other brother: Hare (Bierhorst 1995, 9, 30–31, 38–39). The identification of the good twin with Hare is interesting because it suggests the possibility of some distant connection between Sky Holder and Nanabozho—the Great Lakes Algonquian trickster-hero whose name is said to mean the Great Hare (Bierhorst 1985, 213). In a number of versions from the upper Great Lakes region, Nanabozho fights a brother, often made of flint or named Flint, in a manner resembling the Iroquoian plot. A similar sibling rivalry is sporadically documented for Gluskap, the Algonquian culture hero of the Northeast.[2]

In addition to the rival twins and the earth-diver sequence, the core similarities of earlier Huron and later Iroquois accounts consist of two other sequences or subplots designated by folklorists as motifs: "The Woman Who Fell from the Sky" (Thompson 1929, motif A21.1) and "Earth from Turtle's Back" (motif A815, pp. 278–79). These motifs are often regarded as the quintessential creation myth of the Northeast. Clearly, they are characteristic of Iroquoian speakers: Iroquois, Hurons, and Wyandots. However, they were also shared by the Iroquois's immediate neighbors (mostly to the south), the Algonquian-speaking (west to east) Shawnees, Delawares, and Mahicans (Bierhorst 1985, 200; Flannery 1939, 158–59).

Dean's creation account identifies the principal gods—malicious grandmother and compassionate grandson who is the good twin—known to the Hurons 150 years earlier. The identical pair reigned supreme among the Caughnawaga Mohawks near Montreal during the early 1700s (Fenton and Moore 1974, 168). Thus, three apparently independent sources testify to the belief's wide geographical distribution and to its persistence for at least a century and a half. Although we cannot assume these two were characteristic of Iroquois religion everywhere, this mythic tradition clearly was of considerable stability and antiquity. The grandmother and her good grandson, it was widely believed, lived on after Flint's

2. For accounts from the upper Great Lakes in which Nanabozho fights a brother, see Barnouw 1977, 74–77; Chamberlain 1891; and T. Michelson 1917, 5–23. For Gluskap's sibling rivalry, consult Leland 1992, 15–17; and Rand 1894, 339–40.

death. They intervened in mortal affairs and were credited with opposite dispositions.

Good opposed to evil seems to be a key concept in the Iroquois-Huron cosmogony of the seventeenth and eighteenth centuries. This polarity may be distinctively Iroquoian; certainly, it is unusual in the native mythology of North America as a whole (Boas 1914, 394; Thompson 1929, 280; Hultkrantz 1981, 187–88). Some argue, on the other hand, that this duality reflects nothing more than the bias of Western observers (see Cave 1999 and Paper 1983) because well-defined binary systems of abstract ethics are not supposed to be characteristic of Native American thinking (see Dundes 1964, 72; Wasson and Toelken 2001, 193).

It seems likely that a dialectic of good versus evil was indeed autochthonous and pre-European among the Iroquois. The context of such a pattern, however, suggests an important qualification: good and evil were understood in terms more relative than absolute.

Beyond his role as grandson and sibling in the creation epic, Sky Holder was a tutelary deity who taught his folk, watched over them, and smote their enemies. In this capacity, he was unapologetically parochial and ethnocentric on behalf of his own people. This deity was the Sky Holder Norton said was the Iroquois's great patron (Klinck and Talman 1970, 97). The French Jesuits knew him as the great god of the Iroquois (Thwaites 1896–1901, 53:253), the principal deity "they acknowledge as a divinity, and obey as the great master of their lives" (54:65).

In an Iroquois account of 1827, Sky Holder is remembered as the god who led the Iroquois in their tribal wanderings. He protected his people from monsters such as Stone Giants and a mammoth mosquito. In the latter instance, the mosquito slain by Sky Holder broke into tiny parts that became the small pests known today (Beauchamp 1892, 11–18).

Sky Holder also championed his people in war. This act made him a war god to the extent the Iroquois were concerned with war. The way Norton put it in 1801 was that the Iroquois have a god of war named Sky Holder who also presides over the affairs of men (Boyce 1973, 293). Speaking these words through a man's dream in 1656, Sky Holder said, "I preserve men, and give victories to warriors. I have made you masters of the earth and victors over so many nations" (Thwaites 1896–1901, 42:197). Sky Holder as tribal god, therefore, was certainly and tangibly good. His goodness, however, was apprehended in relation to proximate situation and tribal interest.

The theme of the twins' rivalry in the late eighteenth century seems to be food and ways to get it. Flint, armed with Turtle's flint-tipped arrow lethal to the largest beasts of the forest, is the only brother capable of supporting a household composed of the grandmother and himself. Sky Holder later achieves a sort of food-getting parity when Turtle gives him corn, then frees animals Flint had imprisoned for his own use (Norton 1 and 2). In the final struggle, Flint flails helplessly away with vegetal materials as Sky Holder prevails by applying the substance of the hunt against the hunter (arrowheads were fashioned from antlers and flint).

This contest is a sibling match in which the brothers signify food-getting pursuits competing for dominance in human life (Long 1963, 192). Flint, of course, is the archetypal hunter, Sky Holder the personification of horticulture. As a culture hero responsible for giving corn to humankind, Sky Holder's role resembles the function of Iouskeha, the Hurons' source of food.

Although both protagonists are male, this allegory of subsistence established the dominance of horticulture over hunting in terms compatible with the Iroquois gender-based division of labor. Flint practices acts of violence probably considered quintessentially male. Sky Holder, his bark-tipped arrow suggestive of domesticity, is identified with female responsibilities, including planting, tending, weeding, and cooking corn (in Norton 1 and 2), and with maintaining the brothers' shelter. Bruce Trigger discerns comparable gender association at work in the Huron creation story (1969, 93). Similarly, Claude Lévi-Strauss surmises that women, agriculture, and cooked food stand opposed to men, hunting, and raw food in Iroquois mythic thought (1987, 82).

Nineteenth-Century Transformation

In the early 1800s, the creation account changed rapidly, reconfigured to emphasize the importance of the brothers, rather than one brother and the grandmother. The ancient polarity of good versus evil now comprised the twins, and, as the new central duality, their competition was redefined as a struggle over creation. Once rivals over food and food-getting, the

twins of the modern era now compete to fashion an earthly setting customized for people. Sky Holder (usually recast as the Good Spirit) creates
creatures and features for the benefit of people (Barbeau 1914, 301–3;
Bierhorst 1985, 199). Flint, now the Evil Spirit, objects to such easy living
and tries to negate his brother's acts.

Typically, the Good Spirit brings forth plant species of medicinal and
food value (such as the red osier dogwood, berries, fruit, and maple trees).
The Evil Spirit stunts them or creates noxious counterparts such as thistles
and poison ivy. When the Good Spirit creates birds and game animals, the
evil one offers up bats, flies, and such dangerous animals as grizzly bears
and rattlesnakes. The Good Spirit creates rivers simultaneously flowing in
two directions for ease of human travel. The Evil Spirit changes the current
to a single flow, then throws in such impediments as falls and rapids for
good measure. Some incidents known to be ancient are retold with new
meaning in the context of creative rivalry. For example, the Evil Spirit im-
prisons the game animals; the Good Spirit liberates them for human use.

Earlier, human origin did not require explanation. If people were ac-
counted for at all, they simply emerged from the ground. In creation stories after the early 1800s, however, people resulted from a deliberate act
achieved in specific fashion. Iroquois writer David Cusick made this point
as early as 1827: "When [the Good Mind] had made the universe he was
in doubt respecting some being to possess the Great Island; and he formed
two images of the dust of the ground in his own likeness, male and female,
and by his breathing into their nostrils he gave them the living souls"
(Beauchamp 1892, 3). Attempting to imitate his brother's creation of
human beings, the Evil Spirit produced grotesque reflections such as apes
(see ibid., 3–4; and Hewitt 1974, 214, 514).

This change in cosmological thinking evidently took place in a context
of Iroquois demoralization in the wake of military defeat, land loss, and
unceasing pressure from nonnative people. In this time of despair, the Iroquois found their traditions challenged and devalued at every turn.

In 1799, Seneca prophet Handsome Lake began to experience a series
of visions that (ultimately) revitalized the older Iroquois religion to suit
new circumstances. In Handsome Lake's religion, Sky Holder became a
creator figure (Tooker 1970, 3), a demiurge, and a high god who, in competition with his evil opposite, rendered postmortal judgment in heaven
(Wallace 1972, 251–52, 316).

The creation story does not figure in Handsome Lake's visions, nor is it really a part of the Handsome Lake religion. Yet the cosmogonic narrative changed in conjunction with and perhaps because of the new direction in religious worldview effected by Handsome Lake. And, like the new religion, creation stories of the modern era (since the early nineteenth century) often take on a moralistic coloration and warn of postmortal consequences. The longest creation stories, authored at the turn of the twentieth century by John Arthur Gibson and Seth Newhouse, are of this sort, as are many other versions of recent times (Hewitt 1974). Insofar as the Iroquois creation is a morality play concerning absolute ethical abstractions or creative impulses dialectically confronting destructive ones, it may be of relatively recent date.

The Wyandot creation stories Horatio Hale collected from southeastern Ontario in 1872–1874 (1888) and the ones C. Marius Barbeau obtained in 1911–1912 from Oklahoma (1915, 37–51) also account for the creation of humans, and all feature the twins as morally opposite demiurges engaged in a creative contest to establish the condition of the world. Presumably, Handsome Lake was not responsible for Wyandot twins in the Far Midwest coming to resemble the nineteenth-century Iroquois twins. More likely, we see here parallel mythic developments as responses to similar conditions in two or more locations, conditions that surely included the exertion of strong Christian influence everywhere.

Oneida Creation Stories of the Early Twentieth Century

The creation accounts documented by Hope Allen belong to what I consider the modern era of the Iroquois creation epic. Indeed, the majority of written creation stories date after 1880—the period when oral narratives of every sort were being documented throughout Iroquois country (Abler 1987). So, in addition to offering scope for examining a myth over time, the modern Iroquois myth of beginning furnishes abundant material for inquiring into the contemporaneous distribution of story elements. In the remainder of this chapter, I turn from a historical to a comparative focus to ask: What innovations or influences are discernible? Can one identify elements distinct to the New York Oneida versions and therefore indicative of a local school? Did elements or motifs originate elsewhere, and, if so, what is their source? On the other hand, to what extant do innovations arise from an individual storyteller's embellishments? Such questions hark back to an early-twentieth-century research orientation in anthropology and folklore devoted to understanding whether features of culture were independently invented or diffused from elsewhere.

Let us now consider the versions of creation obtained from each of Allen's primary informants. In both cases, the first and longest solicitation was supplemented by subsequent sessions in which Allen tried to obtain material to clarify or elaborate what was originally recorded. The texts that follow are composite versions of my editing in which later material has been added in appropriate places to the original text. Both deal with the same plot segment beginning with the descent of the woman from the sky and concluding with the twins' fight.

LYDIA DOXTATER'S CREATION, CIRCA MARCH 1918

There was another world before this one and in this other world there was a wicked woman. And she had a great swing and in it she used to swing people. In front of the swing was a great rock and if she disliked people she used to roll away the rock and swing them so far out that they would fall down into the great hole that was under the rock and never be heard of again.

Now there was a young girl whom this woman hated very much just because the girl was so good and beautiful. She was very pure, she was a virgin. And one day the bad woman got the girl into the swing after she had opened the trap door (as it were) into the great hole. When the woman swung the girl she sang a song and it said "Mud is going to be the death of you by and by," and swung her out so that she fell off and into it.

Now the hole led down into our world but there was nothing there but water and water animals. When the girl fell they heard the fall and word went forth, "There is a human being on the way down to us." The animals had a council about preventing her from drowning. Then they all said: "How shall we get ready for her? There is no dry land for her to rest on." But the turtle said: "You can use my back as a foundation." The first animal that dived for the soil did come up dying without anything. And the muskrat dived down to the bottom of the sea and brought up some earth to put on the turtle's back, but he made such a fearful effort to do it that he came up gasping and died.

Then all the animals put in and worked just as hard as they could and by the time the girl reached the surface of the water they had enough on the back of the turtle for her to set her feet on and by night they had enough for her to lie down on. And they continued working after that. The birds brought seeds and they all worked together and made the world as we know it.

And the girl's grandmother came and lived with her. (She doesn't know where the grandmother came from.) She was one day sitting making baskets and the girl was asleep on a cot when a man came in and laid two arrows on the girl's abdomen and went away again. She conceived thus. There were good and evil spirits.

After she had twins and one was good and one was bad from the very first breath of life. They talked together before the birth and the bad one said "Let's go out the wrong way and kill her," and the good one said: "Oh brother, what a terrible thing that would be to do." But the bad one did it and she died.

After the girl had been killed at the birth of the twins, the grandmother brought them up and somehow the bad one got around her so that he was her favorite. One was always good and the other was always bad. Just because he was bad the Bad Spirit once cut a woman in two and threw her up in the sky. I understand that the upper part made the moon and the lower the sun. You can still see her face in the moon but the Good Spirit took pity on her and made the light of the sun so dazzling that her nakedness was covered.

The bad one hunted and got all the animals and wouldn't give his brother any so that the brother was just ready to starve. But everyone has a ministering spirit and the fairy godmother of the good one was looking out for him. [One day she met him in the woods] and gave him some popcorn and said to him: "Now you can use this as a bribe to get your brother to tell you where the animals are. He will want some but don't let him have any till he has promised that. If a single grain pops out of the popper when you are popping it, jump for it and keep it away from him till he has promised, even if to do so you have to pull it out of his throat."

Then the good brother took the popcorn and sure enough the bad one wanted some but he wouldn't give it to him and was successful in keeping it till he made his brother tell him where the animals were. It turned out that they were not killed but all fenced in somewhere by the bad brother and now he let them all out.

The bad brother [made] a huge mosquito. The big mosquito sucked the blood of human beings [and] killed so many people. The good one killed it. However our little mosquitoes grew from the spattering of the blood when the big one was killed.

A fairy came and told the animals about dying, etc. It was for the interest of human people they were working. [The] animals were told that if the old ones went to the top of a certain great hill or mountain (are the same thing in Indian) and circled the peak they would renew their youth and if they could all get into a boat and row across the lake to a certain island without making a sound, they would receive the power of living forever as soon as their oar touched the shore.

So they all started out and all went well. They all got into a boat and set out to find the island. They were in sight of land and then the otter laughed and broke the spell. The beaver who was the oarsman was so angry that he slapped the otter with his tail and that is why the otter has had a flat nose ever since. If the animals had done this people wouldn't have died but they have died ever since.

One day he [the good twin] was in the woods and he heard a strange hissing and he saw a little old woman who said to him: "Grandson, your brother is going to open war on you, but first he will ask you what weapon you fear most and you must tell him that what you fear most of anything in the world would be the sharp buds of the beech tree before the leaves come out. And then you must ask him what weapons he fears most and he will tell you he fears the antlers of the deer that they drop in the Spring."

After awhile it happened just as the fairy godmother

predicted. The bad brother got very provoking and opened war on the good one but first he asked him what weapons he feared most and the good brother said he feared most the sharp bud on the beech tree: "Oh, they stick into a man and pierce and there's no getting rid of them," he said and then he asked his brother the same question. And the bad brother said he feared most the antlers that the deer dropped in the spring. Then each got the weapons that the other mentioned and of course the bad brother got beaten.

The name of the good brother, the good spirit, meant, "He who holds up the sky." To-lo-ga-wa—the last syllables are run together breathlessly and the pause after is dramatic and very sweet. Lydia has heard that it was the mark of the good brother's feet at Footprints near Munnsville. (Allen 1948b, principally 19–20, 29–30)

ANNA JOHNSON'S CREATION, AS TOLD TO HER BY SI JOHNSON, INITIAL RECITATION, DECEMBER 18, 1918

There was once a brother and sister living together and one day the sister was looking in the brother's hair and she found two lice and they both laughed real hearty and it disturbed the neighbors. It was Sunday and they disturbed the people who were going by to Meeting. When the brother realized what he had done on Sunday he was so ashamed that it made him sick.

He asked to have all the people called together and said he was dying and would be out of the way. He asked them to take away the rock and take the sister to the edge of the hole and ask her to look in and then knock her in. This they did.

She fell down towards a great ocean full of waterfowls and they rushed together when they knew she was coming. They said: "There is someone coming down and we must prepare some dry land for her. Who will dive and bring up even a handful of earth?"

The first animal that dived could not get to the bottom and he came up dying. The next one came up with a handful of earth in his mouth but he died when he got up.

Then they tried the backs of all the animals for a foundation and finally settled on the turtle's and they put the handful of earth on it and shaped it and got more and it began to grow and by the time the maiden landed it was big enough for her to step on and later it continued to grow.

The woman who fell down from the sky bore a daughter. [She] got her child by combing her brother's head.

Afterwards she [the daughter] was once lying asleep and two sticks were placed across her chest crossed and after that she gave birth to Cain and Abel. One was good and the other was bad from the time they were very little boys. The daughter "got" her twins by having the man lay the sticks across her but Si doesn't know who he was or where he came from. [The] daughter bore twins and died when they were born.

It was the grandmother who brought the twins up and the bad one got the favor of the grandmother by saying the good one had done something which he hadn't done. Once they were out playing and the bad brother stumbled on a hummock and he was so angry that he jumped on it and stamped. Then they heard a voice saying, "You have killed me."

When they went home and told their grandmother she said, "That is your mother's grave. Now she will never come to life again. If you hadn't done that in nine days (or months) she would come to life and there would not have been any more death."

Once the bad brother thought he would make something and it was an owl. The good brother thought he had made an end of it by cutting it all to pieces, pieces large and small, but instead of that all the pieces became owls, little and big.

[Then the bad brother] made an enormous bat and the good brother cut it all to pieces and that is why we have lots of little bats.

Once Cain made another great harmful animal, a great mosquito and Abel cut it all to pieces and that is why we have lots of little mosquitoes. In this way the good brother was always trying to undo the bad works of the bad brother.

The good brother had all the hunting luck till the bad

brother cast a spell on all the animals and got them all away so that the good brother couldn't have any. When the bad brother had shut up the animals in the rocks he used to go for some when he and his grandmother got hungry. He would stand in front and call an animal and tell it to go where he lived and die, and it would do this. But the good brother came upon the bad one in the woods and saw him strike a huge cliff three times with a stick, and say some magic words. And the cliff opened and all the animals were there and the bad brother took out what he wanted. After that the good brother came and did just what he had seen his brother do and the cliff opened and he let the animals all out. When the animals came out the thunder was so great the people thought there was a great storm.

Finally the two fell to fighting and each asked the other what he feared most. What the good brother named were beech drops (they dropped from the beech trees the Indians think) used as whips. The weapons that the bad brother said would hurt him most were antlers. Cain gave the true answer.

Then each seized the weapon the other said he feared most and they chased each other around the wood and they came out into this valley at Munnsville and the Foot Prints are the mark of their feet. This is a very long story and Si can't remember it all. (principally 32–33, 44)

Discussion

Both creation accounts contain much that is recognizably ancient, including the exiling of a woman from a land above ours and her fall into our realm; a council of animals convened to consider her reception; the appointment of Turtle to hold land derived from mud brought up from the depths by an aquatic animal (earth-diver motif); the conception of twin brothers from two arrows placed on their mother; the death of the mother at the birth of the twins; identification of Flint as the better hunter and his grandmother's favorite; penning up then freeing the game animals; the exchange of information about substances that will harm the brothers, including Sky Holder's "deceitful confidence" (Dixon 1909, 6); and the fight of the twins, one armed with antler, the other wielding vegetal material from the beech tree.

Both convey perspectives characteristic of the modern era, especially the focus on the twins as the fundamental dyad of good and evil. Both indicate the twins' rivalry involved a contest over creation, although neither illustrates this theme very clearly. For example, instead of describing the creation of people, both Johnson and Doxtater mention the incident in which the giant mosquito killed by Sky Holder turned into a host of tiny mosquitoes. Johnson, in fact, piles up several examples of the same phenomenon: the disintegration of a large being into the diminutive forms known today. Both versions evince interest in postmortal existence but not in terms of eschatology or heaven and hell. The issue is posed, rather, as the possibility of eternal life lost in mythological time. For Doxtater, the missed chance was connected with the episode of the animals' voyage. For Johnson, it resided in the killing of the mother before she revived.

Both, in other words, seem idiosyncratic in similar ways. These shared oddities may be local traits indicating common sources and neighborhood communication. I think this point is suggested by identical elements in the opening and closing passages of the two accounts—a door between worlds is opened by rolling away a stone; a geological feature ("the Foot Prints") relates the action to the local landscape.

Of course, each account is also distinctive. Of the two, the Johnson version is more attenuated, suggesting that much of the narrative was lost ("Si can't remember it all"). This understanding was not unique to Oneida. The creation story as living oral literature, according to William Fenton, came close to disappearing everywhere by about 1930 (1962, 285).

Even though the version of the Johnsons contains some nonnative elements (a magic wand and spells, for example), it is far more traditional in tenor than Doxtater's account. The Johnsons preserve the grandmother as a link in the genealogical chain and give the more complete rendering of the twins' rivalry. More strikingly, their version preserves a leitmotif of the older creation story—magical impregnation in three generations. Each of those pregnancies, in the older tellings, is followed by unpleasant consequences for the woman: calumny of gossip, exile from the heavens, and death in childbirth. The Johnson account maintains this authentically old pattern in two generations.

Further, the Johnsons name a method of magical impregnation—the female grooms the male's head—which is also consistent with Iroquois narrative conventions. In a general sense, the Iroquois perceived a set of supernatural associations in the act (apparently customary) of a woman combing or delousing a man's hair. Frequently cited in Iroquois folklore, for example, is the incident of a man overcome by a witch after placing his head in her lap for grooming.[3] More specifically, a girl becomes pregnant after combing her brother's hair in Seth Newhouse's creation narrative (Six Nations Reserve, Canada) of 1896–1897 (Hewitt 1974, 256–57).

The Johnson creation shares incidents of plot with a number of Canadian Iroquois versions but probably is closest to the account of Anthony Day, a Canadian Oneida whose account was written down in 1912 (Lounsbury and Gick 2000, 163–68). Both Johnson and Day, for example, begin with an act of incest committed by a brother and sister in the upper world. Both focus, in similar terms, on the mother's second death.

> JOHNSON: Once they were out playing and the bad brother stumbled on a hummock and he was so angry that he jumped on it and stamped. Then they heard a voice saying, "You have killed me."
>
> When they went home and told their grandmother she said, "That is your mother's grave. Now she will never come to life again. If you hadn't done that in nine days (or months) she would come to life and there would not have been any more death."

> DAY: [Flint] had seen where the grandmother had buried his mother; so he said, "I think the head is right here;" then, with a stone ball, he struck her in the forehead and killed her. The grandmother said, "Now you've killed your mother. If you hadn't done that she would have risen in ten days." (Lounsbury and Gick 2000, 166)

As a matter of fact, the storytelling connections between Canadian and American Oneidas were close (Allen 1948b, 17). Anna Johnson, for example, told Allen about Nelson Smith, a famous Canadian Oneida storyteller who frequently visited New York (Allen 1944, 281).

---

3. The incident of the man overcome by a witch after placing his head in her lap is recounted in Curtin 2001, 389, 427; Hewitt 1918, 753–54; and Parker 1989, 30, 254–55.

Lydia Doxtater's creation shows different native influences. As a girl, Doxtater "went with her parents to Saratoga to sell Indian wares, and became friends with Canadian Indians, some of whom were [Algonquian-speaking] Abenaki; from them she obtained variants of the Canadian Indian stories of the Creation" (280). At least one incident in Doxtater likely derives from such a non-Iroquois source: the young girl treacherously swung into our world from the sky.

Claude Lévi-Strauss regards the swing as a vertical axis linking sky and terrestrial planes in North American native mythology (1981, 414). However, as an instrument used to expel a young lady out of one realm into another, Doxtater's swing does not so much connect worlds as separate them. Her swing incident sounds more like what folklorists call "the swing trick" or "the fatal swing" in which an evil woman tries to kill a younger rival by causing the girl to fall off a swing into a pool of water (Thompson 1929, 350; Waterman 1914, 49). Although I cannot confirm its presence specifically among the Abenaki, a similar swing incident is characteristic of Algonquian folklore from the Great Lakes to the St. Lawrence.[4]

Another possible Abenaki influence is (vaguely) detectable in Doxtater's reference to old ones circling a mountain peak to renew their youth. When Allen questioned Anna and Si Johnson about this puzzling detail, she was told, "in the first part of Creation people didn't die but when they got very, very old, they went up to the top of a knoll and lay down and turned into stones" (1948a, L). If Doxtater's old ones on a mountain relate to the concept of turning into stones, it is a notion at home among the Abenakis (Day 1998, 189) and present in Algonquian mythology throughout the Central and Northeastern Woodlands.[5]

Many of the details Doxtater relates seem idiosyncratically treated. For example, the ancient incident in which the mother's body is hurled into the heavens to create the sun and moon is said to illustrate the bad twin's wickedness, then it is slotted into the context of competition be-

4. The broad northern distribution of the swing incident among Algonquian speakers is inferred from Fisher 1946, 251; T. Michelson 1919, 615, 641; Schoolcraft 1999, 52; Speck 1925, 15; and Williams 1956, 258–59.

5. For examples from the Central and Northeastern Woodlands of being turned to stone, see Fisher 1946, 234; Leland 1992, 49, 62; Rand 1894, 292–93; Schoolcraft 1999, 151; and Skinner 1924–1927, 340, 365.

tween the brothers. Not simply garbled or misunderstood, this incident is being interpreted in an unfamiliar way.

Or again, a European-derived fairy godmother shows up to give Sky Holder popcorn and, later, to warn him about the imminent showdown. Clearly, Doxtater did not know about father Turtle who performs these acts in earlier versions. Perhaps sensing something was missing at these junctures, she supplied a character to accomplish acts that would otherwise go undone or seem inexplicable.

Hope Allen regarded both her main informants as exceptionally intelligent women who were natural historians and patient narrators (1948a, G, I, J). But Lydia Doxtater participated more actively in the wider non-Indian community and was the more self-conscious analyst. She, "especially, was always comparing Indian manners and customs" to the ways of non-Indians around her (1948b, 12).

Some features of Doxtater's creation were molded by her need to explain, to have the story she was telling make sense to her. The clearest evidence supporting this reading is interwoven throughout her account. Recall that Doxtater interpreted "Where the Earth Opens" as a story showing "how Nature and men and animals understood each other in the old days. . . . [T]he earth opened, just to help the boy." Similarly, in her account of creation, the most important tasks are undertaken by animals to help humans. Doxtater's world on Turtle's back is created not through spontaneous generation and not by the twins but by the animals working for a person: "Then all the animals put in and worked just as hard as they could and by the time the girl reached the surface of the water they had enough on the back of the turtle for her to set her feet on and by night they had enough for her to lie down on. And they continued working after that. The birds brought seeds and they all worked together and made the world as we know it."

Some creation narratives of the modern era include an episode in which Sky Holder travels with several animals in a canoe to obtain the sun for mankind. When one of the animals (otter or muskrat) makes an inappropriate sound, his face is smacked with a paddle and flattened (Fenton 1962, 294; Hewitt 1974, 208, 318). The curious voyage of animals near the end of Doxtater's story seems to be a variation on this incident. Doxtater asserts the animals undertook this voyage to secure eternal life for people ("It was for the interest of human people they were working").

In 1918, Doxtater and the Johnsons were heirs to an ancient, pre-European mythic tradition probably extending—in the case of such motifs as the earth diver—many centuries into the past. In presenting the twins as exemplars of good and evil and as beings engaged in creative struggle, their versions also reflected emphases in the primal narrative fashionable throughout Iroquois country since the early 1800s.

At the same time, Oneida storytellers told a myth very much of their present. Both accounts situate the story in the local setting, and both share local peculiarities of plot and style. The account from the Johnsons is the more traditional in feel, but it also evinces connections to Canadian Iroquois sources, particularly to the Oneidas of Ontario. Doxtater's is notable for its more cosmopolitan outlook in foreign (non-Iroquois) Indian elements and its rationalistic approach. A clear example of innovation, it demonstrates how changes are introduced from the connections and questionings of the storyteller.

TWINS IN ONEIDA ART

Three objects fashioned by Oneidas long ago seem to depict the same subject: a pair of humans or humanlike faces or figures (ill. 14). This theme is recognizable on a variety of artifacts and materials spanning perhaps 450 years in the Oneida residential heartland, the area defined in 1788 as the Oneida Reservation.

A pipe of fired clay with a bowl about three inches high derives from an early archaeological site possibly dating to about 1350 (ill. 14, upper right). Presumably, it was used for smoking tobacco, an act requiring the smoker to stare into two humanlike faces.

Another object, also about three inches high and carved of antler, depicts two apparent people side by side with hands on upper chest (ill. 14, upper left). Evidently, it was a comb used either to comb the hair or as an ornament worn in the hair. Dating to about 1575–1610, it comes from an Oneida village site about a mile from the Honyoust place, the focus of a landownership controversy in the early twentieth century (see chapters 2 and 8).

A wooden bowl, probably made in the early 1800s, is about five inches high and fourteen inches wide at the mouth (ill. 14, lower center). Said to

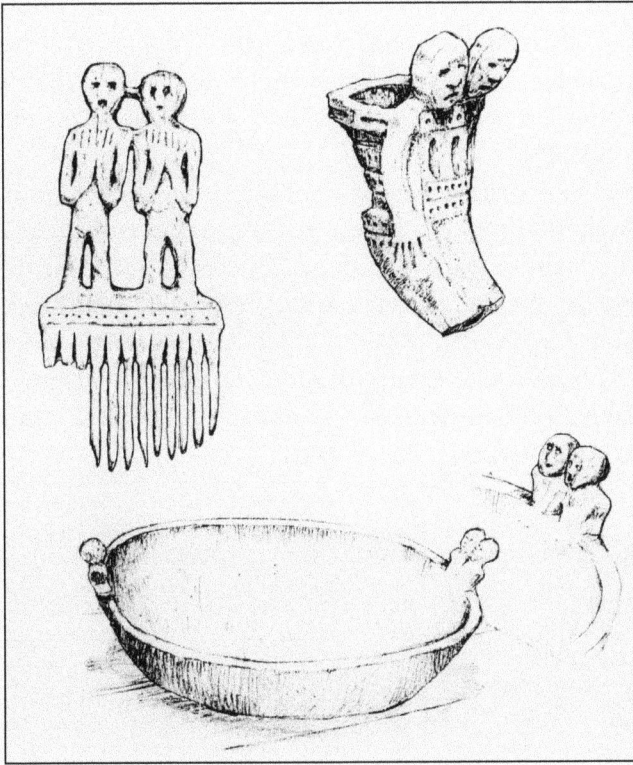

14. Possible twins in Oneida art. Upper right: ceramic pipe bowl from the Schmidka site (after a drawing courtesy of Gordon DeAngelo); upper left: carved antler comb (after a photo courtesy of Longyear Museum of Anthropology, Colgate University, no. 1556); bottom: wooden bowl with carved lugs (after a photo courtesy of the Division of Anthropology, American Museum of Natural History, no. 50.1/1837).

be fashioned from a burl of black ash, the vessel was used "for mixing and serving corn bread, and for general purposes" (accession notes, American Museum of Natural History, New York). On the rim are two handles, each constituting the upper torso of two figures (one is broken off), their eyes represented by tiny white beads of glass embedded in the wood. This object came from a Sherrill location about a mile down the road from Lydia Doxtater's and one-third of a mile from Hope Allen's residence.

My impression is that the artists of all three objects conveyed emotional as well as physical closeness between the figures. On the wooden bowl, for example, the arm of one figure is described as "thrown affectionately about the neck of its neighbor" (not visible in the illustration) (Harrington 1909, 86).

We cannot be certain who or what is represented here, nor whether the same subject is depicted in every instance. Yet in view of the antiquity, centrality, and persistence of the cosmogonic twin story, one would have to nominate Sky Holder and Flint as the most likely candidates. Such an identification suggests that allusion to the creation story was interwoven into a variety of media over some centuries. Oneidas, in other words, liked to be reminded of their culture's key narrative in small things that mattered in the daily business of living.

4

Old Ones of the Forest

Lewis Henry Morgan offered this characterization of the Iroquois folklore he knew in 1851:

> The fables which have been handed down from generation to generation, to be rehearsed to the young from year to year, would fill volumes. These fabulous tales, for exuberance of fancy, and extravagance of invention, not only surpass the fireside stories of all other people, but to their diversity and number there is apparently no limit. There were fables of a race of pigmies who dwelt within the earth, but who were endued with such herculean strength as to tear up by its roots the forest oak, and shoot it from their bows; fables of a buffalo of such huge dimensions as to thresh down the forest in his march; fables of ferocious flying-heads, winging themselves through the air; of serpents paralyzing by a look; of a monster musquito [*sic*], who thrust his bill through the bodies of his victims, and drew their blood in the twinkling of an eye. There were fables of a race of stone giants who dwelt in the north; of a monster bear, more terrific than the buffalo; of a monster lizard, more destructive than the serpent. There were tales of witches, and supernatural visitations, together with marvellous stories of personal adventure. (1962, 166)

Morgan's description rings true today and goes far toward defining what seems distinctive in Iroquois oral narrative. Beyond tales of creation, heroes, wonder, magic, and humor, there lurked a world of supernatural denizens autochthonous to the deep woods. Some were mostly benevolent, but the majority were dreadful most of the time. They are among the most popular characters in Iroquois folklore. Not surprisingly, Hope Allen was introduced to most of the basic supernatural cast—Little People, Flying Heads, Stone Giants, Vampire Corpses—by her Oneida friends.

Little People

When collector Mark Harrington passed through Oneida in 1907 (see pp. 133–34), he acquired a set of grinding stones from Melinda Johnson of the Orchard community (1907, 31 obverse; 1908, 578–79). Harrington was told, presumably by Johnson, "that when a good round stone was needed for a hammer or corn crusher that an Indian would go down to a creek and place an offering of tobacco beneath a flat stone and returning the next day find within the radius of a man's length a stone just suitable for his purposes" (Arthur Parker, quoted in Converse 1908, 101n).

This commerce for mullers occurred between Oneidas and a race of tiny people. Allen did not record whether these dwarf folk were related to the Oneidas' diminutive Thunders (see pp. 112–15). However, in 1919 she obtained from Lydia Doxtater a story of the little folk that told how sexual irresponsibility leads to dire consequences.

LITTLE PEOPLE

The Indians never believed in flirty girls. They didn't like women who took up with every man who came along.

Once there was an Indian girl like this and finally she married a man—Indian fashion—who had just come to the village and went off with him in a boat.

Everyone warned her not to do it but she went even though she didn't know anything about him. She took her basket over her forehead and the little axe and kettle which everyone had in those days and went off.

They rowed a long way until they came to an island and there they spent the night. The next morning the husband went off and left the wife alone and without anything except what she had brought herself. The whole day went on and he didn't come home.

Finally she went out and found some wild potatoes, and ate them. And she found a fine hemlock tree and took her little axe and made herself a little house with bark and with hemlock boughs for a bed.

It was near winter but her husband never came back. She

went out and got enough wild potatoes for the winter and enough fire wood and she once found a deer caught in a tree so that she was able to kill it. She brought it home and cut it up and cured the meat and tanned the hides. And had enough hides and enough meat for the winter (in those days one did all these things). So she lived through the winter.

Once towards Spring she was sitting by a fine fire and suddenly some hands were thrust into the room. They were very chapped and she took some of her good deer's grease and rubbed them with it. Again the next night they were stuck into the room. Again and again she rubbed them with deer's grease.

The third night some little people came in and told her she had been so kind to them in rubbing their chapped hands that they would do what they could for her so they brought her everything good to eat and sang and danced for her. This they did every night till finally some of her own people came over to the island and found her and took her home.

After that she never had any more desire to take up with strangers. (1948b, 65–66)

English-speakers have called this race of supernatural humanoids dwarfs, elves, fairies, and pygmies. Usually, however, they are called simply "the little people." In Oneida, they are *tehotikal:luhe'* (Abbott 1996, 418). In Seneca, according to Arthur Parker, they are the *Djogeon*,

little people who live in caves. They are a tribe by themselves and live in houses as men do. They frequent deep gulches and the borders of streams. In some ways they are tricky, but in general do not injure men. They are not successful hunters and are grateful for the fingernail parings of human beings. These are saved by the thoughtful and tied in little bundles which are thrown over cliffs for the Djogeon to gather as "hunting medicine." They also require tobacco and when they require it they will tap their water drums in their meeting places. The observant then make up little packages of tobacco which they throw to them. Out of gratitude for favors they frequently warn men of danger or assist them to fortune. (1989, 18)

Parker distinguished three types or tribes of Little People: ones devoted to hunting, ones promoting plant growth, and ones who deal most with humans (332). This latter, generic, sort is the subject of most folklore.

Perhaps two feet high, the Little People are visualized as a miniature race of Indians dressing and living in traditional fashion. They appear or disappear at will and are supernaturally powerful. They seem to dance and drum a great deal and are sometimes seen traveling in canoes. They are fond of squirrel meat and appreciate human help in dispatching those animals (Randle 1953, 633; see also Cornplanter 1986, 34). Whether or not Little People are poor hunters, they seem to have mystic connections with the forest animals. They know where the game is and can bestow hunting success (including the ability to call deer) on humans (Beauchamp 1922, 43; Hewitt 1918, 452–53; E. Smith 1983, 39–40).

Although mischievous and not to be trifled with, Little People are kindly disposed toward people. In the earliest account known to me, Little People are the enemies of all monsters "prejudicial to man" (Myrtle 1855, 122). Their specific nemesis, as Morgan heard, is a species of giant subterranean buffalo that Little People slay far to the south, evidently at the Big Bone Licks in Boone County, Kentucky (see E. Smith 1983, 19–20). In later accounts, the Creator charges the Little People to aid humans and to help cure human illnesses (Fenton 1987, 95–97).

In non-Christian Iroquois communities, Little People are thought to combat human sickness through the offices of a medicine society ("Pygmy Society," according to Parker) and a ritual called the Dark Dance, a curing ceremony held anytime to treat illnesses of a general sort (Kurath 2000, 13–14; Parker 1913, 119–21; Speck 1995, 109–11).

Doxtater's story illustrates how Little People typically behave in Iroquois oral narrative: they help humans in trouble, they feed children, they dispatch a monster bear chasing people, and they rescue a group of human hunters who, owing to their own profligacy, are starving (Curtin 2001, 426; E. Smith 1983, 20–22; Weitlaner 1915, 310).

Widely though sporadically documented across North America, the Little People are especially at home in eastern forests.[1] Although belief in

1. For a sense of Little People throughout the East, see Bierhorst 1985, 209; 1995, 10, 61–62; Lankford 1987, 132–34; Rand 1894, 431–33; Simmons 1986, 235–46; Swanton 1929, 149, 247–48; Thompson 1929, 356, motif F495; and Witthoft and Hadlock 1946.

small folk of some sort is attested all over the Northeast and Southeast, the lore of the Cherokees and the Wyandots seems particularly close to the stories of the Iroquois.

Cherokee dwarfs are handsome mountain people with very long hair and a love of music and dance (Mooney 1995, 333–34). An ancient and magically potent race, these small folk are capable of conferring hunting success on humans but, in comparison to Iroquois Little People, are perhaps more to be feared for their mean-spirited pranks (Witthoft and Hadlock 1946).

Even closer to Iroquois thinking are Wyandot notions of Little People. Living in rocky places, Wyandot Little People also enjoy dancing and drumming, and may give their human friends hunting success. They were created by the good twin to assist in the struggle against the evil twin and *his* minions, the Stone Giants. The Iroquois and Wyandot share some of the same narratives about these folk, including the story of a giant witch buffalo killed by Little People at the salt licks in Kentucky.

Flying Heads

Flying Heads seem polymorphic and perhaps polysemous in Iroquois thought. On the one hand, they belong to a class of spirits called the Common Faces of the Forest. At least some of these beings are bodiless heads said to flit from tree to tree (Fenton 1987, 121), and they furnish one explanation for the origin of the False Face medicine society. Disclosing themselves to hunters or to dreamers, the faces instruct people "to carve likenesses in the form of masks, promising that whenever anyone makes ready for the feast, invokes their help while burning tobacco, and sings the curing songs, supernatural power to cure disease will be conferred on human beings who wear the masks" (27).

On the other hand, Flying Heads personify the power of wind, cutting a swath of downed trees through the forest. In this sense, they are called (in Seneca) *Dagwanoenyent*—meaning cyclone or whirlwind (Hewitt 1918, 796 n. 116).[2] This Flying Head is the one commonly encountered

2. In a 1937 story, Cornplanter equated this form of Flying Head *(Da-gwa-nonh-enh-yen)* with the god or spirit of the West Wind, a being ordered by the Creator to bury the Stone Giants in a ravine (1986, 49–51).

in turn-of-the-twentieth-century folktales: a great head without a body, a being with terrible eyes and long hair (Parker 1989, 13).

The earliest written reference to Flying Heads occurs in Tuscarora David Cusick's *Sketches of Ancient History of the Six Nations,* probably published in 1827. This history, the first written in English by a native Iroquois person, is, in large measure, a compendium of oral narrative themes then current among the Iroquois (Judkins 1987). Cusick described Flying Heads as a race of cannibal monsters who suddenly invade Iroquois country. After one of them sees what he thinks is a woman eating coals (actually acorns) out of a fire, they draw off in fear (Beauchamp 1892, 14; Johnson 1881, 54).

Iroquois Flying Heads sometimes battle Stone Giants (Hewitt 1918, 481–85) but, more frequently, chase after humans (Randle 1953, 623–24; see also Fenton 1948, 114–17). They have been known to massacre whole villages (Curtin 2001, 494–95). Wyandots, the only other people I know of in the East who share this concept, have Flying Heads who behave in the same belligerent fashion (Barbeau 1915, 313).[3]

Two Flying Head stories were fairly standardized. In the first, a Flying Head proves surprisingly helpful to a group of brothers preyed upon by a witch. Here the head is featured as a benevolent creature who destroys the villain and resuscitates the slain siblings (Curtin 2001, 482–86; Hewitt 1918, 485–90; E. Smith 1983, 13–16).

Running truer to form in the second plot, the Flying Head is depicted as an evil wizard. Jeremiah Curtin (2001, 379–80) and Erminnie Smith (1983, 45–47) documented the same story of this type that Lydia Doxtater told in 1918:

FLYING HEADS

Once there was a boy who lived alone with his grandmother. She had to work very hard getting food and was away all day but

---

The Senecas call the Common Faces of the Forest *Hodigohsóska'ah* (Fenton 1987, 116). Cusick knew the Flying Heads as *Ko-nea-rau-neh-neh,* a term that Beauchamp said was *Ro-nea-rau-yeh-ne* in Onondaga (1892, 60).

3. Other peoples have rolling skulls, to be sure, and one can sometimes find bodiless, cannibalistic heads (see Radin 1948, 100–101). My point is that disembodied heads as flying creatures seem confined to the Iroquois and Wyandots.

before she would go out she would point out a certain direction and say, "You must never go that way. If you did great harm would come to you."

The boy got very dull being alone and one day he decided to go in the direction he had never been in but he waited until his grandmother was out of sight before he started.

After he had gone some distance he heard a voice from above although he saw nothing. The voice said, "What would you do if it should rain forks?" The boy laughed and said "We should run away." But when he went home and told his grandmother, she was very much afraid and said "Oh, what a terrible thing you have done; now we are lost." And then it began to storm and storm harder, and harder. And forks began to fall but the boy saw a big stone and as he was very strong, he lifted it up and he and his grandmother climbed under it and were safe but their tepee was blown down.

But the next day the boy started again in the same direction as soon as his grandmother had gone out and again he heard the voice. This time it said "What would you and your grandmother do if it should rain manure?"

And again the boy laughed and said "I should run away," and again he went home and told his grandmother and again she was very much afraid and said, "Oh, what a terrible trouble you have brought on us" and sure enough then it began to be stormy and to rain manure. But again the boy who was very strong, lifted up the stone and crept under it with his grandmother and they were safe.

But the next day the boy started out the third time in the dangerous direction and heard the voice but this time Lydia doesn't remember what it did storm but again they were safe under the stone from the deluge and again the next morning the boy started out the same way.

This time he was determined to get the best of the voice so when he was near where he had heard it, he took care to get there by a direction he had never come from before and spoke first and said, "Uncle, how would you like it if it should blow a great wind and break down all the crotches of the trees and leave nothing of them?" Then he saw high up in a tree a great head with a great deal of hair but no body and the voice said, "Oh, nephew, nephew, that is a terrible wish, don't wish that." And then it began to blow and blow and sure enough it broke down all the crotches of the trees and left nothing of them and the great head was never heard of any more and the boy and his grandmother lived and prospered. (Allen 1948b, 23–25)

The Curtin and Smith versions begin with the same warning—don't go in a certain direction—which the boy hero ignores in the same fashion. Initiating a tale with an act of disobedience is one of the most widespread patterns in North American Indian folktales (Dundes 1964, 64). In an analysis based on V. Propp's structural description of Russian fairy tales (1968), Dundes defines the sequence as one of interdiction followed by violation. This convention initiates both Oneida Thunder stories (see pp. 112, 114) and is said to be characteristic of hero tales (compare with the opening of "Where the Earth Opens" in chapter 2; and Dundes 1964, 91).

The Oneida narrative of the Flying Head tells of a contest between wizards, another theme widely known throughout native North America. Among the Iroquois, a common characteristic of the story line is to oppose the "magic power of a hero to the magic power of some wizard or witch, and the hero is often called 'a wizard' for he is the possessor of magic power, and because his magic is superior to that of his opponents he is able to overcome them" (Randle 1953, 615). Broadly speaking, a story such as "Where the Earth Opens" is of this type. However, the classic wizards' duel of the Iroquois highlights the showdown as the focus of the plot and features a stock set of contests in the struggle. Typically, the wizards match powers in a footrace, an ordeal of endurance, or a contest of hiding, dream guessing, or shape changing (see Parker 1989, 241–52; and Sanborn 1888, 196–99).

The Oneida story illustrates one form of this duel sequence in which it is essential to see one's opponent first. The villain initially succeeds in doing so, then causes spears to rain from the sky. Surviving by hiding under a rock or turning his house to stone, the hero subsequently gets the drop on the other, then counters with a magic force that kills the opponent. Thought of as a wizards' duel, this plot does not require one of the parties to be a Flying Head (Curtin 2001, 167–75, 327–50).

The story Allen recorded apparently differs from others of the genre by invoking forks instead of spears. This difference, however, was a purely linguistic desideratum. As Doxtater later told Allen, she meant to say pitchforks. Later still, she indicated the same Oneida word was used for fork, pitchfork, and spear (Allen 1948b, 25).[4]

Wizards dueled throughout Iroquoia, but only in Oneida country did they operate under a cascade of manure. Doxtater told Allen "that once in the rain Aunt Sally Johnson came by their house and her mother called out 'You going to Oneida in this rain?' Aunt Sally said 'Yes, I shall go if it rains manure.' Her mother answered, 'Will you go if it rains spears?' and Aunt Sally answered, 'No, I think I shall stop at that' " (Allen 1948b, 40).

Stone Giants

"Several days ago," Hope Allen wrote on December 26, 1918, "Lydia told me a story of a 'Stone Giant' " (1948b, 41–42).

STONE GIANTS

She said once a man and his wife and little girl lived by a creek where there was a great deal of game. The man was a very fine hunter and used to go off hunting a great deal. Once his wife was alone with the baby and the door opened and a man walked in. He at once made himself very agreeable and seemed to take a great fancy to the little girl and took her on his knee and patted her.

After awhile the husband neared home and as he came in sight of his house he was struck with terror for he saw what seemed to be a stone man standing in front. He was so terror stricken that he ran away as fast as he could.

Soon the stranger said to the wife: "I think your husband is come home and he has been terribly scared and he thinks he is running as fast as he can but really he is just jumping up and down where he is."

---

4. Clifford Abbott kindly confirmed this point (personal communication). An Oneida word used for spear, fork, or pitchfork is *á:shekwe*.

So he opened the door and what had scared the husband was his coat of a stone giant which he had left standing in front when he came in. Then the husband came in and the stranger lived with them all winter and ate what they ate.

Stone Giants really are cannibals and Lydia used to be terribly afraid of them when she was a child, but when he took his stone shirt off he was like other men.

When Spring came he said that he had left his wife because she was a very domineering woman and used to oppress him, but that now she was coming to find him and would soon be there. He told them that he would fight with her and she would get the best of it if they didn't help him.

He said they were to go down to the creek and get a good size piece of dogwood and when they saw her getting the upper hand they were to put that under her feet and trip her. This would give him a breathing spell so that he could get the better of her.

It happened just as he said. The woman came complaining loudly because her husband had left her children all winter and they had nearly starved. "You have got nothing for me," she said, "and now I have come to fight you."

So they fought but the man and his wife tripped her and she fell and her husband conquered.

Lydia said her grandmother used to tell this story when she was in her dotage and doze over it, and she said that the Stone Giant's wife came across the stream covered with silver brooches. (Allen 1948b, 41–42)

David Cusick's 1827 history describes Stone Giants (also called Stone Coats)[5] as another race of fierce cannibals who once swept out of the North to terrorize the Iroquois. Rendered impervious to human weapons

---

5. Their Seneca name, *Genonsgwa* or *Genonska'*, may be translated as Stone Coat, Stone Shirt, Stone Giant, or Monster Man, according to Hewitt (1918, 812n. 457). Cusick called them *Ot-ne-yar-heh*, which Beauchamp identified as Oneida (1892, 15, 61). He was surely correct, inasmuch as the Oneida word *atn'yálhu* is glossed as "giant, boogeyman" (Abbott 1996, 120).

by their lithic exteriors, the giants had an easy time of it until Sky Holder came to the aid of his people. That deity assumed the aspect of a Stone Giant, lured them into a ravine near Onondaga, then buried all but one under a torrent of boulders (Beauchamp 1892, 15–16).

Stone Giants were great favorites of folklore, the stories about them tending to be standardized into three story types. Cusick's plot, the first of the recurrent patterns, was documented throughout Iroquois country around the turn of the twentieth century (Curtin 2001, 122–23; Hewitt 1918, 682–85; Johnson 1881, 55–56; Parker 1989, 340–41, 394–96, 425–26; E. Smith 1983, 13). In later tellings, the supernatural who intervenes on behalf of humanity is the Creator or the Great Spirit, rather than Sky Holder.

To explain the origin of "Stonish Giants," Cusick referred to what he called a Shawnee tradition that these brutes had started out as human beings but had become increasingly large and savage. They acquired their hard skins by rolling around in the sand (Beauchamp 1892, 15). The woodcut he composed to illustrate this passage depicts two large people brandishing clubs and wearing what look like seamless, hooded bodysuits of very bumpy texture (Bryden 1995, 62). Each of their heads (or hoods?) rises up to form an odd-looking knob projecting forward from the top of the skull.

A number of later sources agreed these beings had pointy heads (Cornplanter 1986, 47; Fenton 1987, 127; Turner and Hickerson 1952, 12). The idea that their hard coverings resulted from rolling in the sand was familiar also to Arthur Parker (1989, 394),[6] and, though not univer-

---

6. But, as Parker noted, "there appears to be some confusion as to the origin of the stone coats" (1989, 402). The greatest confusion, I think, was Hewitt's, and it grew out of his conviction that Stone Giants were an unfortunate abstraction resulting from an Iroquois misunderstanding of their own language and myth (1918, 806n. 303).

The quintessential deity connected with stone, Hewitt reasoned, was Flint or Tawiskaron—the evil twin of the cosmogonic myth. Stone is "poetic license" for flint, which, in turn, meant ice. Interpreting the creation myth as metaphor for seasonality, Hewitt convinced himself that Flint (that is, Tawiskaron) personified winter. Indeed, he was *the* Winter God.

In the thinking of the Iroquois, Hewitt asserted further that "the Flint-clad Man-being became separated and distinct from the Man-being of the Winter. At this point the fictitious Man-being who was Stone-clad parted company forever with the personified nasally agreed, most storytellers insisted the giants' stone coverings were garments taken off at night (Curtin 2001, 122; Hewitt 1918, 683; Parker 1989, 335; Randle 1953, 631). Parker thought such coats were made of flint (1989, 18).[7]

Stone Giants were credited with extraordinary strength and with such magical powers as the ability to disable humans with a shout (Beauchamp 1892, 28–29; Goldenweiser 1914, 474). Seducers of lonely hunters in the North Woods, Stone Giant women could be strangely alluring. Most consistently, however, Stone Giants (like Little People) were considered to have mystical ties with game. They were highly accomplished hunters capable of conveying luck in the chase to humans (Curtin 2001, 216, 511; Hewitt 1918, 437; Parker 1989, 336–39).

The second standardized plot about these creatures (also appearing for the first time in Cusick) concerns an Iroquois hunter chased by a Stone Giant. When the hunter climbs a tree, the giant stands beneath it perplexed. This incident highlights an important trait of this race: they cannot look up because of the inflexibility of their necks. The Stone Giant pulls out a magic pointer or game finder: a human hand or finger (alternatively, a stone finger). Pointing upward, the object's behavior puzzles the dim-witted giant whose hesitation allows the hunter to seize the pointer and race away. The man may keep the charm or return it. In either event, the man benefits in some fashion, usually as the recipient of luck in hunting (Beauchamp 1892, 28–29; 1922, 41; Curtin 2001, 123; Parker 1989, 337–39; E. Smith 1983, 17–18).

The chase scene of this scenario often has the man crossing and recrossing a river while the Stone Giant lumbers slowly across on the river bottom. This sequence allows the human to gain a lead on his pursuer and seemingly accounts for his name—Skunniwundi, one translation of which

---

ture force or process that was frost-bearing and ice-clad [Tawiskaron]. The former was gradually reduced to a peculiar species of mankind—the stone giant, for he was represented as stone-clad, while the latter retained his first estate as one of the chief characters in the Genesis myth of the Iroquoian peoples" (1918, 63–64).

7. Hewitt (1918) also thought Stone Giant coverings were made of flint. Moulton and Abler believe Stone Giants and Flint, the evil twin, are mythological reflections of prehistoric stone-tool technology (1991).

is "Cross-the-Creek" (Parker 1989, 334–39; 1994, 21). The same incident showcases another characteristic of these stone-clad beings: they cannot swim. Emerging from the water, the giant often encounters a stone ax left by the man. Spitting on it or rubbing the blade with his finger, the Stone Giant unwittingly imparts to the ax the power to split rock. When the man regains the tomahawk, its effectiveness becomes obvious to both parties. This story segment concludes with the Stone Giant fleeing or being dispatched with the ax (Beauchamp 1922, 146–47; Curtin 2001, 509–10; Goldenweiser 1914, 474; Parker 1989, 334–35; Randle 1953, 626–27).

Lydia Doxtater's story belongs to the third type of Stone Giant tale. A young family out hunting is visited by a Stone Giant who, in all versions other than Doxtater's, is female (Beauchamp 1922, 148; Curtin 2001, 511; Hewitt 1918, 437–39; Parker 1989, 335–36; E. Smith 1983, 16–17). The visitor helps the family achieve hunting success and often aids in other ways—for example, she provides a prodigious amount of firewood. When the Stone Giant's husband shows up, the two monsters engage in mortal combat. Because the spouse is stronger, the Stone Giant woman requires human assistance. Generally, one of the people has to spear the male brute in the back or anus. Here is a theme of human intervention that will recur in the next chapter: a supernatural needs human help to overcome an enemy.

The reason the Stone Coat woman visits this nuclear family is that, earlier, she had formed a bond with the human male. That man, as it happens, was an irresponsible young person avoiding marriage—another situation we will encounter again. Hunting alone the previous year, the man had fallen prey to the Stone Giant's seductions, and, now, she returned to present him with his child (Hewitt 1918, 555–64; Turner and Hickerson 1952, 11–12). Subsequently, the human wife will desert the hunter, and no other woman will have anything to do with him. Thus, the story exemplifies a moral suggested by the story about Little People: terrible things happen to those individuals who "refuse to participate in normal human sexual conduct" (Randle 1953, 625).

The Iroquois Stone Giants closely resemble the Wyandots' flinty giants, who also lose their human-finger pointers to more nimble humans and run from axes they unwittingly sharpened. The name of the Wyandot human who perplexes the giant by repeatedly crossing the stream is about the same as the name of his Iroquois counterpart: Skadawa'ti, or "Always on the Other Side of the River" (Barbeau 1915, 60–63).[8]

The Iroquois creatures have something in common with "Dressed in Stone," the Cherokee cannibal whose magic cane indicates the direction of human game (Fogelson 1980; Mooney 1995, 319–20, 469). Additionally, there are similarities between the Stone Giants and various races of northern cannibal monsters familiar to neighboring Algonquian peoples, including Wendigo of the Chippewa and Ojibwa and Chenoo of the Micmac (Barnouw 1977, 120–31; Bierhorst 1995, 12). But because the Algonquian ghouls are not necessarily stone-clad or gigantic, the striking commonality is a thematic one. A recurrent plot describes how one of these creatures shows up at a human family's hunting camp and becomes their friend. When a fellow cannibal monster attacks, the first monster needs human aid to dispatch the second (see Bierhorst 1995, 59–60; Morrison 1979, 58–61; Parsons 1925, 59–60; and Rand 1894, 190–99).

Closest to the Iroquois case may be the Passamaquoddy (Maine-New Brunswick) Kewahqu'. This creature equips itself with an exterior covering reminiscent of the Stone Giant: "In summer time they rub themselves all over with . . . fir balsam, and then roll themselves on the ground, so that everything adheres to the body,—moss, leaves, and even small sticks" (Leland 1992, 247). Among Kewahqu', the female is the more fierce and powerful. Hence, in the scenario requiring human assistance, people help the more domesticated male Kewahqu' to conquer the attacking female. This detail, of course, is what makes Doxtater's account of the Stone Giant's visit seem so idiosyncratic in an Iroquois context. It is further evidence of New England Algonquian influence showing up in Doxtater's repertoire (see p. 82).

---

8. The occurrence of the same name in the same context in Iroquois and Wyandot versions is, to my mind, proof of the word's primary meaning.

Fenton referred to Skanawundi as a trickster figure in Iroquois folklore (1947, 386), a character Randle thought was the Hare (1953, 626). Parker employed the word in the title to his book of animal stories for children, *Skunny Wundy.* In that work, he implied that Skunny Wundy might be a rabbit or raccoon (1994, 13–22). Elsewhere, Parker characterized Skunniwundi as a great warrior and "a great name" (1989, 334), whereas Jesse Cornplanter maintained that Ska-nonh-wonh-dih designated a braggart (1986, 49). All of these names presumably are variant spellings of the same word.

The monstrous guest described by Doxtater instructs his hosts to obtain "a good size piece of dogwood" with which to trip the hostile Stone Giant. Knowing that dogwood usually meant the red osier dogwood (see chapter 6), Allen was puzzled by the description and use of this wood (1948b, 42). In this instance, however, Doxtater probably remembered a different tree—the basswood (genus *Tilia*), "reputed in legendary lore as having the power of depriving a Stone Coat of strength and life" (Hewitt 1918, 807n. 305). In general, the Iroquois overcome Stone Giants not by locating a secret vulnerable point on the body or the hiding place of a removable heart, but by wielding a weapon made of basswood (330–31, 803n. 228). When a Stone Giant needs human help in overcoming one of its kind, the Seneca friend will spear the enemy with one or several fire-hardened basswood poles (Hewitt 437–39, 555–64; Parker 1989, 336). Doxtater's chunk of wood, however, sounds more like the block of "lynnwood" Wyandots employ to beat flinty giants to death (Barbeau 1915, 8, 64; see also Hewitt 1918, 807n. 305). The Wyandots' lynnwood must be linden *(Tilia)*—that is, "linn or basswood" (Mooney 1995, 421).[9]

Vampire Corpses

The favorite story of Iroquois people everywhere at the turn of the twentieth century may have been a blood-curdler often called the Vampire or Cannibal Corpse (Beauchamp 1922, 13–15; Parker 1989, 298–300; E. Smith 1983, 47–48). Describing it as a historical incident that took place in Oneida country, Tuscarora David Cusick was again the first to set the tale to paper:

9. The Cherokee "Dressed in Stone" is also said to be vulnerable to basswood in some versions (Fogelson 1980, 150n. 15; Lankford 1987, 131–32). Among the Iroquois, basswood has some seemingly minor medical applications. Otherwise, it is prized in Iroquois culture for its easily worked wood, from which False Face masks are fashioned (Herrick 1995, 21, 146). This use may explain the thinking behind Parker's unusual explanation for the False Face medicine society: the souls of dead Stone Giants reside in basswood trees (1989, 396–401). Although Parker attributes his story to a Seneca informant, he may have drawn at least part of it from the generally unreliable Harriet Maxwell Converse (1908, 76–78).

VAMPIRE CORPSES

About this time a strange thing happened near the village of Kaunehsuntahkeh, situated east of Oneida creek: a man and his wife and another person returned from hunting, but before they reached the village the night was getting late; they went into a house to stay over the night; the house where the dead bodies were deposited; they kindled a fire and went to sleep, but when the fire was out, the room became dark, the man heard something was gnawing: the man kindled the fire, he discovered the person was dead eaten by a ghost; he was so frightened that he trembled; he immediately told his wife to quit the room as soon as possible; he remained a few moments and also left the house and followed his wife and overtook her, but she became faint and could not run fast; they saw a light coming and supposed the ghost was chasing; fortunately they gained the village. The next day the people went and burnt the dead bodies. This important event was soon made known among the five nations, and afterward changed their mode of burying, by setting posture face to the east. (Beauchamp 1892, 30)

Hope Allen encountered it among the Oneidas more than ninety years later as one of the first stories given her by Anna Johnson:

VAMPIRE CORPSE

It began with all the Indians going to a great gathering—perhaps a council—in every way they could. Some went on horse back, some drove, and one couple with a child went on foot. These walked as hard as they could all day and when night came they were so tired—first the one would carry the child and then the other—that they dropped down into a cabin they came to about dark, and went to sleep on the dirt floor. Towards morning the man woke up and heard crunching on the shelf above. And then he saw that the child was gone. Through whispering he and his wife decided to leave and he told her out loud to go out to the spring for water to make them their morning drink and come back. She did not come back and about noon he said out loud that he wondered what had become of her and he must go and see. As soon as he found her they began to run—as fast as they could and they ran all night. Finally she got so tired she dropped and then he told her to lie close to a stump as if she was part of it. They had been hearing the terrible cry of the spectre getting nearer and nearer.

So he went on, and came in sight of the great dances and the platform where all the people were dancing—by the light of pine knots. They had been running all night. At last he got the attention of the crowd and they came out and ran back to catch the ghost just as day [dawned]. They found a corpse with a bloody mouth.(1948a, D)[10]

Allen's account does not develop a moral, but she must have heard one in the original telling. "My gentle Indian char-woman tells me a terrible ghost story told her by her grandmother [Dolly Antone]," Allen noted about 1918, "which was founded on this custom"—that is, abandoning a dwelling in which a death occurred (Hirsh 1989, 59–60).

"This is one of the most popular Iroquois stories," Martha Champion Randle observed, "and is found in practically all of the collections. That so many versions were collected at Six Nations about 1915 [Waugh recorded five] shows how well-known it was at that time."

> The story is simple: a group of people, two or more men, or a married couple with or without a child, stay overnight in a lodge on the trail. During the night one of the party is attacked and eaten by a vampire, for a sorcerer's corpse has been left in the shack and has turned vampire. The remaining member or members of the party attempt escape, usually talking first in matter-of-fact tones so that the vampire shall be deceived as to their knowledge of its deed. Some member of the party effects his escape and reaches a community where he relates his experience. The next day a party is sent out to investigate and finds the corpse with blood upon it. A further destruction of the corpse, by tomahawk, by burning, or by earth burial, then takes place.

10. The last sentence is added from a different passage (Allen 1948b, 9), where it is identified as the concluding sentence of this story.

"Generally," Randle concluded, "this story is accompanied by a discussion of the various forms of burial, and is given as one reason why the ancient custom of burial in a bark case inside a shack or on a scaffold in the trees was abandoned" (1953, 632).

As we have seen in connection with "Where the Earth Opens," Iroquois people maintained "the story was always an illustration of some moral or principle" (Johnson 1881, 220). Indeed, no oral narrative more clearly illustrates this tendency than the Vampire Corpse, which nearly always inspired the narrator to expiate on changes in burial practice. Here, for example, is part of one such passage concluding a Seneca version of the story during the 1870s:

> Taking down the bark box, they looked at the skeleton of the dead man and found his face and hands bloody. The chief said it was not right to leave dead people in that way; therefore they dug a hole, in which they buried the man-eating skeleton, and took the bones of the other man home. The chief had him buried and ordered that thereafter all dead people should be buried in the ground. At first the dead were put on scaffolds, but the people used to see sights which frightened them, for the dead would rise and run after the living. Then it was resolved to build bark lodges for the dead and to put them on shelves therein. This plan did not work well, as the foregoing story shows. (Hewitt 1918, 459)

The Vampire Corpse may be unique to Iroquois folklore, although the Wyandot have similar stories about the buried undead that are also given in explanation of changing mortuary customs (Barbeau 1915, 113–15, 152–53).

How Old?

At the turn of the twentieth century, Oneidas enjoyed telling stories about a suite of supernatural beings, including Little People, Flying Heads, Stone Giants, and Vampire Corpses. Two of these races were closely associated with forest animals and hunting magic, but all four species were very much at home in the woods.

Quite possibly, as beings at home *only* in the deep forest, they were native to and ancient in the eastern woods. We cannot, however, establish them as particularly old through documentary means. Three were initially mentioned in Cusick's history of 1827; the fourth appeared a quarter century later.

Nevertheless, an age comparable to the age of the creation story is implied by comparative considerations presented in this chapter. In all four instances, the closest affinities lie with the Wyandots of Oklahoma. Indeed, in the cases of Flying Heads and Vampire Corpses, the Wyandots furnish the only similarity I can identify. Resemblances are numerous, are present in virtually every case, and are often identical as to specific details. Not only, for example, do Wyandots and Iroquois visualize Little People in similar ways and tell similar stories about them, but both also speak of a giant buffalo killed by Little People at salt licks in Kentucky. Or again, not only do both enjoy similar stories about similar stonish giants, but both also tell a story about a giant who runs from an ax he unwittingly sharpened and loses his human-finger game pointer to a nimble human who bears the same name in Wyandot and Iroquois languages. Further, no other group in the intervening area shares anything like the stock of mythic material held in common by Wyandots and Iroquois.

How can one account for Iroquois and Wyandot forest monsters so closely resembling each other? Did Iroquois and Wyandots independently make up the same characters and stories? Did each group remember only those stories they happened to swap only with each other during the 1600s and 1700s? Did each group adopt identical monster stories at the same time from some unknown third group?[11]

Linguists recognize strong evidence for a historical relationship when they find pervasive similarities between two widely separated languages. If they can rule out alternative explanations (borrowing, chance, or independent development), the conclusion becomes unequivocal: such resemblances must be cognates descended from common ancestry (see Fiedel

---

11. Or, one could logically ask, is Iroquois folklore derived from Huron captives adopted into the New York Confederacy after the destruction of the Huron Confederacy? If so, Iroquois and Wyandot similarities result from a common Huron-Wyandot stock but not from a Huron-Iroquois stratum prior to 1650. Such a scenario requires earlier Iroquois lore to disappear, suddenly displaced by a massive influx of new oral narrative from a single source. This scenario seems wildly unlikely and inconsistent with evidence for the presence of a (specifically) Iroquois creation story predating 1650.

1991 and Mithun 1984). Franz Boas advanced this sort of argument in 1891 to explain the occurrence of the same story (which, after all, is a particularly complex linguistic package) in two distant locations (1940, 441–43). The cognate explanation also is the most parsimonious and historically appropriate reading of the Iroquois-Wyandot case.

The earliest cosmological myths of the Iroquoian-speaking Iroquois proper (New York) and Huron seem closely related on an early-seventeenth-century time level (see chapter 3). Iroquoian-speaking Wyandots are descended from the Huron and neighboring Petun tribes from the eastern shore of Lake Huron. After being dispersed in the mid-seventeenth century, some of these folk reconstituted themselves as the Wyandots and ended up near Detroit early in the eighteenth century. Descendants of those people were induced to move to Oklahoma by 1845 (Tooker 1978b).

In this instance, therefore, similarity in folklore content is attributable to the same ancestral stock of oral narrative. We have seen that the creation stories of the Hurons and Iroquois were closely related centuries ago (see chapter 3). And, in large measure because of that common stratum, creation stories told by Wyandots in Oklahoma and Iroquois in New York around 1900 resembled one another closely. Similarly, concepts of Little People, Flying Heads, Stone Giants, and undead ghouls must be coming out of the same source. That logic suggests these supernatural beings may well date to the early 1600s when Iroquois, Huron, and Petun presumably shared such concepts.

Concluding that Iroquois and Wyandot oral narratives are very similar is nothing new (Fenton 1947, 390–91), and, in fact, students of the subject often assumed they were identical. Both Erminnie Smith (1983, 9–10) and William Beauchamp (1922, 118–21), for example, casually included the same Wyandot story in their Iroquois compilations.[12] Presumably, they sensed it *should* be an Iroquois tale because it embodied "the

---

12. The story was one Horatio Hale collected from a Wyandot informant in Ontario in 1874. It tells of a young Wyandot man abandoned to die by his comrades after being wounded on the warpath. Unexpectedly, the warrior is nursed back to health by a mysterious old man. Learning from a Thunder that his host is actually a giant porcupine, the human lures his benefactor into the open where the Thunders kill him. The human then goes on to help the Thunders locate and slay another of their enemies (1891).

most ancient and widespread beliefs of the tribes of the great Huron-Iroquois family" (Hale 1891, 289).

What seems odd is that no one found such similarity to be remarkable, or pointed out that it might carry implications for dating in historical research. Granted, as a dating method, this form of analysis is not free of bias and is not applicable, with any confidence, to any single narrative in contextual isolation. Further, acknowledging that oral narrative changes over time, one must always allow for the possibility of separate narrative trajectories developing out of a common origin. Nevertheless, the apparent common ancestry of Iroquois-Wyandot material is an important analytic tool that, if used judiciously, allows one to illuminate reaches of time otherwise inaccessible.

HUMAN FIGURES ON ONEIDA POTTERY

"The most intriguing item in any Oneida pottery collection is the effigy face or figure," an archaeologist observed of the humanlike depictions characteristic of ceramics from about the late 1400s to the mid-1600s (Whitney 1971, 12). Similar representations occurred on pottery of the other Iroquois nations in New York also, but the tradition was especially strong among the Oneidas and may have centered in Oneida country (ills. 15–16) (Wonderley 2002). These consciously fashioned images were of obvious conceptual importance to the users of the pottery. For us today, they remain the single greatest source of information about material symbols important to Oneidas long ago. What did these mysterious representations mean?

Iroquoian peoples everywhere employed vessels of fired clay to prepare the mainstay of their diet: a mush or gruel or boiled maize. Because some cooking vessels were decorated with effigies, the images were daily present on the hearth, and everyone must have known what they meant. Yet they were most resonant to the ones who grew, harvested, and stored the corn; prepared the corn to eat; and created the pots in which corn was cooked: the women. If, therefore, the meaning(s) of effigies had anything to do with how they were made and used, one would have to guess they related in some fashion to corn and perhaps femaleness and domesticity.

I think an analysis of the effigies as an artistic tradition leads to the

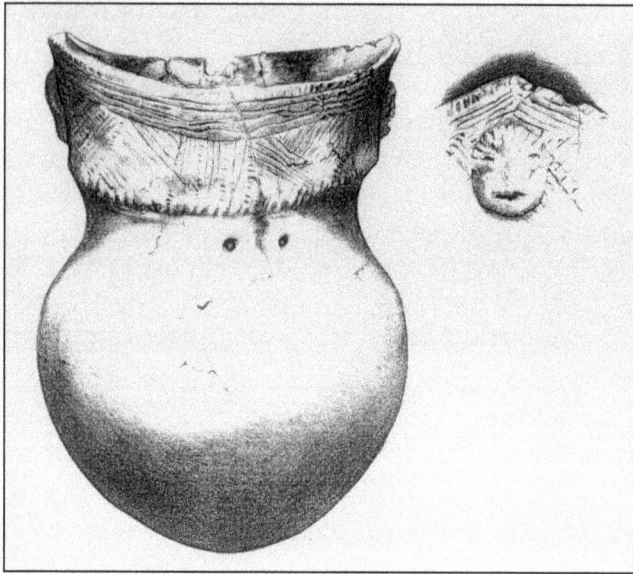

15. *Oneida pottery vessel with effigy (only one of two faces intact), about eleven inches high, circa 1500 (Longyear Museum of Anthropology, Colgate University, no. 2087).*

same conclusion. At first, only faces were shown (see ill. 15). Then bodies, characterized by sets of parallel notches called hash marks, were added over time as though to sharpen the recognition of whatever was being depicted (see ill. 16). Remarkably uniform, the subject matter itself is a tightly patterned cultural expression focusing on one humanoid or a limited set of anthropomorphic representations. Further, this humanlike image could occur at only one location: on the vessel exterior at or below a castellation (an upward flaring point at the top of the distinctive neck or collar of an Iroquois vessel).

The hash marks of the effigy figures were also characteristic of the "ladder motif" found throughout the Iroquoian world and occurring far more commonly than humanoid depictions. The ladder motif consisted of a strip of clay applied at the castellation and decorated with the parallel indentations (ill. 17c). The apparent identity of hash-marked design on both humanlike effigies and the ladder motif has been remarked by other researchers (Cervone 1991, 274; Kent 1984, 144). In the Oneida con-

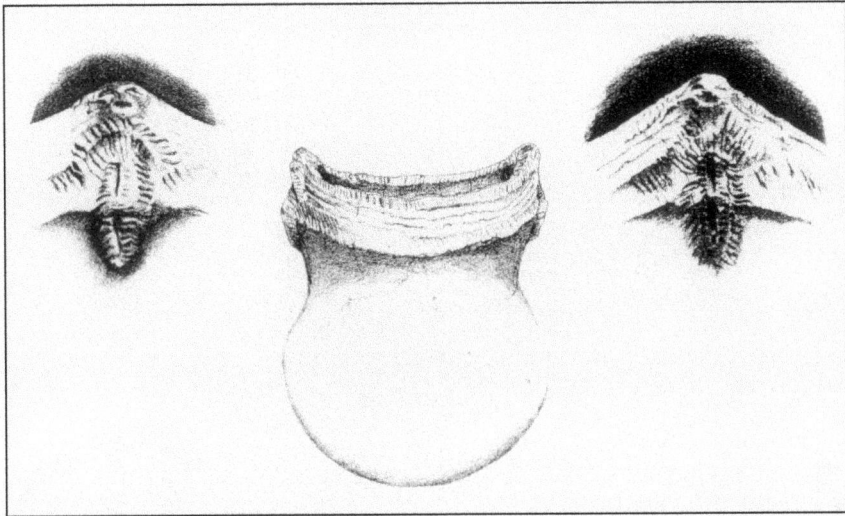

16. Oneida pottery vessel with two effigy figures, about 6.5 inches high, circa 1630 (Longyear Museum of Anthropology, Colgate University, no. 2426).

text, the resemblance seems particularly clear, inasmuch as the body of the fully developed anthropoid figure was typically constructed out of two apparent ladder motifs (ill. 17a).

But what were the hash marks meant to convey? Charles Wray et al. observe that the ladder motif resembles an ear of corn removed from the "corn ear" design (ill. 17e), the most obviously representational decoration found on the pottery of the St. Lawrence Iroquoians, an archaeologically known people along the St. Lawrence River in New York and Canada (1987, 79). Not an effigy attached to a castellation, the corn-ear design was a series of raised, vertically oriented ridges placed continuously around a vessel's rim. Similarly, George Hamell (1979, fig. 7 caption) suggests hash marks depicted corn-husk or corn-stalk materials.

In Oneida pottery after about 1500, hardly any design elements at the castellated effigy position departed from the figural theme. The few that did illustrate all the remarks made above. It looks as though the anomalies pertain to the ladder motif and perhaps even to a naturalistically depicted ear of corn (ill. 17a-d). The most plausible interpretation is that the Oneida humanoid effigy had something to do with corn.

Because no European documentation of ceramic effigies has survived,

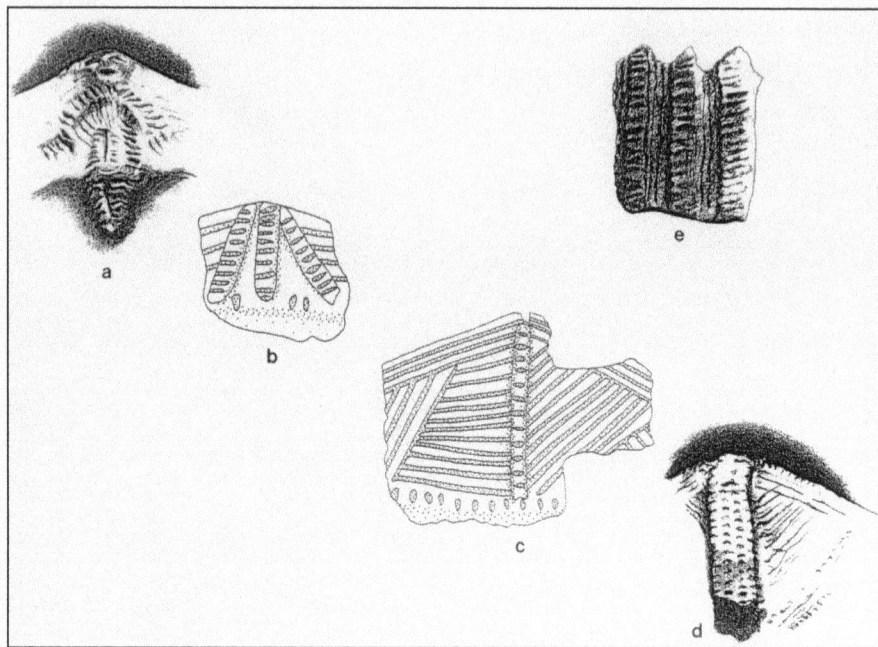

17. Forms of Oneida effigy designs (a-d) and the "corn ear" rim design (e).

we cannot consult the historical record to confirm or deny a link between pottery imagery and corn. However, we can try to establish the image's identity by searching the literature of Iroquois ethnography and oral narrative for some being who meets the criteria suggested by contextual and iconographic inquiry. The most likely candidate would be one encompassing full-figure imagery related to corn, and conformable with domesticity and femaleness. I think the subject most clearly satisfying these criteria is a race of beings responsible for the present-day Husk Face medicine society among the Iroquois, mythological cornhusk people for whom great antiquity is suspected (Fenton 1987, 444; Tooker 1970, 152).

Diminutive beings personifying plant fertility, cornhusk people are an industrious agricultural people especially concerned with growing corn, and it is cooked corn food that they crave. Cornhusk people are regarded as messengers of the Three Sisters who prophesy bountiful crops and many children (Fenton 1987, 383–404; Shimony 1994, 150; Speck 1995, 93–96; Tooker 1970, 72). Their leadership is dominated by women, and the cornhusk folk are strongly linked to women (Fenton 1987, 105, 408; Kurath 1968, 49, 182).

Stories about cornhusk people specify an appearance completely covered over by corn tassels or cornhusks: these beings "dress in cornhusks" (Fenton 1987, 399). This characteristic still came through in the origin myths for the Husk Face Society collected at the turn of the twentieth century. Husk Face knowledge in such tales derived from a hunter's encounter with a cornhusk person dressed up in corn tassels (Speck 1995, 96). The hunter was informed, "you must tell your people that you and they must prepare something with cornhusks which shall resemble the form of my body" (Fenton 1987, 387).

Insistence on full-figure bodily appearance seems consistent with the appearance of Oneida effigies. But I am even more intrigued by the manner in which the later folklore might clarify the logic behind effigy development. Over time, Oneida effigies increasingly defined the anatomical details of a complete figure, a figure decorated with hash marks very possibly related to corn. This evolution accomplishes exactly what the hunter was told to do.

5

⊹△⊹

Thunders

Thunder Stories

In early 1918, Hope Allen recorded that Lydia Doxtater's uncle, Daniel Webster, "who lived over on the West Road said that once he was haying over there and he lay down on a hay mound and looked up at some thunder caps overhead and as he looked he heard a clap of thunder and then he saw a little man walk out over one thunder cap and pass into another and then there was another clap of thunder" (1948b, 13). Webster's vision above the Windfall community was of one of the Thunders or Thunderers, celestial humanlike beings responsible for rain and lightning as well as the thunder.

The close kinship Oneidas felt for Thunders is implied in a story Doxtater told Allen about the same time:

THUNDER'S CHILD
Once there was a young girl who lived with her grandmother. The grandmother told her she must never walk in a certain direction but one day she disobeyed and did so.

She came to a beautiful spring and while she was there a man appeared before her—"a fine looking Indian." He asked her to marry him and she consented.

He wrapped her in his blanket and carried her away. She was all covered up so that she could not see where they were going but they went so fast it seemed as if they were flying. Finally he set her down and undid the blanket and she found herself in front of a tepee by a water and an old man sat in front of the door making fish nets. This was the new home of the maiden and the old man was her father-in-law.

The place all about was wonderfully beautiful. She lived there some time and was very happy. Then one day the old man said to her, "You are going to have a child and you must go home but when your child is grown, you must never let it play with other children for if you do, they will quarrel, as children do, and he may hit another child and something terrible will happen." Then again, her husband wrapped her all about in his blanket and carried her so swiftly it seemed that they were flying and she was set down at home.

There she lived and her child was born. And she tried to keep it away from other children but one day it was playing with others and as children will, it struck one and the child who was struck fell dead. Then the sky darkened and came a clap of thunder and the clouds seemed to stoop to the earth and take up the little boy, for he was the son of the Thunder God.

Lydia says that was why he couldn't hit another child without killing—"he was so full of electricity." She says that when after a thunder clap, a low rumble sometimes follows, people say, "That is the Thunder Boy." (15)

Allen mentioned another Oneida woman who had no fear of violent storms because "we have a relative there who makes the thunder" (13). The sentiment was widespread. Mohawks of the time believed the thunder was caused by seven men in the sky, one of them a mortal who "prevented them from harming Indians. Thus it is that no Indian is ever struck by lightning" (Beauchamp 1922, 116).

The theme of a human woman having a child by a Thunder who, in turn, is taken up to the sky to become one of the Thunders is found in folklore throughout Iroquois country. It dates to at least the mid-nineteenth century, to judge by the narrative as recorded by Lewis Henry Morgan among the Senecas (1962, 159–60). Morgan's form of the story includes the information that the Thunder lived behind Niagara Falls, and this belief was also shared by the Oneidas: Thunder "lives behind the waterfall and comes out in the sky" (Allen 1948b, 8).

Often the motif of the woman with her Thunder child is part of a longer story pitting Thunders against enormous horned serpents that live underwater. Thunders were regarded as patrons protecting the Oneidas from these monsters in a struggle played out across the local Oneida land-scape. Doxtater remembered "hearing the old women tell when she was a child that a sea serpent lived in one of the lakes near Pine Woods [about twelve miles south of Doxtater's home] because once when some people were camping there a man went in swimming and was never seen again but his blood came to the surface" (60). Similarly, William Rockwell wrote a note to himself to elaborate this memory: "Indian Story of Thunder Storm. It kept the serpents down under the water of the great lakes. I re-member how my grandparents used to tell us the serpents must be trying to get out onto the land when there would be several heavy thunders one after another" (n.d., bII c3 f12).

The enmity between snakes and Thunders figured in a story Doxtater told in January 1919.

THUNDER KILLS SNAKE

Once there was a girl living with her grandmother who told her not to go in a certain direction. But she did and as she was sitting by a spring she met a fine looking young man who asked her to marry him. She consented and he took her away to his home. She was one that you would call fast; when any stranger came to the village, she would be the first to go with him. So she consented to marry this stranger the first time she saw him.

When they came to his home (which was probably a cave) an old man was sitting there. In a few days the husband turned into a great snake and the girl was very frightened and the old man reproached the husband for scaring her by showing himself in his true form so early. She was very miserable but she could not get away.

One day she was making corn soup which has to boil all day and constantly have [*sic*] to have the water renewed. She went out to the spring for some water and there she met a man who said he was a thunder man and would help her get away from her husband. He told her to come back for some water for her soup as soon as her husband had left the house and then to run away from the spring as soon as possible.

This she did but she had not got far when her husband came home and missed her. He was very angry and went to the

spring for her and when he saw her not there he started
after her.

He first had to raise himself full height to see her and he was
a terrible sight when he did this, and threw himself again on the
ground and crawled as a snake does. He kept raising himself to
keep her in sight in this way and then crawling on.

When he got near her she commenced to weaken under his
baleful influence and then there came just a little cloud in the
heaven and out of it a terrible flash of lightning which killed him
instantly. Then soon two thunder men appeared (they are a small
race) and began cutting him up saying that this was their food.
The girl went home again and knew enough not to take up with
strangers again. (Allen 1948b, 51)

If combined with the first story, Doxtater's narrative would exemplify
the most popular type of Thunder story told throughout Iroquoia. A
young woman married to a serpent is rescued from her unfortunate matrimony by a Thunder. She has a child by her rescuer who becomes a Thunder himself (see Hewitt 1918, 228–29, 268–70; and Waugh n.d., H.
Printup 200 f36, S. Hill 201 f28, and E. Cook 202 f23).

In Doxtater's version, the young woman seems to end up marrying
the snake as punishment for having been promiscuous. The more general
Iroquois theme emphasizes how a young person (generally female), too
haughty to accept a spouse in a timely fashion, ends up with a snake as a
mate (Randle 1953, 625). As more than normally libidinous beings constantly searching for human mates, serpents are cast in the role of correct-
ing improper conjugal behavior. This fate is illustrated in "The Serpent
and the Thunderers," a tale attributed to an Oneida living on the
Onondaga Reservation, about forty miles west of Oneida.

THE SERPENT AND THE THUNDERERS

Sa-go-na-qua-de, "He who makes every one angry," told me this
story, which I reproduce nearly in his own words. An old Oneida
came into his aunt's house at Onondaga Castle and after all had
given him the customary tobacco, the story-teller's fee, he
related the following tale.

A long time ago, in an Indian settlement, were two wigwams

not far apart, and in these lived two squaws who were very good friends. They had two children of about the same age, who played together, and when they had little bows and arrows they shot together. As they grew bigger they wanted stronger bows and arrows, and their uncles made some for them. They used these every day, and became skilful in killing birds and small game, and then asked for some still stronger, that they might kill larger animals. They were now young men and good hunters. One of them, being handsome and kind, was very much liked by the women and some of the maidens would have married him, but he refused all offers. At last his friend talked with him, and told him he had better marry, or something might happen for which he would be sorry. This troubled him, and he said he would soon choose a wife, but first they would have a long hunt together.

They got ready for this, telling their mothers they were going away on a great hunt, far from their village, and might be gone many days. So their mothers took some corn and roasted it, and then pounded this into meal in their wooden mortars. This was light and would keep a long time. The young men filled their sacks, took their bows, and went to their hunting-ground. They walked all day and camped in the woods. They walked all the next day, and camped on the hunting ground, where they soon built a wigwam.

After this they hunted every day, and one was lucky and brought home a great deal of game, but the one whom the girls liked came home without any, and said very little. This happened for several days, and the one who had been so happy and such a favorite seemed sorry all the time. Every morning they went off to hunt in opposite directions, and one day his friend thought he would follow him and see what he did. They went out as before, and after he had walked a little way the lucky hunter turned back into the other's path. He soon saw him running very fast through the woods and hurried after him, calling to him to stop, but he did not. They ran till they came to a lake, and the first one plunged into the water and swam across, while his friend went around the shore. The swimmer got there first, paying no attention to his loud calls. They ran on to a second smaller lake,

where they did the same, but this time the one on shore got
ahead. The sorry young man then turned back, and his friend ran
past both lakes, and was hiding in the bushes when the other
came ashore. As the swimmer entered the woods the other
jumped out and caught him, asking him what was the matter and
why he acted so strangely.

At first the young man could say nothing and seemed to
know nothing, but soon came to his senses. He told his friend
that he was going to be married and must leave him all alone, for
he could not go back to his home. If he wished to see him at any
time, he might come to the lake, bringing fresh Indian tobacco
and clean clay pipes. These things he must lay on bark just from
the tree, and must then say to the lake, "I want to see my friend."

So he went off another way, and married the big serpent in
the lake. When he had gone his friend went back to the wigwam,
and he, too, was very sorry, and did not wish to hunt. He built a
fire and sat down alone.

It was very still for a long time, and then he heard some one
coming. When he turned around a young man stood in the
doorway, dressed in white and with white feathers on his head.
The visitor said, "You seem to be in trouble, but for all that you
are the only one that can help us. My chief has sent me to invite
you to our council." Then he gave him wampum, to show that he
brought a true message. The hunter said, "Where is the council?"
The young man in white answered, "Why you came right by our
wigwam in the woods, though you did not see it. Follow me, and
you will find it quite near." So he went with him, not very far, till
he saw smoke rising from the ground, and then a wigwam. Going
in, he saw eight chiefs sitting quietly on the ground. All had white
feathers on their heads, but the principal chief had larger feathers
than the rest. They gave him a place, and the hunter sat down and
smoked with them. When the pipe came round to the principal
chief, he rose and spoke to the young man.

"You have come to help us, and we have waited for you a long
time." The young man said, "How can I help you?" The chief
answered, "Your friend has married the big serpent in the lake,
whom we must kill. He has told you how to call him when you

want to see him, and we will furnish the tobacco and pipes." The chiefs then gave him clean pipes and fresh tobacco, and the hunter took these and went to the lake. The principal chief said also, "When your friend comes you must ask to see his wife. She will want to know if the sky is clear. When she comes you must take them a little way from the lake and talk to them there. The chiefs will come in the form of a cloud; on the lake, not in the sky."

So he took the fresh tobacco, the clean bark and pipes, and laid them by the shore. Then he stood by the water and called loudly for his friend, saying he was going away and wished to see him once more. Soon there was a ripple out on the lake, and the water began to boil, his friend coming out of it. He had a spot on his forehead, and looked like a serpent and yet like a man. His friend talked with him, asking what he should say to his mother when he got home. Then he asked to see his wife that he might tell his mother what she was like. The serpent man said that she might not wish to come but he would try. So he went to the shore and lay down, placing his lips to the water and beginning to drink. Then the hunter saw him going down through the water, not swimming like a man but moving like a snake. Soon the water boiled again and he came back, saying that his wife would come, but she did not. Then he looked around to see if the sky was clear; and went to the shore once more, drinking again and going down in the water like a snake.

Now a greater sight was seen. The lake boiled again, not in one spot but all over, and great waves rolled up on the shore as though there had been a strong wind, but there was none. The waves grew larger, and then the serpent man's wife came out of the water. She was very beautiful and shone like silver, but the silver seemed like scales. She had long hair falling all around her, as though it had been gold and silver glittering in the sun. Her husband came with her through the waves and upon the shore, and all three sat down on a log and talked together.

The hunter remembered the chief's words, and at last saw something like a cloud a great way off, moving upon the water and not through the sky. Then he asked them to go into the woods, where the sun was not so hot, and there talk with him.

When they did this he said he must step aside, and then he ran away, as the chiefs had told him. As he ran, a great cloud came at once over everything, and terrible thunder and lightning followed where they had sat, with rain everywhere.

At last all was quiet again and the hunter went back to the lake, where a big and little serpent lay dead on the ground. They were the serpent woman and his friend. The eight chiefs were there, too, and had a dance, rejoicing over their dead enemy. When this was over they cut up both serpents, making eight equal bundles of them. Each chief put one on his back, and then they were ready to go. All thanked the young man for what he had done, and told him he should always be lucky, saying, "Ask us for what you want at any time, and you shall have it." Then they went off through the woods in Indian file, and as he looked they seemed to step higher and higher, until they went up to the sky. Then there was a great thunder storm, for the chiefs were the Thunderers.

The hunter went back to his wigwam, but it was quiet and lonesome and he was sad; so he took down part of his meat, carrying it a half day's journey into the woods, where he hung it up on the trees. Then he returned for more, doing the same with the rest until he got home, where he told the story to the mother of his friend. She was very sorry for the death of the son whom she had loved, but adopted him in his place, and so the young man had two mothers.

So far, the old Oneida said, it was "all a true fact," but he had an opinion about the place which was not a part of the story. He thought Crooked Lake, in a group of lakes far up the valley, was the first lake the young man swam across, and Round Lake the second. This seemed likely to him, but it was only his opinion. (Beauchamp 1888b, 44–48; 1922, 15–19)

Thunders in Folklore and Mythology

Like Doxtater's story, this one insists that Thunders ate the snakes they killed—a common Iroquois view of the matter (Hewitt 1918, 791 n. 10).

Tobacco plays a prominent role in the Onondaga Oneida's story as something linked to the serpents. Elsewhere in Iroquois folklore, however, tobacco is quintessentially the substance of Thunders. "*Hi-nṹ* [Thunder] was considered a great lover of tobacco, but always in want of it" (E. Smith 1983, 31). According to one story, the Thunders used tobacco to cleanse themselves (Hewitt 1918, 270). Humans were to remember and thank Thunders with tobacco offerings (Beauchamp 1922, 117; Hewitt 1918, 627).

The white feathers worn by Thunders in Beauchamp's story have an echo in Morgan's account, the earliest description (1851) of Thunder appearance. Hé-no the Thunderer was visualized as a man "wearing the costume of a warrior. Upon his head he wore a magical feather, which rendered him invulnerable against the attacks of the Evil-minded" (1962, 158).

Morgan's Thunder carried on his back "a basket filled with fragments of chert rock, which he launched at evil spirits and witches, whenever he discovered them, as he rode in the clouds" (ibid.). In 1912, John Arthur Gibson said the Thunders attacked serpents by hurling thunderbolts shaped like stones resembling spinning tops (Waugh n.d., 200 f11:32). Generally, however, people thought of Thunder as shooting an arrow seen by the people below as a flash of lightning (see Harrington 1906, 129).

Iroquois accounts of the modern era do not mention wings and do not worry much about how Thunders get around. With the exception of what is *not* said, however, it would be difficult to list physical aspects of Thunder accepted as standard everywhere. Morgan, for example, said there was one god of thunder who had three assistants. Elsewhere, that god may be the father of Thunder sons (as in an Allen account) or the chief of a group of Thunders (as in the Beauchamp account). The very idea of hierarchical ranking could be set aside to describe an egalitarian set of seven or some other number of beings (Hewitt 1918, 803n. 229, 805n. 281). Thunders could be young or old; they could be of normal human appearance or particularly small, as occurs simultaneously in the Oneida tales recorded by Allen.

Thunders might also be associated with the game of lacrosse and with war. At any rate, today's Thunder ceremony (a summer religious rite held to induce rain) features that ball game and the war dance as its key observations (see next section). There is at least one link between lacrosse and

Thunders documented in a story about two boys receiving help from a Thunder in a lacrosse match (Waugh n.d., D. Jack 201 f 24). As for war, one of the tales in which mortals assist Thunders in the killing of a monster occurs in the course of a war party against Indians in the Southeast (Curtin 2001, 218–19; Parker 1989, 426–30). Based solely on the evidence of Iroquois folklore, however, it is difficult to imagine that one could identify lacrosse or war as activities specifically dedicated to Thunders.

The reason Iroquois Thunders battled snakes was explained in Iroquois mythology, particularly in the creation narratives dating to the turn of the twentieth century (see Hewitt 1974, 197, 243–44). The most fully developed mythic charter, the work of John Arthur Gibson in 1900, indicated that Flint had created monstrous beings that he sent to devour Sky Holder's creations (including human beings). Rounding up the evil creatures, Sky Holder imprisoned them in the cave Flint had used earlier for penning the game animals. Before the brothers came to blows, Flint declared that his beings would have the humans as food. After the fight, Sky Holder ordained that the Thunders would protect people by keeping Flint's creations confined under the earth (519–55; cf. 805–6 and Hewitt 1918, 619–20).

According to Seth Newhouse (version of 1896–1897), Sky Holder told Thunder:

> Do not then ever fail to do thy duty. Thou must, of course, ever be vigilant; if at whatever time it be there come dangers to the lives of men because great serpents move from place to place in the depths of this earth and also in the sea; if it come to pass that at some time these great serpents desire to seize people as they severally travel from place to place, thou must at once kill such serpents, and when thou killest them, they will be that on which thou shalt feed. Other animals also, equal in otkon orenda (malefic magic power) to these, all such shall fare like them. (Hewitt 1974, 338–39)

In Parker's more contemporary English, Thunder said, "I shall slay evil monsters when they escape from the under-world. . . . I shall shoot all otgont beings" (1989, 72).

The belief in evil snakes underground is documented as early as 1640: "The Hurons believe that there is a kind of monstrous serpent which they call *Angont,* which brings with it disease, death, and almost every misfortune in the world. They say that that monster lives in subterranean places, in caverns, under a rock, in the woods, or in the mountains, but generally in the lakes and rivers" (Thwaites 1896–1901, 33:217).[1]

In battling these enemies, Thunders often needed human help. The second most popular Thunder story described a mortal able to locate monsters concealed from the Thunders (Curtin 2001, 218–19; E. Smith 1983, 8; Waugh n.d., J. Jamieson 201 f 29, E. Cook 202 f 24). Frequently, this man also had the power to slay (or help kill) the evil creature(s), often using weapons made of red willow (see next chapter).

This story commonly provided an alternative explanation for the presence of a human Thunder: the sky beings, unable to locate or dispatch the beast themselves, gratefully initiated the man into their order (Hewitt 1918, 622–24; 1974, 809; Parker 1989, 421–30; Waugh n.d., J. Gibson 200 f 11, J. Jamieson 201 f 6). This story, in fact, served as the origin myth for the ceremony devoted to Thunders:

> At one time a particularly harmful [snake] roamed the Allegheny region.
> This snake could not be killed by man, nor had the Thunderers, who ordinarily control snakes, been able to kill it either. The Thunderers therefore enlisted the aid of a mortal . . . who was instructed to shoot with a

---

1. Note how the same word—*otkon* in Seneca, *angont* in Huron—is used differently in these passages. The Huron word seems to be applied specifically to the underground serpent(s). Much the same meaning is preserved in a contemporary Oneida word for snake, *otku"* (Abbott 1996, 388). More frequently, the word is said to mean "evil power" or "witch" (Chafe 1963, 59; Mithun 1984, 278).

Certainly, that sense is how Hewitt (and Parker, presumably after Hewitt) used the word, as in "otkon orenda (malefic magic power)." William Fenton, however, never met a Seneca who knew the word *orenda* (1987, 98). Could Hewitt have coined the word to designate inanimate power inhering in certain beings and things? When I asked Fenton what Seneca word would best describe this concept, he replied " "otkon," meaning power with no implication of being good or evil (personal communication).

Fenton's definition would seem to return us to an older meaning of the word. The earliest dictionary of an Iroquois tongue (Mohawk, late seventeenth century) defines *atkon* as "demon" (or perhaps "devil") and as a quality associated with a bold man for whom nothing is difficult (Bruyas 1863, 36). This definition suggests the word then meant exactly what Fenton now seems to mean: "magical power or potency in humans or other-than-human objects" that can be employed constructively or destructively (Hamell 1998, 266).

bow and arrow at the red spot near the ear of the snake. He shot 12 red-willow arrows, killed the snake, and was taken by the Thunderers to be one of their number. (Shimony 1994, 162)

Thunders in Religion

Lewis Henry Morgan regarded Thunders as central to Iroquois religious practice around 1850. Though scarcely mentioned in the sermon he quoted by a Handsome Lake preacher (1962, 231–59), Thunders were invoked as important gods in the course of the annual ceremonial round. Morgan said the Senecas dedicated seed-planting and crop-harvesting ceremonies to the Thunder and, in time of drought, held a special ceremony to implore Hé-no for rain (158, 196–97). The Onondagas were even more assiduous in their attentions to the sky beings, according to Beauchamp (1888a, 199–200). One day of each of the major annual ceremonies (what Beauchamp called Midwinter, Planting Feast, Strawberry Feast, Green Bean Dance, Green Corn Dance, and Thanksgiving Feast) was dedicated to the Grandfather Thunders.

Thunder, as Morgan observed, has its own ceremony. At Six Nations Reserve during the 1930s–1950s, it was a one-day rite scheduled anytime during the summer, and, as noted earlier, its central rituals comprised a lacrosse game and a war dance (Shimony 1994, 163–65; Speck 1995, 117–18). The Thunder ceremony of 1850, in contrast, included neither lacrosse nor the war dance. Instead, the major activities described by Morgan were characteristic of the church of Handsome Lake: public confession, the Thanksgiving or Skin Dance, and the rite of personal chant *(Ah-dó-weh)*, the latter said to be "peculiarly acceptable to *Hé-no*" (1962, 196).[2]

So if Morgan and the twentieth-century anthropologists were talking about the same ceremony, the connection between the Thunders on the

---

2. Possibly Morgan had no firsthand knowledge of the Thunder ceremony and did not know the rite well. Yet he certainly knew what the war dance was, insisting that it was the most popular Iroquois dance and had nothing to do with religious activities (1962, 263, 268–79). In the 1820s, Seaver said much the same thing (1990, 153). Therefore, even if Morgan got the Thunder ritual wrong, it seems to me unlikely the ceremony then included the war dance.

one hand and the performance of lacrosse and the war dance on the other evidently occurred after Morgan's time. Michael Foster believes Handsome Lake or the Handsome Lake religion has toned down the warlike features of Thunders (1974, 69). Perhaps more accurately, the Handsome Lake religion domesticated the violent war dance by placing it under the beneficent Thunders.[3]

The Thanksgiving Address, the all-purpose ceremonial speech opening and closing all religious (and most public) occasions, testifies to Iroquois views of Thunders 100–150 years ago within the setting of the Handsome Lake faith.

CA. 1846:

We return thanks to our grandfather *Hé-no*. We thank thee, that thou hast so wisely provided for our happiness and comfort, in ordering the rain to descend upon the earth, giving us water, and causing all plants to grow. We thank thee, that thou hast given us *Hé-no*, our grandfather, to do thy will in the protection of thy people. We ask that this great blessing may be continued to us. (Morgan 1962, 220; cf. 243)

1890s:

So now, too, this assembly of people, such as it is, is giving thanks this day. He willed, "I shall place a duty on certain persons to care for and watch over the earth, and they shall cause rain to fall habitually, and the rain shall prosper all the things that grow out of the earth, and these persons shall habitually approach from the west, and people will call them Our Grandsires, whose voices are heard from place to place—the Thunderers." (Hewitt 1918, 635)

1906:

Now again the smoke arises
To you who were born of Earth,
To you who dwell in the sky!

---

3. This occasion appears to have been the second in which a dance performed in the Thunder ceremony had been so domesticated. Morgan's Thanksgiving or Skin Dance originated as a performance for boasting about military deeds. Iroquois tradition insists it was Handsome Lake who transformed this activity from one of war to one of thanksgiving (Fenton 1991, 103–4; Speck 1995, 138; Tooker 1970, 106).

Now they come from the west.
Ti'sot we call them,
Our great grandfathers the Thunderers;
You did make them our relatives.
They were placed in a high position
That they might care for the earth
And feed the waters that flow over the world and purify them,
And freshen all things that grow.
A certain season was appointed for their activity
The season when the earth commences to become warm again.
(Parker 1913, 91; cf. 98)

One striking feature emerging from these statements is that, in terms of religious address, Thunders were not primarily agricultural gods acknowledged as responsible for crops—that is, such domestic foods as corn, beans, and squash. Rather, the sentiment focused on giving thanks for rain sustaining all of nature and for freshening and purifying the earth.

A second notable aspect is that Thunders generally were not credited with the job of striking down horned serpents. They cared for and watched over the earth, and they protected people. But the idea that Thunders were entrusted with the duty of suppressing Flint's evil minions seems to have remained almost entirely within the province of folklore and myth, not of formal religious address.

Both of these attributes of the Thanksgiving Address, I believe, remain true today. Thunders are still regarded as servants of the Creator responsible for bringing fresh water to replenish and purify the earth, and for assisting generally with plant growth. And still today, the duty of Thunders to keep the great snakes imprisoned seems to be mentioned infrequently (cf. Chafe 1961; Foster 1974, 68–69; Shimony 1994, 137). Perhaps the Handsome Lake religion toned down the idea of monsters teeming beneath our feet in much the same way it domesticated the wild war dance.

Comparisons

Wyandot Thunder lore, not surprisingly, is virtually identical to the lore of the Iroquois. Wyandot Thunders compose a race of humanlike sky beings, "all called Hino, who may (for the Wyandots rarely use the plural of nouns) be regarded as one god or many—the Thunderer or the Thunderers" (Hale 1891, 293). Wyandots, like Iroquois, feel close to their Thunders and enjoy telling stories about them. And just as Wyandots use the same word to denominate these deities, so their Thunder stories present the familiar Iroquois themes. Some are variants of the most popular Iroquois plot. After rejecting mortal suitors, a disdainful young woman marries a giant snake. She is rescued by a Thunder who kills the serpent and becomes the father of her son. Too powerful to be left among human playmates, the son is taken up into the sky where he becomes one of the Thunders (Barbeau 1915, 53–56, 340–41). Another tale (mentioned at the close of the previous chapter) emphasizes how a mortal assists the Thunders by finding one of their enemies, a giant grub. Their mission, as they explain to the man, "was to keep the earth and everything upon it in good order for the benefit of the human race. If there was a drought, it was their duty to bring rain. If there were serpents or other noxious creatures, they were commissioned to destroy them; and, in short, they were to do away with everything that was injurious to mankind" (Hale 1891, 291).

There are, to be sure, differences. Whether Wyandot Thunders are connected with lacrosse is unclear. But, on the other hand, Wyandot Thunders are linked to war, and they actively dispatch enemies of the Wyandot (Barbeau 1915, 282–83). Further, one of the Wyandot creation stories regards Thunder as a tribal god, roughly equivalent to Sky Holder in the capacity of patron deity (see chapter 3). In this guise, Thunder watches over his people as they emerge into this world from an underground cavern (Connelley in ibid., 303–11).

Delaware Thunders, like their equivalents for the Iroquois and Wyandot, are responsible for watering the earth and for doing battle with horned water serpents (Harrington 1921, 29–31, 193; Speck 1937, 70). For the Delawares also, Thunders were a favorite story topic. They know the Iroquois-like story of a young woman rescued by a Thunder from a marriage with a serpent (Bierhorst 1995, 48–49). Possibly, they are familiar with the tale of the mortal who, after helping the Thunders dispatch their enemy, becomes a Thunder himself (37; Curtin 2001, 206–10). Delaware Thunders are associated with the ball game and seem generally humanlike. Apparently equipped with wings, however, there is a suggestion of avian qualities reminiscent of Thunder appearance farther west or of the bird form attested among the Hurons in the early 1600s (Bierhorst 1995, 11).

Beliefs in Thunders and horned serpents characterized native folklore over a vast area of the middle and eastern United States. For many people of the Great Lakes regions, however, these terms existed within a larger dichotomy emphasizing enmity between "birds of the sky and underwater animals. There was a kind of feud believed to exist between these two classes, especially between thunderbirds and snakes, although thunderbirds were also enemies of underwater panthers, lions, or lynxes" (Barnouw 1977, 133). When this distinction focused on a struggle between snakes and Thunders, the latter were birds or at least creatures most frequently visualized in avian form.[4]

Among the Menominis, for example:

> Far, far away in the West where the sun sets, there floats a great mountain in the sky. . . . [O]n the summit of this mountain dwell the Thunderbirds. They have control over the rain and the hail. They are messengers of the Great Sun himself, and their influence induced the Sun and the Morning Star to give the great war-bundle to our race. They delight in fighting and great deeds. They are the mighty enemies of the horned snakes, the Misikinubik. Were it not for the Thunderers these monsters would overwhelm the earth and devour mankind. (Skinner 1911, 140)

Lacrosse among the Menominis is also associated with these Thunders.

In New England, Kathleen Bragdon discerns the theme of Thunderbirds on prehistoric objects (1996, 188–89, 211–12). It is unclear whether Thunderbirds existed in the nineteenth-century folklore of the region (Flannery 1939, 159), but there was certainly a wind bird (Fisher 1946, 238; Rand 1894, 360–61; Speck 1917, 480) and a giant carnivorous bird (Simmons 1986, 70)—neither obviously associated with thunder or snakes. Although snakes are an important topic of native New England, and the theme of sex between women and snakes is well developed, few of these stories make reference to thunder (Leland 1992,

---

4. For some examples of Western Algonquian views of Thunders emphasizing the avian aspect (thunderbirds), see Chamberlain 1890; Michelson 1919, 111–13, 185, 191–92; Radin 1926, 23–24; and Schoolcraft 1999, 183–90, 240–48.

268–80; Parsons 1925, 95–96). Thunders seem to be winged anthropo-morphic beings who play ball across the sky and are associated with moun-tains (Leland 1992, 259–66). But they do not seem as clearly defined (and perhaps not as important?) as they are among the Iroquois (see Fewkes 1890, 265–66; and Rand 1894, 116). At least one story, however, features something resembling a classic Iroquois plot: a woman raped by a snake is aided by humanlike thunders; she has a child who apparently becomes a Thunder (Leland 1992, 266–67).

Unlike their beneficent counterparts, Thunders in the Southeast are unconcerned with safeguarding human existence (see Grantham 2002, 33–34; Swanton 1929, 124, 184–85, 239–41). They are, however, an-thropomorphic, and, among the Cherokees, the concept embraces major sky-dwelling figures of the cosmogonic myth as well as little people living in rocky places on the earth (Witthoft and Hadlock 1946).

As in New England, it is difficult to relate southeastern Thunders to a mythic paradigm in which sky beings battle snakes. On the one hand, fre-quent antagonism between a Roc-like bird and a monstrous serpent is not obviously related to thunder (see Grantham 2002, 24–26, 199–234). On the other, some enmity between Thunders and snakes can be inferred from the recurrence of a story in which a mortal helps a Thunder to kill a snake, then becomes a Thunder or obtains thunder power (Bierhorst 1985, 203; Lankford 1987, 79–80; Mooney 1995, 300–301; Swanton 1929, 7–9). In most of the lore, however, Thunders do not hunt snakes; rather, they wear them as adornment or ride them as steeds. This point is emphasized in a series of Cherokee stories in which a young man visits Thunder, usually in hopes of marrying the latter's daughter or sister. The mortal is subjected to various ordeals with snakes and must play the ball game with the Thunder's two sons (Mooney 1995, 311–15, 345–47; Witthoft and Hadlock 1946, 419).

Thunder's sons, known to the Cherokees as the "Thunder Boys," are regional manifestations of a classic North American Indian theme, Lodge-Boy and Thrown-Away (Thompson 1955–1958, 5:564, motif Z210.1). Taken from the body of a slain mother, one brother is raised by the father, and the other grows up wild. After the father and first son catch the sec-ond, the brothers engage in adventures they have been forbidden to un-dertake. Invariably, the brothers triumph over a series of supernatural dangers and enemies (Voegelin 1984, 642). Though possibly centered in the Plains region, the story of Lodge-Boy and Thrown-Away is widely distributed throughout much of native North America (Lowie 1908, 139–42; Reichard 1921, 272–74; Thompson 1929, 319).

The southeastern variants of the theme, however, include a feature apparently unique to the region: the brothers let loose game animals impounded in a cave or under the ground. This incident figures prominently in the Lodge-Boy and Thrown-Away narratives recorded among the Cherokees, speakers of an Iroquoian language (Mooney 1995, 242–48); the Creeks, speakers of a Muskogean language; and the Natchez, speakers of a linguistic isolate (Swanton 1929, 2–7, 222–30). Among the Iroquois, in contrast, freeing the game occurs as a detail of the twins' rivalry in the cosmogonic myth (see chapter 3). Is it possible that incident could also be related to thunder in Iroquois country?

A History of Thunders

The earliest documented Iroquoian views on the subject were the ones of the Hurons, who believed thunder was a bird (Wrong 1939, 183). It was a very big bird, LeJeune added, one that ate snakes and produced its characteristic noise as flatulence (Thwaites 1896–1901, 6:225). In 1628, a Huron sorcerer claimed a Christian cross frightened "thunder, which they pretend is a bird," and thereby prevented the arrival of rain (10:45). Elaborating on this belief, Jean de Brébeuf stated:

> *Onditachia* is renowned among the Tobacco Nation [or Petun, Iroquoian neighbors of the Hurons who, with the Hurons, were ancestral to the Wyandots], like a Jupiter among the heathens of former times, from having in hand the rains, the winds, and the thunder. This thunder is . . . a man like a Turkey-cock; the sky is his palace, and he retires there when it is serene; he comes down to earth to get his supply of adders and serpents, and of all they call *Oki* [spirits], when the clouds are rumbling; the lightnings occur in proportion as he extends or folds his wings. If the uproar is a little louder, it is his little ones who accompany him, and help him to make a noise as best they can. (195)

Some eighty years later, Lafitau said some Indians visualized thunder as a winged humanlike figure, but the majority "hold that it is an extraordinary species of bird" (Fenton and Moore 1974, 102). This passage apparently referred to the Mohawks of Caughnawaga, a Jesuit reserve near Montreal. But it could as easily pertain to Canadian Indians more generally, that is, speakers of Algonquian as well as Iroquoian tongues. Certainly, that conception was true earlier. The Hurons' Thunderbird was a concept shared with surrounding Algonquian peoples (see Thwaites 1896–1901, 12:25–27).

Among the Iroquois of New York, references to Thunders are very sparse—curiously so for such important figures. The oldest documentary evidence for thunder beliefs dates to about the 1670s. In the Gallinée version of the creation story, Sky Holder, like Thunders of a later era, killed a great serpent. The latter, it was said, had destroyed the first humans (Margry 1876, 361). When Sky Holder looks down from heaven, according to the Hennepin creation narrative, he "rattles his thunder from time to time over his unhappy brother's head" (Thwaites 1903, 452).

These passages suggest thunder was simply another attribute of the protean Sky Holder. Here, then, is a possible Iroquois connection between liberating the game animals and thundering: both were things Sky Holder did. This evidence suggests mythological comparability between at least some features of the Iroquois creation narrative and the corresponding southeastern tale Lodge-Boy and Thrown-Away. By the age-area principle, we should suspect not only that the concept of emancipating the pent-up game is ancient, as Robert Hall suggests (1997, 139), but also that freeing the animals had associations with thunder and possibly rain.

Sky Holder, however, must have begun to delegate his responsibility for storm making to a humanlike associate before the end of the eighteenth century. In Norton's extensive Onondaga creation (Norton 2), Sky Holder designates a young person to "take the Thunder in charge" (Klinck and Talman 1970, 97). A few years later, David Cusick mentioned the same incident: Sky Holder appointed Thunder to water the earth, after which Turtle Island became fruitful (Beauchamp 1892, 3).

The conceptual shift from Sky Holder as a thundering one to Thunder as Sky Holder's appointee emerges clearly from comparison of the same passage as it occurred in the writings of Cusick and Elias Johnson, two Tuscarora chroniclers writing about half a century apart. Cusick, in 1827, wrote: "About this time a great horned serpent appeared on Lake Ontario, the serpent produced diseases and many of the people died, but by the aid of thunder bolts the monster was compelled to retire" (Beauchamp 1892, 11). The identity of the one wielding thunderbolts is made clear several pages later: "The lake serpent discovers the powerful operations of the Holder of the Heavens, instantly retreats into the deep places of the lakes" (16).

Johnson generally followed Cusick very closely. Indeed, when composing his mythological passages sometime before 1881, Johnson must have had a copy of Cusick open before him. In this instance, however, Johnson not only clarified Cusick's passage, but also fundamentally altered its meaning:

> A great horned serpent also next appeared on Lake Ontario who, by means of his poisonous breath, caused disease, and caused the death of many. At length the old women congregated, with one accord, and prayed to the Great Spirit that he would send their grand-father, the Thunder, who would get to their relief in this, their sore time of trouble, and at the same time burning tobacco as burned offerings. So finally the monster was compelled to retire in the deeps of the lake by thunder bolts. (1881, 42)

Between 1827 and 1881, in other words, the idea that Sky Holder, rather than Thunder, shot thunderbolts at a monster water snake had become unfamiliar and in need of correction. Evidently, Thunder was codified in its present form during that brief half century of the 1800s, a standardization that must have occurred prior to Morgan's researches at midcentury.

Among the New York Iroquois, then, the earliest documentary references to Thunder (late 1600s) describe manlike beings. That Thunders were conceived more as people than as birds during the 1600s is also implied by the virtual identity of Iroquois and Wyandot Thunder lore. This comparability is another consequence of the cognate reasoning advanced in chapter 4: where we have two societies sharing similar content and common past, the resemblances probably date to the time of the earlier shared condition.

Whether the Iroquois, like the Hurons, believed in a bird of thunder is unknown. Certainly, by the turn of the twentieth century, however, they knew of an avian figure who assisted the Thunders:

The Dew Eagles wheel in flight among the clouds beyond the sight of mortals. . . . They are the greatest and highest of all the creatures of the air. Dew Eagle collects a pool of dew in the hollow in his back between his shoulders and when the Thunderers fail in their duty of watering the earth, Dew Eagle tilts his wings and the mists descend to refresh the crops. For the Seneca, Dew Eagle divides the tasks of refreshing the earth with "our grandfathers," the Thunderers. (Fenton 1991, 114)

The Seneca Dew Eagle, however, has little to do with snakes or, for that matter, with thunder. Likewise, beliefs about the thunderbird documented among the Hurons in the 1620s–1630s have nothing to do with eagles. So although the Dew Eagle may attest to the survival of an ancient Iroquois belief in an avian thunder, it is more likely to be a newer concept, one perhaps introduced into Iroquois life with the foreign Eagle Dance in the early 1700s (Fenton 1991; Kurath 2000, 62, 67).

⊣△⊢

The Oneidas regarded Thunders as celestial beings of rainstorms and terrestrial neighbors living behind nearby waterfalls. Protecting humans from evil beneath the ground, these humanlike supernaturals were benevolent. Their enmity toward horned serpents may have been primal and timeless, but it was not abstract. That battle was waged actively across the Oneida landscape.

Oneidas felt close to the Thunders, and their folklore established a kin relationship with those beings. Oneida lore cautioned young people that they might end up with a serpent mate if they were too finicky about taking a spouse. Other Iroquois told stories about humans assisting the Thunders against their enemies. These themes of Thunder lore were fairly standardized across the Iroquois area.

Some of these motifs and plots were shared with the neighboring Delawares. Virtually all were held in common with the more distant Wyandots, the near synonymy strongly suggestive of a considerable age for thunder folklore that we cannot otherwise document.

The connections of Oneida folklore were widespread, and its roots went deep into the past. "There is here," Michael Foster observed of Iroquois Thunders, "a link with one of the most widely diffused mythic themes in North America and northeastern Asia, that of the Thunder Bird and the serpent" (1974, 69). No doubt that is true. The battle played out between Oneida Thunders and snakes must preserve some mythopoeic opposition from a remote American past, whether Thunders were anthropomorphic or ornithomorphic or both or something altogether different. Yet such a link can be difficult to define, partly because thundering does not occur with every mythic pairing of bird and snake, as illustrated, especially, by New England and Southeast folklore.

One rather surprising linkage of Oneida belief may lead toward the Southeast, where thunder gods included a pair of brothers responsible for letting loose game animals penned underground. A similar Iroquois incident is connected with the twin brothers of the creation narrative. Prior to the development of the Thunder or Thunders familiar today, Sky Holder was vested with Thunder attributes and perhaps even served as an Iroquois thunder god. Thus are Iroquois country and the Southeast united in possession of a common mythic theme, presumably an ancient one, relating thunder to a pair of brothers and to the freeing of the game.

DAN WEBSTER'S WAMPUM STRING

Lydia Doxtater's uncle, the man who saw the Thunder being in the sky, lived on the West Road in the Windfall, the western Oneida community (map 4, see residence of "D. Webster"). When he passed away, the local obituary read:

> Daniel Webster, the oldest Indian residing on the Oneida Reservation, died at his home Saturday afternoon. . . . He was born and had always resided here. As near as can be learned, he was 88 years of age. He was a familiar figure on the streets of Oneida, his stalwart and upright figure attracting attention. He was respected and esteemed. He was an inveterate hunter and trapper and the room in which he died was hung with his heavy rifle and numerous traps. His wife, a [daughter] of Chief Beachtree, died three years ago. (*Oneida Democratic Union*, October 5, 1907)

Very shortly before his death, Webster was visited by Mark Harrington, a young anthropologist then traveling through Iroquois reservations

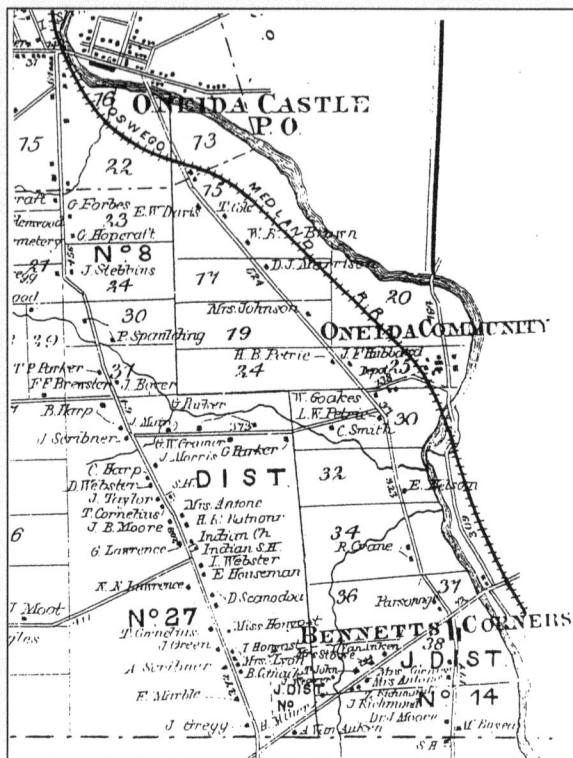

Map 4. *The Windfall Community, 1875. Map showing the community, located within the area marked "DIST. No. 27." The house of "D. Webster" is shown on the west side of the road, left of the "DIST." legend; Beers 1875, 53.*

hoping to buy old artifacts for museums. He found one at Webster's house, a string of wampum he bought for $5.84 (ill. 18). Harrington recorded that this object, called *Oni go' l*ʰ in Oneida, represented "the chieftainship of the turtle clan . . . once held by Chief Chrisjohn Beechtree" (1907, 175). The previous owner of Webster's house had been Beechtree (ca. 1804–1869) who, as noted in the obituary, was Webster's father-in-law. Chrisjohn Beechtree, "head chief of the Oneidas," had been among those people listening to William Tracy's dedicatory address in which burial space was offered to the Indians beneath the newly located Oneida Stone ("Consecration of Forest Hill Cemetery," *Utica Daily Gazette,* June 15, 1850).

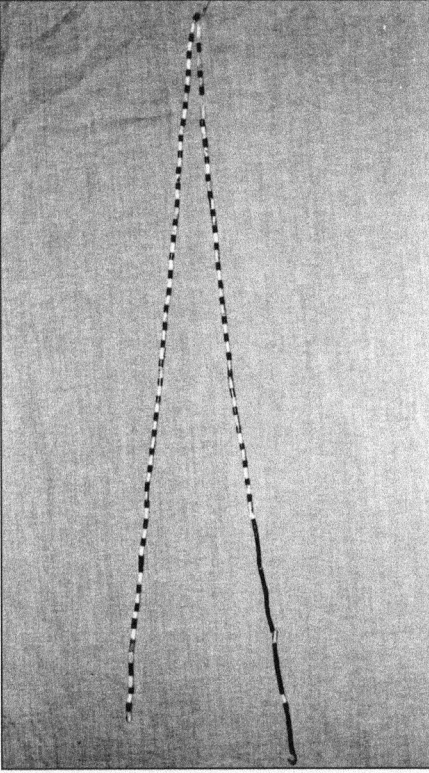

18. Dan Webster's wampum string measures some twenty inches from the top to the tip of the longer strand.

Tradition had it that the League of the Iroquois had started out with a council of some fifty chiefs or sachems drawn from the five member nations. The names of the original chiefs came to be regarded as permanent offices or seats of the confederacy council, each being passed on to a new officeholder at the death of the previous one. Nine of these names or titles belonged to the Oneida Nation, three assigned to each clan. Within a clan, the title was considered to be the property of a particular extended family or matrilineage. The matron of that family unit determined which of her male relatives would succeed to a vacated sachem position and assume that sachem name. Hence, the fifty names had long since become hereditary chiefly titles extending into the distant past.

In one of the oldest texts recorded on the subject of league traditions (ca. 1900), it is said that a wampum string of mixed white and purple beads shall be "an official emblem of the title of each chief" (Fenton 1998,

222). Evidently, it was one of these material symbols of office that Harrington acquired from Dan Webster, a string to one of three ancient leadership titles belonging to the Turtle clan of the Oneida Nation. Today, a title wampum string may be made up for the occasion (168), presumably because few strings of any age survive. The Beechtree-Webster title string is among the oldest documented anywhere.

What Harrington recorded of the string indicated its use as credentials. Chief Rockwell of the Windfall knew this meaning but added that the word Harrington heard also connoted "mind of knowledge" (n.d., bII c5 f1). This connotation implies that the Oneida view of the object also comprehended duties of the office and, perhaps, the character of the officeholder.

Iroquois culture is notable for attaching a strong sense of physicality to the spoken language. Words that were true and important in Iroquois councils, as Daniel Richter observes, were accompanied by presents of symbolically charged items. "Indeed, to Iroquois minds, the gift and the word seem to have become inseparable" (1992, 47). For about four hundred years, the preferred substance accompanying and standing for speech has been wampum (see pp. 8–9), its general amount offered in proportion to the proposition's importance and accepted in acknowledgment of the proposition's truth. Thus, the Thunder in Beauchamp's story gave wampum to the mortal "to show that he brought a true message."

Wampum played an important role in Iroquois folklore as a substance of great worth often originating in the intimate effluvia of magically charged human bodies. For example, a hero frequently demonstrates his power by spitting out wampum beads from pipe smoke. Or, in another common scenario, witches torture the hero's relatives with fire, the victim's tears turning to wampum.[S1]

Iroquois tradition about the founding of the confederacy defined wampum as the thing necessary for restoring the grief-stricken to productive social life. In that sense, wampum is fundamental not only to the Condolence Ceremony, but to every Iroquois ritual of adoption, mourning,

---

S1. For the hero expectorating wampum beads from smoke, see Hewitt 1918, 262–66, 516–17; Parker 1989, 187; E. Smith 1983, 58; and Waugh n.d., T. Smoke 201 f27. Tears from a tortured victim turning into wampum beads are described in Curtin 2001, 189–90, 301, 339–40, 358; and Randle 1953, 617.

and alliance making as well. The league tradition also equates the confederacy's beginning with the first wampum. Indeed, the earliest such narrative recorded in an Iroquois language (1912) has Hiawatha inventing wampum just outside the Oneida village (Woodbury, Henry, and Webster 1992, 139–50).

Wampum continues to be emotionally resonant for Oneidas today, a fact recognized by the American Museum of Natural History in repatriating the wampum string acquired by Harrington in 1907 to the Oneida Indian Nation in 1999. Under the terms of the 1990 federal Native American Graves Protection and Repatriation Act, the New York City museum acknowledged that the Beechtree-Webster wampum string was an object of cultural patrimony, that is, a thing of ongoing historical, traditional, or cultural importance to the Oneidas that could never have been *rightfully* alienated by an individual.

6

⧉

Something New and Some Things Very Old

In chapter 3, I tracked the creation story almost four centuries back in time to the limit of written evidence in the Northeast. I argued further that, in the absence of documents, we can infer about the same age for incidents and plots that are common to Iroquois and Wyandot folklore (see chapters 4–5). Clearly, however, the narrative of beginning is older than its earliest mention by Europeans, and parts of it may be very ancient. Is it possible to follow oral narrative further back in time?

In this chapter, I focus on a thoroughly European story, a seemingly improbable vehicle for preserving ancient tradition. Yet within this foreign and recent tale, one can detect two distinct layers of mythological content far older than European presence in the Americas. In the case of the first layer, an incident called obstacle flight, I draw on premises of the age-area principle to infer its antiquity. In the case of the second, an allusion to red willow, it appears the Iroquois themselves date it to an earlier time. As native testimony to relative age, it is a claim meriting serious consideration.

⧉

On December 18, 1918, and January 3, 1919, Anna Johnson told Hope Allen the following story:

THE MAGIC BULL

Once there was a rich man, an Indian. His first wife died and left him with a little boy and after awhile he married again. His second wife wanted to have all the property and she hated the little boy and treated him very badly. Every night she used to tell the father bad things she said the boy had done, and after awhile the father didn't love the boy as well as he had. She didn't give him anything to eat and he almost starved.

138

One day one of the cows "came in" and a bull was born and the boy asked his father if he could have it and the father said "Yes—it doesn't give any milk." So the boy took the bull and fattened it and it grew well.

Time run on and one day he (the boy) was very hungry and miserable and he went out beside the bull and cried. Then the bull spoke and asked him why he was crying. The boy said he was crying because he was hungry. Then the bull said: "Whenever you are hungry take a stick and tap me above the ear three times but be sure no one sees you."

So the boy tapped the bull above the ears three times and his skin opened and a man stepped out with a tray full of good things to eat on it. After this the boy got his food in this way whenever he was hungry and he began to pick up and get fat.

Time run on and his step-mother began to notice the change and wondered. Finally she decided to watch the boy and one day she hid and saw what happened. Then she pretended to be very sick and one day she said to her husband that she had a dream— she would be cured by eating the flesh of the bull. The bull told the boy to consent, but to insist that the woman had to come out to kill him herself. He said, "You stand in the middle of the field with your legs far apart. Perhaps I will come and perhaps I won't, but you must be there."

When the time came the boy was there and the stepmother and the bull came too. The stepmother had a hammer to knock out his skull but every time she tried to use it, he leaned far forward and caught her on his horns and tossed her in the air. He did this three times and the third time she was killed.

Then the bull said to the boy, "You jump on my back and we will run as fast as we can." This they did and all the people chased them. They all ran on and on and finally the people began to fall out and at last there wasn't anyone left but a fierce great lion, that belonged to the boy's father.

When the bull began to grow weaker and the lion nearer, the bull gave the boy a feather and said to him: "You stick in the ground ahead of us this feather of a wild pigeon and make the wish that the wild pigeon build a nest of feathers that will stretch from one end of the world to the other." The boy did as he was told and there sprung up a wild pigeon nest, feathers that stretched from one end of the world to the other. The lion came up to it and thought it was a forest and he ran to the end of it and back, that is to the end of the world and back. When he came back to where he started from, the nest was gone and the road was clear so he went ahead.

After a little he gained on the bull and boy again and then the bull gave a stone to the boy and said: "You drop this stone and wish for a stone wall." So the boy did as he was told and a stone wall rose up and when the lion came to it, so eager for the chase that he did not see where he was going, he ran against it and was knocked senseless. But when he came to his senses the wall was gone and he went on.

About this time they came to a creek and the bull said to the boy: "I am about worn out and I can hardly get across the stream, but you cut seven whips of red willow. When you see me begin to sink, begin to whip me with the whips one at a time and throw each one away when it is worn out."

Then they plunged into the stream and when they were only a little way across the bull began to sink till only his head appeared above the water. Then the boy took the whips as he had been told and used them one by one. He got to the last one a long way from shore and they were afraid they would never make it but they got there before the bull gave out. He said: "I can go no further. We must fight it out here for I am too weak to go any further. You climb a tree and watch us."

The boy climbed a tree and it seemed to him that neither won, for when they stopped fighting the lion went one way and the bull another. The boy followed the lion and after a little he came to some bushes and there the lion was lying dead. He came back and went after the bull and he found him dying. The bull said to him: "When I am dead you must cut out of my hide the white stripe that runs from the tip of my nose to the end of my tail and save it and it will help you to do anything."

He died and the boy did as he was told though he did not

quite know what he was to do with the length of skin. He went on with it and after a little he came to two armed men and one barred his way and demanded payment, though the other was willing for him to go on. He took his stripe and hit the unwilling one with it and he dropped down at once. The boy saw that he could make any use he wished of the hide so the boy went on. After a little he came to two more men, both of whom were unwilling that he should go on. This time he hit them at once with his stripe and they dropped down. After that he came to a village.

Near this village was a terrible snake, which demanded every year a young girl to eat up. This year the young girl chosen was the daughter of a rich man, the richest in the village. The boy came to the village and heard all this and offered to kill the snake. The people urged him not to try for it would be certain death, but sure enough he had only to hit the snake with the stripe to kill him. Then the boy came back to the village and married the rich man's daughter. (1984b, 34–35, 47–48)[1]

One might suspect a story featuring an Old World bovine is Old World in derivation, and that is the case. Folklorists know much of this as "The Little Red Ox," a type of story distributed from India to Europe (Thompson 1981, 178, motif A511A). However, the Oneida story is also related to at least three other similar narratives then popular among native people, all themselves of European derivation.

First, a segment of "The Magic Bull" is virtually identical to the beginning of "The Steer and the Ill-Treated Step-Son," a Wyandot story recorded in Oklahoma in 1912 (Barbeau 1915, 215–24).[2] Like the Oneida animal, the Wyandot steer opens up to release human waiters car-

---

1. The text is another composite version I edited from the two sessions with comparatively minor changes. I standardized the sex of the beast (defined as a heifer in the first telling, as a bull in the second) and supplied the title.

2. The Oneida story also resembles a Chippewa tale, "The Magic Ox," documented later in time (1940) than the comparisons emphasized here. That story is also attributed to French Canadian sources (Barnouw 1977, 207–9, 225).

rying food. After the steer bears the boy to safety, it perishes in battle with an adversary named Starvation. The dying animal tells the boy to remove a strip of hide running down the middle of the beast's back. This object magically aids the boy in a series of fairy tale-like episodes resulting in wealth, power, and a wife for the hero.

Second, that part of the "The Magic Bull" concerned with the leather strip also resembles "A Wonderful Bull's Hide Belt," a Micmac story (New Brunswick, Canada) of 1871 (Rand 1894, 369–74). It tells of a magical strip of hide, cut from the top of a bull's back, which enables its young owner to acquire great wealth.

Third, the chase sequence of "The Magic Bull" is similar to one described in "Louis and the Gray Horse," a 1912 story of the Maliseets (Maine and New Brunswick) featuring a boy on horseback pursued by the devil (Mechling 1913, 247–55). Like the Oneida boy, the Maliseet youth has to revive his flagging mount and tosses objects behind him that become impediments delaying the pursuer.

As a group, the Oneida, Wyandot, Micmac, and Maliseet stories demonstrate that native people were attracted to some European wonder tales, presumably those stories offering "new difficulties and new means of overcoming obstacles, for their own heroes" (Fisher 1946, 233). French Canadian sources lie behind the Maliseet tale and at least part of the Wyandot story (Barbeau 1915, 217; 1916, 15; Thompson 1919, 357), a provenience consistent with the locale of Micmac storytellers, and perhaps with the diverse Canadian connections of Oneidas. The Wyandots may have acquired the French Canadian content before leaving the Great Lakes region prior to the 1840s. If so, we should suspect native people throughout the Northeast were adopting certain foreign magic motifs by the early nineteenth century.

Obstacle Flight

When Indians told European stories, one can usually sense a native aspect, even when the tale seems thoroughly foreign in character. In the case of "The Magic Bull," the stepmother's wish attributed to a dream is a nice Indian touch. The maiden who has to be rescued from a serpent may be another. But the most obviously Iroquois portion of this story is the motif

Arthur Parker called "obstacles-produced-magically," in which the "hero is beset by a witch or monster and flees. Upon being pressed the hero creates obstacles by dropping a stone and causing it to become an unsurmountable [*sic*] cliff. He casts pigeon feathers and conjures them into a great flock that makes a slime that is impassable" (1989, 26).

This incident, as episode or story, was one of the most popular themes in Iroquois folklore around 1900.[3] The classic Iroquois plot demands a hero chased by a supernatural being—most frequently a monster bear, although a rolling head, a flying head, a sorceress, or a cannibal serve equally well. In longer versions, the hero employs such tricks of deception as shape changing or self-propelled magic moccasins to elude pursuit. Always, however, the hero tosses behind objects that magically transform into impediments that slow the approaching enemy. Almost always, as Parker noted and Allen documented, these objects comprise a stone and a pigeon feather. The fleeing party often receives help from an "uncle" who slows down the pursuer with a net. In the end, the hero typically arrives at the house of his mother or mother-in-law who kills the villain with boiling bear oil.

The earliest reference to this incident in Iroquois context appears within the pages of Cusick's *Sketches of Ancient History of the Six Nations* (Beauchamp 1892, 8). But it is much older than 1827. In fact, the Iroquois magic chase is but one example of the obstacle flight—one of the most widely distributed motifs in world folklore (Thompson 1929, 333, motif D672). Understood as a chase sequence in which the fugitive throws objects backward to magically impede the pursuit, the obstacle flight spans a considerable part of the globe, including a band across Eurasia from Siberia to France (Barbeau 1915, 31; Swanton 1929, 270–71).

Recall that the age-area principle requires a vast amount of time to account for a trait so widely distributed. Munro Edmonson speculated the obstacle chase might date to the Mesolithic age, presumably in the neigh-

3. The Iroquois version of obstacle flight can be found in Curtin 2001, 303–6, 371–73, 422–26, 443–47; Hewitt 1918, 675–76; Parker 1989, 264–65, 295–96, 347; Waugh n.d., J. Echo 201 f25, E. Cook 201 f28; and another instance in Waugh identified by Randle (1953, 623–24).

borhood of ten thousand years ago (1971, 61). In early-twentieth-century discussions of New World origins, the obstacle flight was often cited as evidence attesting to Asian connections via the Siberia-to-Alaska route (see Aarne 1930, 138–41; Wauchope 1962, 84). In addition, Franz Boas claimed (1940, 518) the geographical distribution of the chase incident indicated the direction from which it had come:

> Transmission between the Old World and New has been proved by the occurrence of a set of complex stories in both. The most notable among these are the Magic Flight (or obstacle myth) [and others]. . . . The area of well-established Old-World influence upon the New World is confined to that part of North America limited in the southeast by a line running approximately from California to Labrador. Southeast of this line, only weak indications of this influence are noticeable. Owing to the restriction of the tales to a small part of America, and to their wide distribution in the Old World, we must infer that the direction of dissemination was from the west to the east, and not conversely. (Boas 1914, 384)

One can sense in this passage a tone of doctrinaire certainty in what some regarded as an impressionistic analysis of complex phenomena (Goldenweiser 1933, 144; Thompson 1946, 349, 387). But whether or not Boas exaggerated the certainty of his conclusion, we are still left with the following conundrum. Iroquois people in New York and Canada told the same obstacle-flight story at the turn of the twentieth century. Why? Surely, no one would argue the story had been created independently in six Iroquois communities. Presumably, the situation resulted from ongoing interaction among communities sharing a common cultural heritage. Granting that premise, it is reasonable to project the same principles onto a larger canvas. But how large can the canvas plausibly be?

Since Boas's time, a line demarcating the presence of the obstacle chase in America would have to be extended south. Nevertheless, the substance of his insight about distribution remains true today. The obstacle flight is a mythic theme typical of North America but not of Central or South America. In terms of the age-area principle, this point has interesting implications for today's debates about the age and origins of the earliest American people. Possibly, the mythic chase was part of the intellectual baggage of the second (or a succeeding) group of newcomers—immigrants, that is, who arrived after at least one earlier wave fanned out farther to the south.

The Eldest Medicine

I mentioned earlier that "Louis and the Gray Horse," the 1914 Maliseet story, describes an obstacle chase and even includes the detail of reviving a tiring mount being overtaken by a supernatural pursuer. The Maliseet youth reinvigorates his horse by feeding him kernels of black corn (Mechling 1913, 249–50).

In contrast, the Oneida boy achieves the same result by lashing the bull with red-willow whips. An identical action occurs in a contemporaneous Seneca story about a horned serpent who rescues a young woman stranded on an island (Parker 1989, 223–27; cf. Cornplanter 1986, 58–65). Placing the woman on his head, the snake carries her to the safety of the land while under attack by a pursuing Thunder. Fortunately, the snake had equipped the woman with twelve "osiers" with which she lashed him as he tired in his swimming. The scourging revived the serpent's strength just sufficiently to reach land.

This same story is well known to Oklahoma Delawares, except that their plot includes no switches and no whipping (Bierhorst 1995, 63–64, 98–99). A very similar Ojibwa tale of Fort William, Ontario, likewise contains no allusion to osier switches (Michelson 1919, 185, 383–85).

We have, then, two instances in which much the same story can be compared in Iroquois and non-Iroquois settings. In both, the Iroquois telling adds the same odd detail: a human restores the vigor of a weary supernatural by whipping the being with lashes said to be of red willow or osier.

These terms in an Iroquois context—red willow, osier, and often dogwood and willow—almost certainly refer to the same plant: red osier dogwood, *Cornus sericea* (formerly and synonymously *C. stolonifera*), a native deciduous bush, commonly growing six to twelve feet high (ill. 19). At home in a northern habitat of swamps and marshy soils, the shrub is remarkable for its wildlife value. Its small white fruits are eaten by bluebirds, cardinals, kingbirds, bobwhites, ruffed and sharptail grouse, and several species of woodpecker. Deer, elk, moose, cottontail, and snowshoe hare eat its twigs. Its most notable feature, however, is its color. As new growth occurs during the late spring and summer, its branches are green. In the

19. Red osier dogwood at winter's end.

late fall, they begin to turn red and become progressively redder over the winter. By early spring they are a deep bloodred. This plant catches the eye and dominates many a winter landscape.[4]

More generally, red willow—probably meaning several species of *Cornus*—is well known ethnobotanically in much of the United States as medicine for eye and respiratory ailments (Moerman 1998, 178–80). Frequently, it is mentioned in connection with making arrows. And, throughout the eastern United States, red willow is best known as an important—possibly the principal—ingredient of kinnikinnick, an Algonquian word for smoking material made from wild plants often used with tobacco (Springer 1981, 220; Yarnell 1964, 181). Native people may have

4. For the biology and natural history of red osier dogwood, see Dirr 1990, 247–48; Flint 1983, 130; Hightshoe 1988, 550; Petrides 1972, 77; Soper and Heimburger 1982, 359; Sternberg and Wilson 1995, 89–90; and Whitcomb 1983, 295.

been smoking kinnikinnick prior to the appearance of tobacco in the region, possibly about 500 B.C. (Hall 1977, 513–14; Rafferty 2001; Yarnell 1964, 86). In any event, the word for "pipe" long predated the word for "tobacco" in the reconstructed proto-Iroquoian language (Mithun 1984, 274–76).

Among the Iroquois, red osier dogwood occupies a respectable niche in medicine, although apparently it is not ranked among the most powerful medicinal plants (Herrick 1995, 21, 91–92). Its primary medical applications are to respiratory problems, and it is used as an emetic in the winter and spring by, among others, lacrosse players (Fenton 1942, 524; Herrick 1995, 178–79). No medicinal listing will tell you, however, that whipping your supernatural ally with red willows will revive him when you and he stand in the greatest mortal danger.

As Lydia Doxtater put it, "the red whips are supposed to be magical" (Allen 1948b, 39). One sees this principle applied to the arrows in folklore that never miss—often they are specified to be of this material (see Curtin 2001, 33, 346; and Waugh n.d., G. Davis 201 f29, E. Cook 202 f23). George Hamell characterized another context: wherever one encounters a magic wand in Iroquois folklore, it is likely to be a twig of red osier dogwood (1979, fig. 2 caption). An osier switch enlarges a table and makes food appear (Waugh n.d., J. Davis 201 f25). A wand of this material enlarges or shrinks a dog, then transforms the canine into a monster bear to do your bidding (Hewitt 1918, 672–79). It is the tool for changing logs into giant men, for lengthening one's legs in a fight with a supernatural enemy, and for animating a manikin who then provides advice (Curtin 2001, 346; Waugh n.d., T. Smoke 201 f29). Red-willow poles mark off the course of a footrace against an evil sorcerer in which death awaits the loser (Curtin 2001, 31). And if your pond is blighted by a giant bloodsucker, you induce the monster to rise to the surface by scattering scrapings of red-willow bark around the water's perimeter (Waugh n.d., J. Jamieson 201 f29).

If you had touched that water, you would have been poisoned, and your cure would require body purification. In 1915, when John Jamieson Jr. of the Six Nations Reserve told Frederick Waugh about the giant bloodsucker, he included directions for the cleansing: induce vomiting by drinking a decoction made from the bark scrapings of the red osier dogwood. This kind of use may relate to William Fenton's observation that red willow is used to cure a nosebleed after seeing False Face (1987, 156). In both examples, a cure becomes necessary after coming in contact with the supernatural.

One of Waugh's informants thought red-willow switches were very powerful in matters of witchcraft (n.d., "Ooksayik" 201 f26). If so, virtually nothing has been recorded of osier in this context beyond a brief Oneida anecdote of 1919: "Once a woman that wasn't good fell in love with a young man and his people didn't like her but she gave him some love powder and he fell in love with her. His family felt very bad and his grandmother cut three red whips and stewed them and gave him to drink and he was cured of his craze" (Allen 1948b, 73). Possibly, this antiwitchcraft beverage counteracted the love powder as an emetic, causing the victim to vomit out the poison.

A familiar vignette in Iroquois folklore has the hero demonstrating his power by converting tobacco smoke into wampum beads (see sidebar, chapter 5). Red-willow kinnikinnick is remembered in the same fashion (Hewitt 1918, 262–66, 516). Also like tobacco, the burning of red willow can be efficacious apart from pipes. Another incident in Iroquois folklore has the hero rising on the smoke of burned red-willow shavings so he can overtake some witches making a getaway (Curtin 2001, 188; Waugh n.d., "Ooksayik" 201 f26).

Naughty Iroquois children are lashed with whips of red osier dogwood (Fenton 1987, 167; Shimony 1994, 209–10). Another Oneida story of 1918, one given by Lydia Doxtater, helps to explain how this application might relate to magic and medicine:

THE NAUGHTY GIRL

Once there was a little girl who was very naughty but her mother never punished her and in time she died and her mother was very sad.

She was buried and one day a man was going past the cemetery and he saw her hands sticking out of her grave. He told her mother who was terribly broken up over it and went to see the minister about it.

The minister asked if the child had ever been punished. The mother said no. She had been very naughty but never punished.

Then the minister asked how old she was and the mother said she was 12.

Then he told her to get 12 red whips and whip her hands with one at a time and then throw it away.

She got them and the hands began to draw back as soon as she began with the first whip and when she had used the whole 12 they had entirely disappeared. (Allen 1948b, 38)

Like the story opening this chapter, this tale seems distinctly European and for equally good reasons: it is straight out of the Brothers Grimm.[5] But here again—just as with the Oneida magic bull and the Seneca horned serpent—the Iroquois retelling adds a lashing with red osier dogwood switches.

The tale may reflect the sentiment "Spare the rod, spoil the child." However, it also implies that the effectiveness of red willow on children (as well as on magic bulls and horned serpents) has little to do, mythologically speaking, with corporal punishment. Instead, the power of dogwood whips resides in their capacity to draw out the offending substance. Evidently, red willow soaks up the evil (or the fatigue, or the sickness, or the wrong) like a sponge and, by so doing, removes the malefic influence.

That must be why the whips have to be applied one at a time (the action is gradual and cumulative) and why the switches have to be carefully set aside and individually disposed of (they have now absorbed the noxious substance causing the problem). Possibly, that is also why the Iroquois regarded the whips as "medicine" for youthful disobedience (Shimony 1994, 210)—a kind of action consistent with a property of

5. This Oneida narrative is very similar to the Grimms' "Willful Child," story no. 117 of their 1857 large edition: "Once upon a time there was a child who was willful, and would not do what her mother wished. For this reason God had no pleasure in her, and let her become ill, and no doctor could do her any good, and in a short time she lay on her death-bed. When she had been lowered into her grave, and the earth was spread over her, all at once her arm came out again, and stretched upwards, and when they had put it in and spread fresh earth over it, it was all to no purpose, for the arm always came out again. Then the mother herself was obliged to go to the grave, and strike the arm with a rod, and when she had done that, it was drawn in, and then at last the child had rest beneath the ground" (Grimm and Grimm 1944, 534–35).

red willow already noted: it cures by cleaning out; it purges the body of poison.

The effect of taking away weariness or sickness is to restore health, revitalize, and regenerate. This principle is vividly illustrated in a story about a human who steals a magic game pointer from a Stone Giant (see chapter 4). The game pointer is a severed human hand that does not work when it dries out. Consequently, the owner must restore its magical life by soaking it in a solution made from red willow (Beauchamp 1922, 147).

Probably the most common use of red willow in Iroquois folklore is in killing supernatural enemies, a notion well documented at Oneida and Cattaraugus (Allen 1948b, 41–42; Curtin 2001, 426). But, by far, the greatest number of stories illustrating this application derive from Waugh's work at the Six Nations Reserve during the 1910s.

·A boy shoots a cannibal bird with a bow and arrow of red willow.

·A hunter kills a monster bear with twelve arrows of red osier dogwood.

·A man aids a white bear in mortal combat with a giant lizard by spearing parts of the lizard with twigs of red willow as they fly off to prevent them from reassembling.

·A person kills a magical animal called "It Eats All" with red osier dogwood switches.

·A human armed with red willow bow and arrow aids a bear in mortal combat against her wizard husband.

·Ten human hunters, each armed with three arrows of red osier dogwood, overcome a monster cricket.

·A stone ax, hafted with red osier dogwood, is used to kill a witch.[6]

And so on. The giant bloodsucker in the pond mentioned earlier was destroyed with Thunder's lightning and with a boy's two red osier dogwood arrows (Waugh n.d., J. Jamieson 201 f29). In the previous chapter, I mentioned the mortal who helped the thunders by shooting a giant snake with twelve red-willow arrows (Shimony 1994, 162). Waugh heard a similar story about forty years earlier (n.d., S. Hill 201 f28).

Waugh also documented a version of what is probably the best-known

6. These allusions to red willow, all occurring in Waugh n.d., are: P. John 201 f6, D. Jack 201 f24, Mrs. P. John 201 f27, T. Smoke 201 f27, D. Jack 202 f23, and E. Cook 202 f24.

Iroquois serpent story. In 1918, Elias Cook told him about an odd-looking pet snake who matured into a monstrous man-eater. Eventually, the serpent overwhelmed the people of a nearby village who ended up walking into the creature's open jaws. Fortunately, the last survivor managed to kill the snake with red osier dogwood, and, when several people emerged alive from the carcass, they immediately ingested a purgative made from red osier dogwood (202 f24).

In the 1880s, Jeremiah Curtin collected at least two variants of this story among the Senecas (Hewitt 1918, 106, 420–21). In one of them, a two-headed serpent encircles the settlement in such a way that both heads converge at the gate in the village palisade. This element was the essential feature of the story as known to David Cusick in about 1827, who added that the incident occurred at a historically known Seneca town (Beauchamp 1892, 20–21). Indirectly, the same plot can be traced back nearly a half century earlier to Horatio Jones's boyhood captivity among the Senecas. The story attributed to Jones has the last survivors being two orphan children who "were informed by an oracle of the means by which they could get rid of their formidable enemy": shoot it with a bow and arrow "made of a kind of willow" (Seaver 1990, 143).

Possibly the Jesuits made reference to this story among the Hurons in 1640. The Indians suspected sickness emanated from an evil snake ("a certain serpent of which their fables make mention") kept hidden from them by the French missionaries (Thwaites 1896–1901, 19:97). In any event, the plot (though not necessarily the allusion to red willow) is likely to be older than the late 1700s because it was present among the Oklahoma Wyandots (Barbeau 1915, 146–48).[7] This fact constitutes one more instance of identical Iroquois-Wyandot content implying a common origin in the seventeenth century.

---

7. The serpent pet of the Oklahoma Wyandots who grew up to devour a village was killed by arrows made of a substance translated as "a switch of dogwood" and "a dogwood stick" (Barbeau 1915, 147; Pearson 2001, 136). Hence, the Wyandot and Iroquois stories are essentially the same, and the concordance of Wyandot dogwood with Iroquois red willow seems very close. One cannot be certain, of course, that the Wyandots meant red osier dogwood. Further, the Wyandot word for dogwood in the phrase cited above—*u-"gyohara"*—does not seem to be cognate with the corresponding Oneida term (Michael K. Foster and Bruce L. Pearson, personal communications). In Oneida, the plant is rendered as *o-nikw'htala"* (red) *nika-kwil-ó-t^* (willow; kind of whip) (Lounsbury and Gick 2000, 75).

The story is still told today. Recently, an Iroquois journalist published it as the traditional tale of two environmentally destructive serpents named Canada and the United States who are slain by a Mohawk boy armed with a special bow of willow (George-Kanentiio 2000, 30–34). So after perhaps four centuries, the mythic imagery of the tale apparently remains vigorous. Most remarkably, the contemporary telling still retains at least a vestigial allusion to killing evil ones with red willow.

Memories of red osier dogwood some two hundred years old are retained in the Iroquois creation story as a tradition that it was the first plant on earth, springing up at water's edge around the circumference of Turtle's back. In an Oneida account of 1971, the woman who fell from the sky sees that the "first two things that came to be growing were the red willow" and something else the narrator could not remember. A 1912 Oneida account insists on the same incident: "The earth began to grow bigger, and [the woman] could see the red osier dogwood bushes" (Lounsbury and Gick 2000, 40, 165). So did Mohawk Seth Newhouse in 1896–1897: "At that time she looked and saw that willows had grown up to bushes along the edge of the water" (Hewitt 1974, 288). Around 1876, Seneca Esquire Johnson related the plant to the creative activities of the Good Spirit: "and at once the earth was made beautiful with the green grass. He then made the red willow grow on the wet lands" (Caswell 1892, 232). The Oneida account of James Dean (see chapter 3) probably permits us to extend osier back into the late 1700s: "The earth continued to expand and soon formed a small island, skirted with willow and other aquatic shrubbery" (1915, 3).

Admittedly, this tradition sometimes seems to be one in which the narrator is unsure of the detail. That perception is precisely the sense in which we receive red willow from John Arthur Gibson in his Onondaga creation epic of 1900. Gibson, the greatest synthesizer of mythic lore of his age, handles this topic inconsistently. His Sky Holder creates grass, the sunflower, and then red willow, yet repeatedly insists the red willow was the first plant to grow on this earth (Hewitt 1974, 544, 573). "Here," the good twin announces after creating it, "I have planted a medicine which then shall be the eldest one of all those that shall continue to grow here" (491).

Exactly what Sky Holder intended the medicine to do is unclear, although, a little further on, he wafts his grandmother up to the sky on red-willow smoke. Then, turning to the first human couple, he says that, in the future, only the word and mind will be able to go up, and they only on tobacco smoke (552–53). Thus, Gibson mythologically dated red willow to an age earlier than the age of humans and tobacco use.

Apparently, it was difficult to remember much about red willow's sacred aspects by 1900, possibly because osier was divorced from religious practices of the day. I can find no reference to the plant in Thanksgiving Addresses, all recorded since the mid-nineteenth century (Chafe 1961; Foster 1974; Hewitt 1974, 568–70, 594–96; Morgan 1962, 218–21; Parker 1913, 85–100). And although Seneca prophet Handsome Lake forbade the whipping of children, red osier dogwood is not mentioned in the Handsome Lake texts published by Lewis Henry Morgan (1962, 233–59) or Arthur Parker (1913). The Longhouse religion evidently did nothing to encourage or preserve the topic, but, on the other hand, I can find no evidence that red willow played a role in religious observations prior to Handsome Lake. If what we see in oral narrative reflects former religious importance, it must have been something that long predated written documentation.

Handsome Lake aside, however, allusions to red osier dogwood pervaded Iroquois folklore and mythology at the turn of the twentieth century. These references add up to an extraordinary bundle of ideas. Red willow removes poison or diminishes a life-threatening state. When applied to the body as a whip, it purifies from the outside in. Its switches are medicine that removes malefic influence by drawing out an offending substance—be it fatigue, sickness, evil, wrong, or even childish disobedience. Used as an emetic, it cleanses and purifies as a purgative from the inside out. Either way, red willow renews health, strength, vigor—it replenishes and revivifies. Further, a human being can derive great power from its smoke, inhaling from a pipe in the form of kinnikinnick or experiencing its fumes emanating from a fire. Finally, red willow is the weapon of choice against otherworldly foes.

A couple of motifs or plots specifically linked with red willow can be dated, through documentary means, to the late 1700s and perhaps even earlier. In asserting that red willow was the first plant in our world and that it predated the use of tobacco, however, the Iroquois claimed the subject to be far older than the eighteenth-century references.

How old could that be? Dean Snow draws attention to the apparent conceptual importance of red stone to Paleo-Indians in the Northeast twelve thousand years ago (1980, 132–34). Red ocher, evidently indicative of mortuary symbolism, has been found on burials spanning the Early and Middle Archaic (some ten to five thousand years ago) in the Northeast (Robinson 1996). However, the strongest association of red ocher with graves occurred in connection with various so-called burial cults characteristic of the East during the Late Archaic and Early Woodland periods, roughly five to two thousand years ago (Tuck 1978, 41–42).

Probably an archaeologist's first guess would be that Iroquois notions of red willow might relate to the Meadowood phase or culture, dated approximately from 1000 to 500 B.C. Meadowood included a highly developed manifestation of red mortuary symbolism in the territory that would later be Oneida and Iroquois.

Meadowood burials, as first described by William Ritchie, were sited on knolls overlooking lakeshores and riverine marshes (suitable habitats for red willow) (1968). They were associated with blocked-end tubular pipes signaling the apparent onset of ritual smoking in the area (consistent with red willow's identification with kinnikinnick and the efficacy of its fumes). They contained the thin preforms of chert used to make the diagnostic Meadowood projectile points, which may indicate the first appearance of the bow and arrow (Wright 1994, 59–62). This theory would also be in conformity with red willow's use as arrow-shaft material and with the Iroquois predilection for employing osier against supernaturals (Hall 1989, 276–77). And they were characterized by the extensive use of red ocher interpreted by Ritchie as indicating vitalization and restoration of life (congruent with the color and connotations of red willow). Because the biology and ideology of red willow are keyed to winter's end—that is, one specific and presumably datable time of the year—the proposal that Iroquois concepts are applicable to ancient mortuary ceremonialism may well be archaeologically verifiable (cf. Granger 1978, 105; and Hall 1997, 35, 157).

In the meantime, a literal application of age-area premises would indicate that the Iroquois package of red-willow beliefs is unlikely to be of great age because it seems unique to the Iroquois. Its distribution not being particularly great, no substantial time depth is evidently involved.

Yet the matter is not so simple. Much of the apparent originality of the Iroquois in the matter of red willow resides more in the synthesis than in the content. Attitudes and ideas organized around the osier theme in Iroquois country *do* occur elsewhere, but seem to be packaged differently. For example, a mythic charter for red willow as a smoking material is characteristic of the Great Lakes region where the Algonquian trickster-hero Nanabozho typically punishes his rear end for its failure to keep watch while he sleeps. Blood from Nanabozho's self-induced wound stains the osier bush red, which, hereafter, shall be available for humans to smoke (Michelson 1917, 113, 179, 415; cf. Barnouw 1977, 29–30; and Skinner 1924–1927, 340). This detail, however, has nothing to do with using red willow as a weapon against supernatural antagonists.

On the other hand, a red plant is commonly employed against otherworldly foes in the Midwest, but it is not necessarily red willow and not necessarily linked to kinnikinnick. For Wyandots in Oklahoma, such a plant is the redbud tree (Barbeau 1915, 315). Elsewhere, red cedar and other plants are named in similar context (see Barnouw 1977, 122, 132–37). Robert Hall has long argued that red willow is connected with concepts of immortality, to kinnikinnick and ancient rituals involving sacred smoke, and to a symbolism of weaponry employed to make peace (1983, 40–41; 1997, 157–59). In the midwestern setting of his arguments, however, red willow is only one of several reddish plants imbued with the symbolism of life continuity, the others being red cedar, bearberry, and sumac (1977, 505–6). Hence, although we encounter familiar ideas in the Midwest, red osier dogwood does not loom as large in the oral narrative of that region, nor are its associations identical.

Perhaps the strangest aspect of all the Iroquois views on red willow is the idea of purifying or strengthening the body through whipping. However, the "notion of whipping or striking an object to give it special power" evidently exists in the Wyandot language (Bruce L. Pearson, personal communication). And the same concept may have been known to the Iroquois's southern neighbors, the Delawares. Frank Speck cites a possible allusion to whipping in the course of a ceremony in 1670 (1937, 8). Around 1750, nativistic Delaware prophets "pretended that stripes were the most effectual means to purge away sin. They advised their hearers to suffer themselves to be beaten with twelve different sticks from the soles of their feet to their necks, that their sins might pass from them through their throats" (Zeisberger quoted in Harrington 1921, 58).

A Delaware folktale collected in Oklahoma in 1912 tells of a boy with thunderbird power who teams up with Wehixamokäs, a trickster-warrior character. The latter gets into a fight with giants who all but subdue him. "So this friend of his, this boy, had more power than Wehixamokäs had. So he helped Wehixamokäs. He horsewhipped Wehixamokäs because he was scared and was getting overpowered. So by his assistance, Wehixamokäs and he managed to escape from those giants" (Bierhorst 1995, 115). If the Delaware indeed engaged in whipping similar to what was defined in Iroquois oral narrative, the material used for the switches is unknown.

The Iroquois form of whipping may be more distantly related to southeastern "dry-scratching," the custom of drawing blood with a sharp comblike implement. This act is regarded as preparatory to engaging in such acts of religious importance as learning sacred texts or playing in a ball game (Mooney 1995, 230, 476). More generally, the Southeast is home to a philosophy of purificatory emetics similar to another concept familiar from red willow (Hudson 1976, 340–41, 415–16). Redroot, from willow, is a sacred plant of that region taken to induce vomiting prior to ceremonies. Such purgations "render the user pure and properly prepared for participation in his ritual encounters with the sacred" (Grantham 2002, 55).

In sum, a mythic charter for red willow as a smoking material is characteristic of the Great Lakes. Perhaps the concept of employing a red plant with or against supernatural beings should be sought to the west also. Whipping as purificatory action may have analogues to the south. Certainly, faith is strongest in the Southeast that an emetic—often a red plant substance—prepares one to enter the realm of the numinous. It is as though the themes and symbolic functions intersecting in Iroquois culture around the subject of red willow occur elsewhere separately, sometimes disconnected from the specific botanical referent. In any event, such themes as smoking red willow and purging for spiritual effect have a real distribution vastly greater than Iroquois territory and must be of proportionately great antiquity by the tenants of age-area.

REIFIED NARRATIVE?

For the Iroquois, tobacco smoking was quintessentially a male activity, performed by the individual with his own pipe in a solitary fashion. Even in a group setting, an Iroquois man typically sat "smoking his own pipe incessantly" (Fenton 1991, 111). One European attending an Iroquois council in 1669 described it this way: "It is their custom, on entering, to seat themselves in the most convenient place that they find vacant, without any consideration of rank, and at once get some fire to light their pipes, which do not leave their mouths during the whole time of the council, and they say that 'Good thoughts come while smoking.' " "This," William Fenton concludes, "is a persistent theme in Iroquois political life" (1998, 22).

Not surprisingly, fired clay pipes are rather common in the Iroquois archaeological record. The majority, being plain or decorated with geometric designs incised and punctated into the clay fabric, are not obviously representational. Some, however, depict birds, mammals, reptiles, humanlike figures, and other subjects in an apparently naturalistic fashion. Almost every one of these images was created on the bowl to face the smoker (Brasser 1980). In the vast majority of such effigy pipes, the smoker confronted one such image (one owl or one bear, for example), or, if more than one, it was still a relatively simple iconic composition (such as twins; see sidebar, chapter 3).

The most complex composition found on Iroquois effigy pipes occurred on examples attributable to the Oneidas (ill. 20h, 20i), Mohawks (ill. 20g and a—a carved antler comb), and Onondagas (ill. 20f); to the Wyoming Valley region of northern Pennsylvania (ill. 20b; vicinity of Tunkhannock south of Binghamton, possibly referable to the Iroquoian-speaking Susquehannocks); and to the St. Lawrence Iroquoians, chiefly of present-day Jefferson County, New York (ill. 20c-e). The latter are thought to have been speakers of Iroquoian languages inhabiting that area from about 1350 to their disappearance about 1550 (Abel 2001; Engelbrecht 1995; Pendergast 1991).

The complete composition visible on these pipes (and at least one comb) consists of four design registers:

1. Three or four humanlike faces are depicted in a row, each with a raylike feature projecting vertically upward from the top of the head (ill. 20a-d, f, h-i).

2. A platformlike element occurs horizontally beneath the heads and rising to frame them on each end (ill. 20d, f, h-i). It resembles a cutaway view of a box or boat, or a squarish letter *c* lying on its back.

3. Two circles or circular depressions are depicted beneath the platformlike feature (ill. 20a-c, f-g, i). They tend to be relatively large, some-

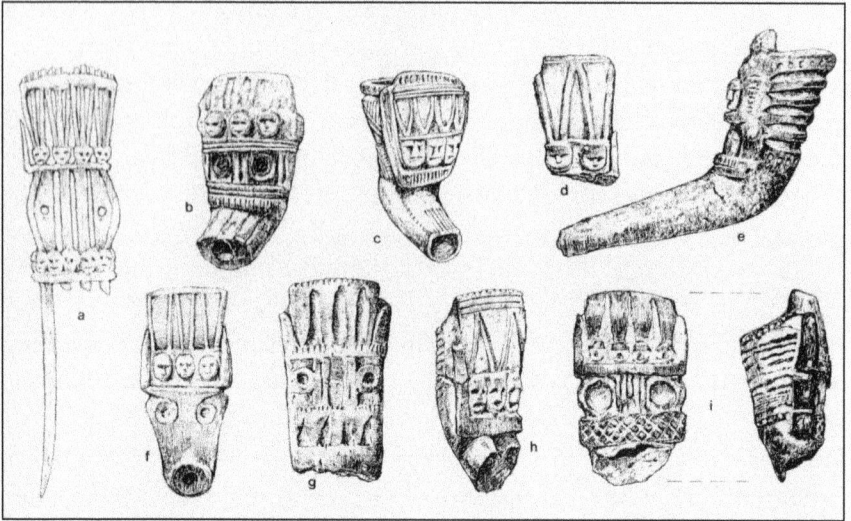

20. *A complex design on eastern Iroquoian pottery pipes and an antler comb. Not to scale but shown at approximately the same relative sizes. Comb at left (a) is about 6.5 inches high; pipe bowl at lower right (i) is about 2.5 inches high.*

(a) carved bone comb, probably from the Mohawk Valley, N.Y. (after a photo courtesy of James Walsh; Rochester Museum and Science Center, no. 6542/177); (b) stone pipe bowl, Wyoming Valley, Penn. (after Kent 1984, fig. 28); (c) ceramic pipe bowl from Putnam site, Jefferson County, N.Y. (after Skinner 1921, fig. 39b); (d) part of ceramic pipe bowl, Roebuck site, Grenville County, Ontario (after Wintemberg 1936, pl. LXVIII: no. 7); (e) ceramic pipe with eroded register 1 once containing three or four rayed heads, Woodworth site, Jefferson County, N.Y. (after a photo courtesy of the Division of Anthropology, American Museum of Natural History, no. T/2726); (f) ceramic pipe bowl, Onondaga County, N.Y. (after Beauchamp n.d., 10: no. 646); (g) ceramic pipe bowl from the Mohawk Valley region (after a photo courtesy of George R. Hamell); (h) part of a ceramic pipe bowl, Nichols Pond site, Madison County, N.Y. (after Pratt 1976, pl. 6: no. 31); (i) ceramic pipe bowl from the Dougherty site, Madison County (Madison County Historical Society, no. I 57).

times resembling the goggle eyes of the Mesoamerican water god, Tlaloc. Vertical lines generally separate the two circles; sometimes they resolve into two vertical strips.

4. The least documented and apparently the most variable, the lowest register shows what look like several vertical strips in one instance (ill.

20g), a crosshatched design zone in another (ill. 20i), and, in the third, a row of faces similar to the ones of the first register but lacking the raylike appendage (ill. 20a).

Presentation of this visually complex composition seems to require that a two-dimensional surface, a plane performing the service of a plaque or small billboard, be added. The registers or friezes of this composition are always presented hieratically from top to bottom in the numbered order. Evidently, not all the registers need be present, a phenomenon suggestive of the metaphorical process called synecdoche—a figure of speech in which a part makes reference to the whole. Nevertheless, even presented partially, whatever registers are shown must conform to the same numbered order. Register 2, for example, must be placed below register 1 or above register 3, or between registers 1 and 3 if both are depicted.

This elaborate composition presents the viewer with a sequence of images reminiscent of linear syntax necessary to narrative plot. Because the incidents of a story are temporally related—one precedes and is the precondition of the next—the story must be presented in chronological order. The pipe design is also suggestive of some hierarchically constructed cosmogram or *weltbild,* a picture of the world order conceived in vertically stacked layers. Either way, the sequentially structured image could well illustrate a myth.

If there was such a narrative, it was one shared by certain men in the Oneida, Mohawk, Onondaga, Jefferson County Iroquoian, and Susquehanna River regions. It was a myth these men agreed should be given concrete form because, presumably, they thought it was worth thinking about individually or alone together as they puffed away on their pipes in council during the fourteenth and fifteenth centuries.

I know of no surviving myth offering a simple register-by-register reading of this visual work. But I can suggest a partial and speculative reading on the assumption that the hieratic space of the composition relates, at least in part, to a depiction of space on a vertical axis. In that case, we might have some humanlike gods or heroes (register 1) above what might be the eyes of an owl or serpent in register 3. Owls, in fact, were very popular effigies at this time, although I have never seen one like this one. If, on the other hand, it was a snake, perhaps it had a great maw sometimes filled with people (register 4). We may have encountered surviving fragments of this hypothetical myth in, first, the memory of the good twin with thunder qualities who smote a great snake in the Cusick and Gallinée accounts of Sky Holder (see pp. 130–31), and, second, as the most famous Iroquois serpent tale that tells of the monster who swallowed a village (see pp. 150–51), or both.

7

⟊

The Fabric of Daily Life

This chapter illustrates the range and spirit of Oneida storytelling at the turn of the twentieth century. Material surveyed here falls squarely within the regional corpus of Iroquois folklore of the time, yet it manifests links throughout native America, including some surprisingly close ties to distant regions. Often European influence is evident, the Old World wonder and fairy tales having been incorporated into the Oneida repertoire and rendered Oneida in interesting ways. At the same time, mythic threads interwoven throughout the cloth of Oneida oral narrative seem likely to be of great antiquity.

Diversity in form is notable. The fifteen or so texts in this section include allegories, fables, and tall tales. They range widely in expression and theme. Some comment on family values and morality; others reflect a keen interest in animals. There are a few scary tales and a marked predilection for humor. What the Oneidas told while holding on and getting by as marginalized people in their own homeland evinces little anger or bitterness. On the contrary, as reflections of outlook and daily experience, these stories demonstrate the Oneidas were surprisingly good-natured.

⟊

Lydia Doxtater told this story during the cold months of 1918:

BEAR AND FOX, OR HOW THE BEAR LOST HIS TAIL

A long time ago the men and animals understood each other. Once a fox met a man driving a load of fish and he wanted some very much. So he thought of a trick to get it by. He ran on ahead and lay down in the road as if he were dead and when the man came along he thought the fox was dead. He took him up saying "How lucky I am today! First, I got the fish and now I find this

161

fine fox." So he threw the fox in the back with the fish. Now this just suited the fox and he commenced dropping fish off the wagon. And when he had dropped off enough, then he dropped off himself and the man never noticed. The fox picked himself up and then ran back and picked up the fish. Just then a bear came along.

Most bears are very fond of fish. The bear said to the fox, "Ha, Cousin, where did you get that good fish?" And the fox answered, "You come and I will show you so that you can catch some the same way." Then the fox led the bear down to a creek that was solidly frozen over for it was winter (Lydia added "It must have been a winter like this one") and he clawed a hole in the ice and he said "Now you sit there and let your tail drop down in the water and the fish will come and take hold of it. That is the way I catch my fish."

In those days bears had long tails. So the bear sat down as the fox told him to and let his tail hang in the water but very soon he got tired of this and he called the fox and said, "Hey, Cousin, I'm feeling my tail very heavy." And the fox answered and said "That is your good luck. How many fish you must be catching!"

So the bear sat on the ice awhile longer but after a little he called the fox again and again complained. This time the fox said, "Well, I'll go and get some of my relatives to help you."

But the bear began to surmise what the fox meant and he said "Oh, no," still the fox went. He ran through the places where there were dogs and when the hounds had the scent, he ran back to where the bear was and right up to him and the hounds came and attacked the bear. And to defend himself he had to pull himself loose from the ice and leave his tail behind and that is how the bear has a short tail. (Allen 1948b, 16–17)

"When I told the story of the bear and its tail to Josiah Johnson (1948—who was an invalid, but by this time had lost his shyness enough to talk sometimes directly to me about the stories)," Allen wrote, "he said there was something at the end about 'gangs' and Lydia afterwards remembered that and this is how the story goes as I have pieced it out from the two of them."

The bear was very angry at the way he had been hoodwinked and lost his tail and he told the fox to meet him and fight it out. And he got the pig to help him.

He and the pig got there first and the bear climbed a tree to see whether the fox was coming and he called down quickly, and saw that the fox was coming up strong. He had two warriors with him. One was picking up stones all the time as he came and the other carried a great spear. Then the pig was very much frightened, and he lay down and covered himself all up with leaves. But when the fox came, with him were only a dog that limped as it walked and a cat that was walking with its tail set up straight. They found no one because the bear was up the tree and the pig was buried in the leaves. But of course the pig had to breathe, and it rustled the leaves and the cat who was a good mouser jumped at that and dug its claws into the pig.

The pig jumped up with a great grunt which so frightened the cat that it jumped up into the same tree that the bear was in and scared the bear so that it began to run and that scared the cat more than ever and the cat and the bear chased each other about the tree furiously. At last the bear fell down and ran away. He told afterwards, "What a terrible time that was when I ran up and down the branches with that great spear after me!" (26)

Rivaled only by "Vampire Corpse" (see pp. 102–4), "Bear and Fox, or How the Bear Lost His Tail" (often including the episode in the fish wagon) may be the most frequently documented Iroquois story of the twentieth century (see Fenton 1948, 112–13; Hinton ca. 1997, 21–22, 62–64; Michelson and Nicholas 1981, 28–33; Parker 1994, 102–8; and Rustige 1988, 48–50). Precisely the same incidents given to Allen (fish wagon, tail in the ice, animals' duel) were recorded at the Six Nations Reserve in the early 1880s (E. Smith 1983, 35–36) and in 1915 (Waugh n.d., J. Hess 201 f26). Obviously, this tale was fun to hear or to tell. "This is a child's story," William Beauchamp observed of the final episode, "allowing spirited action on the part of the frightened bear, but when the narrator imitates the pig's squeal there is intense delight among the Indian children" (1922, 59).

Allen sensed the story originated in Europe, a suspicion shared by

Beauchamp, William Fenton, and Frederick Waugh. Certainly, all three incidents of the Oneida anecdote—fox feigns death and throws fish off
wagon, fox tricks bear into fishing with his tail, the gang fight of cowardly
animals—are well known throughout Europe, where they must be of respectable antiquity. Kaarle Krohn thought the first two may have been
combined first in northern Germany (1971, 155–57); Stith Thompson
believed the third, the "cowardly duelers," may have originated in Germany. In any event, all are thought to have entered the Indian lexicon by
way of French Canada (Thompson 1919, 438–39).

Non-Iroquois examples of the story, however, are not necessarily
about the bear. Some European versions, for example, place wolf or dog in
the bear's place, and in some Wyandot tellings, it is fox who plays bear's
role (Barbeau 1915, 180–82). Does it make any difference?

To the Iroquois it might as a question of near kin. "We, the bears,"
says one of Jesse Cornplanter's characters, "are the most closely related to
your people" (1986, 158; cf. Beauchamp 1922, 58; and Lévi-Strauss
1981, 522).

The rather strange tale that follows was told by Anna Johnson early in
1919:

COUSINS DOG AND GREY SQUIRREL CLAN

Once two men lived together who were cousins. They were
Cousin Dog Clan and Cousin Grey Squirrel Clan. They lived
together in one house but they never spoke to each other except
when one or the other came in. The one who came in would say
to the other: "I have come home Cousin Dog Clan" (or Cousin
Grey Squirrel Clan as the case might be).

In this way they lived a long time till finally Cousin Dog Clan
said to Cousin Grey Squirrel Clan, "The time has come for you
to get married and your wife is waiting for you. You are to go and
get her. You are to travel on foot day and night till you come to
the house of a woman with seven daughters. You are to marry
the youngest but when you go there you are to take her and go
away at once. You must not on any account be persuaded to stay.

Above all you must think of me if you are in any kind of danger and if you only call my name I will be there and help you. Don't ever forget me and you will be safe."

Cousin Grey Squirrel Clan went as he was told and arrived at the house and asked for his wife. His mother-in-law said to him, "Why do you hurry away? Stay with us awhile. There is plenty of time. Anyhow your wife hasn't got her clothes together yet." "No," he said, "I must go on" and he stood outside the door and wouldn't come in.

But he was very fond of popcorn and after awhile she popped a lot of corn and offered him some and he came in. It ended by his spending the night because his wife hadn't got her clothes ready. He forgot all about his Cousin Dog Clan.

In the morning his mother-in-law said to him, "Now you must do something to earn your wife. You must go where a man is building a mud house and stand by the fire by which he is drying it longer than he can stand it."

He had to go to this fire and stand there. Soon it got terribly hot because they kept dropping bear's grease in it to make it flame up. He began to suffer terribly and became very faint and then he remembered what his Cousin Dog Clan had told him.

"If you remember me, Cousin Grey Squirrel Clan, no trouble will come to you and if you are in trouble think of me and if you even speak my name I will be there and help you."

So he began to think of his Cousin Dog Clan and all this time his Cousin Dog Clan was thinking of him and suffering over his suffering. He kept saying, "Why doesn't he think of me. If he only called my name I would be there, even by the time he only said as far as Cousin."

And now at last Cousin Grey Squirrel Clan remembered and called on Cousin Dog Clan and Cousin Dog Clan came before his name was even all said and he took Cousin Grey Squirrel's place by the fire just when he was almost overcome and Cousin Grey Squirrel Clan was almost overcome by the heat and he went outdoors to revive and while he was there the other man died and he was free.

So Cousin Dog Clan saved him and he went back to get his wife and Cousin Dog Clan said, "You must not on any account go in and you must not forget me" and went home.

Then Cousin Grey Squirrel Clan went to the door and asked for his wife and his mother-in-law came and said his wife's clothes weren't ready yet and she asked him to come in. He refused but she brought him a great quantity of popcorn, a great deal more than she prepared the night before, and finally she got him to stay.

He went in and ate a great deal and his wife's clothes still weren't ready and again he stayed the night. The next morning his mother-in-law said to him, "Today you must do something to earn your wife. There is going to be a moose hunt and you must catch the moose." But Cousin Grey Squirrel Clan said "I can't run at all. I am so overloaded with all the popcorn I ate," and it was just as he said. He could hardly move and when he started it was very painful to him and he didn't know what was going to become of him. His Cousin Dog Clan was in his house seeing all this and he was very sad and he kept saying, "Why doesn't Cousin Grey Squirrel Clan call on me? Why has he forgotten me? If he even so much as said Cousin I would be with him."

Then Cousin Grey Squirrel Clan remembered and he began to think of Cousin Dog Clan and he began to call on him and instantly Cousin Dog Clan was there. When he saw the condition Cousin Grey Squirrel was in, first he knocked him to one side and a stream of popcorn came out of his mouth and then he knocked him on the other and a stream of popcorn came out of his mouth, and then he knocked him forward and another stream came out. Thus Cousin Grey Squirrel Clan was lightened and he was able to go and run the race.

Cousin Dog Clan went back home and all the time he was expecting Cousin Grey Squirrel Clan. The foxes used to come to his door and knock and say "I have come home, Cousin Dog Clan" and he would rush to the door and when he would see who it was he would say "Go out and die" and he had so much power that it would happen as he said. They would go into the woods and die.

After awhile Cousin Dog Clan gave up expecting Cousin

Grey Squirrel Clan. It seemed such a long time. And he neglected the house and the room he had prepared for the bride but finally Cousin Grey Squirrel Clan really came home.

He won the moose and went to claim his wife and this time he refused to come in and his mother-in-law couldn't get him. He said he would wait outside till his wife got her clothes ready and when she brought them out they were a pile about a yard high but when he put them on his back they were only a little bundle. So he and his wife set out.

When they got near his house they found the woods full of dead foxes and he began to be very much afraid. "I am afraid," he said, "that something has happened to my Cousin Dog Clan" and he ran all anxious up to the door. But when he knocked and said "I have come home, Cousin Dog Clan," Cousin Dog Clan didn't believe him for he had been fooled so many times by the foxes and he refused to open. Finally he said, "Go out and die" as he said to the foxes and his power was so great that Cousin Grey Squirrel started out as they did and began to feel sick unto death.

But then as at other times when he was in great trouble he began to think of Cousin Dog Clan and thought "I will think of him even now and call on him and perhaps it will help me even yet." So he thought of him and called on his name and he began to feel stronger and was able to get back to the house. Then he knocked again and said, "I have come home, Cousin Dog Clan" and this time Cousin Dog Clan came to the door and saw that it was really Cousin Grey Squirrel Clan but he only let him put his hand in and refused to open the door any further.

He took one of the pieces of leather thong that you use to tie up parcels with (Si and Anna only know the Indian name which is Ha-Ge) and tied in Cousin Grey Squirrel Clan's hand and held him there and then with one hand he swept the floor and with the other he shaved and when he had everything all in good shape he opened the door and welcomed the bride. (Allen 1948b, 56–59)

This narrative resembles a Seneca story (itself unusual) in which a pro-tagonist named Yellowbird receives help in a series of tight spots from his brother, a godlike guardian who tells him, "Think of me and I'll be there" (Curtin 2001, 272–87). Though rarely occurring in an Iroquois context, such psychic summoning seems to be a fairly common device in Micmac stories (Rand 1894, 29, 380, 410–11).

The outstanding feature of Yellowbird himself is his polymorphous nature. Said to be an inchworm, he behaves as a person capable of assuming various animal forms. Something like the same fluidity of shape was evoked in the comment Lydia Doxtater made to Allen about the Dog-Squirrel Clan story: "when she was a child if anyone was specially foolish they would say he was just like the squirrel and needed the dog to help him out of his scrapes. She knew the Dog and Squirrel story as animals, not men" (1948b, 63).

Unlike the Seneca story, however, the Oneida plot centers on a conflict between Cousin Dog Clan and a wicked stepmother, evidently a person of considerable magical power. The theme of a mother subjecting her potential son-in-law to a series of deadly tests is a common one, not only in Iroquois folklore, but also throughout native North America (cf. Hewitt 1918, 811 n. 421; Parker 1989, 23–24; and Swanton 1929, 270).

Perhaps the most curious aspect of the story is a sequence in which foxes trick Cousin Grey Squirrel Clan, then the returning hero sticks his hand through the door where it is tied up. These details are fixtures of many other Iroquois stories. Typically, some older relative (an uncle or grandmother) awaits the hero's return. Animals (usually foxes) imitate the absent one's voice at the door, an apparently malicious trick that angers and sometimes seems to humiliate the waiting one. Because of the deception, the person who is waiting compels the returning one to insert an arm or hand through the entrance to establish the latter's identity.[1] One of the versions collected by Waugh provides a detail identical to an item in the Oneida story: the waiting uncle orders the foxes to go off and die (n.d., E. Cook 202 f 23).

The incident in which an arm is somehow thrust through the door to

---

1. The vignette in which one who is waiting orders a returning person to place an arm through the door is found in Curtin 2001, 46, 191, 390–91, 491–93; Parker 1989, 120–21, 258–61; E. Smith 1983, 59–61; and Waugh n.d., P. John 201 f 6, J. Echo and Mrs. P. John 201 f 26.

prove the visitor's identity was documented as a feature of Huron folklore more than 350 years ago (Thwaites 1896–1901, 10:151). The specific two-step sequence may be unique to Iroquois folklore, although stories elsewhere allude to waiting people, often in mourning, who are tricked by animals or other people imitating the absent ones (cf. Barnouw 1977, 96–97; Michelson 1917, 205, 483; Schoolcraft 1999, 165; and Swanton 1929, 175, 218–19). Wyandots, as is so frequently the case, offer an analogy closest to the Iroquois convention. It is foxes, they say, who fool a man hoping for his nephew's return (Barbeau 1915, 231).

Proprieties

Oneida stories often emphasize strongly moralistic lessons about marriage and sexual behavior. For example, we have seen how Little People and Thunder correct promiscuous behavior (see pp. 88–89, 114–15). We know from Beauchamp's snake tale that horrible things happen to people who do not marry when they should (see pp. 115–19). Similarly, the following two stories discuss behavior proper to married men and women. Both include supernatural incidents, although the magical quality of the occurrences is muted.

The first was told "many years ago by Baptist Johnson an Oneida Indian to his son Josiah, and by 'Si' and his wife to Hope Allen, Dec. 1925" (Allen 1948a, N). Although the story opens on the issue of misogamy, the man's refusal to marry is corrected in short order. More important is his attentiveness and perhaps fidelity to his wife. It is, as Allen put it, "a narrative inculcating family stability" (H).

THE MISOGAMIST

Once there was a young Indian who lived all alone in a little house in the woods. He hated to see people and especially women, and he used to say that he was never going to get married.

One day he was coming home from hunting, and he stopped to drink at a spring, for he was very dry. As he leaned over to drink, a snake coiled itself about his neck, and asked him if he was going to get married. When he said "no," it gripped him tighter;

and when it asked again he said "perhaps he would some day."
Then it loosened, and ran away.

Some time after that he came one day to a little house in the
wood when he was hunting, and a woman lived there and he saw
her and fell in love with her and stayed in her house and forgot
his own home and his own people. After a long time when two
children had been born one day she said to him, "I know you
must be lonesome. You must go home to your own people—but
you mustn't stay long, and you mustn't go to any dances. If you
do, I shall know it and you will never see me again."

So he went away, and when he came to his reservation the
people spoke to him and were glad to see him again, and invited
him to a dance. He went, and while he was there he saw a very
pretty girl he had never noticed before, and she asked him to
dance with her and he did so. Afterwards he went home to his
own little house. And the second night he went to a dance, and
the third he went and danced all night, but in the morning he
went home.

When he got home, he found his house was gone, and his
wife and his children, and when he found this out he was as
unhappy as he could be. Then he started out not knowing where
he was bound for, and he said he didn't care where he was going
or what was going to become of him, for he had lost his wife and
children. He went on and on for days, without food and until he
was so tired he could hardly go. It began to rain and he was just
about to give up when he saw a very small light ahead, so he kept
on. When he came near, he saw a small house, and he went in
and there was a woman he had never seen before, with two
children. She prepared food for him, and said she would give him
a bed on the floor, because she had no other except what she
needed for herself and the children. He went to bed but he was
too tired and miserable to sleep. And then after a time the
children woke up and questioned her about this man who had
come, and after a time they got whiny, and he heard their mother
tell them to keep quiet or they would disturb their father. Then
he knew, and he got up and hugged his wife, and children, and
his wife got up and cooked him some breakfast. (N)

In March 1918, Hope Allen obtained the next story from Mrs. Malinda Skenandoah Johns (1853–1931), another Oneida working in the Mansion House as a domestic. Allen thought Johns showed "the same fine intellectual balance exhibited by Lydia and Anna" (1948a, J). The story was called "The Jealous Woman," the point apparently being that jealousy is an undesirable trait in a spouse (1948b, 6). More generally, the tale seems to inveigh against wifely hectoring or shrewishness that may drive off the game. Like the "flirty girl" aided by the Little People in chapter 4, the woman of this story undergoes the ordeal of being abandoned on an island to die—a common occurrence in North American folklore (see Thompson 1929, 326, motif K1616).

THE JEALOUS WOMAN

Once a long time ago when the Indians lived by hunting and fishing there was a woman who had a brother and she was married. She was so jealous that she would never let her husband go away without a great fuss and when he came back she always accused him of going with other women and was as mean to him as she could be for several days.

Finally when he went out hunting he didn't get anything and it was because he had such a jealous wife. One day he and her brother went hunting a long way across a big water and they took her with them. They rowed a long, long way out of all sight of land but when night came they reached a shore and camped. In the morning they wanted to start but the woman was mean and made a great fuss and kept them waiting a long time.

At last her brother said "She acts so mean, let's go and leave her here" and they went on. She expected them to be waiting for her ahead but when she finally started she went on and on and found no one.

At last night came and she came to a strange man camping alone. She asked him to give her something to eat but he refused angrily and only when he finished eating himself, he threw her some scraps and bone.

In the morning when she wakened the man was gone and again she went ahead all day. At night again she came to a man camping and again she could get from him only scraps and again in the morning he was gone. This happened again the third night but the fourth morning the man whom she had seen the night before was still there.

He then talked to her and told her the way to her own reservation. When she got home at last she found that her husband had taken another wife and he never had anything to do with her again. (Allen 1948b, 6)

✦

Published in the *Journal of American Folklore* as "An Oneida Tale," this piece was told by Lydia Doxtater, probably in 1918:

WHO WILL MARRY ME?

Once there was someone who was going along singing, "Who will marry me, who will marry me?" The owl answered and said, "I will marry you." The man said, "What will you give me to eat?" The owl answered, "I'll give you snakes and mice." "Oh!" he answered, "I couldn't stand that diet," and he went on singing, "Who will marry me?" The frog answered, "I'll marry you." "What will you give me to eat?" "I'll give you worms and flies." "Oh! I couldn't stand that diet," and he went on repeating, "Who will marry me?"

The third time (it is always the third time, Lydia says, in Indian stories) an answer came, "I will marry you." "What will you give me to eat?" "I will give you corn." "Then I will marry you," and he was so delighted, he ran and embraced her. She was corn and he was beans and this is the way the Indians always planted corn and beans. The beans were "pole beans" (they were colored like calico beans, "quail-head beans" some people call them) and they were planted with corn so that they ran up the corn stalks. (Allen 1944, 280–81)

The same story was current among the Senecas, except that corn was male, beans female (Hewitt 1918, 646–49). Likewise, a closely related Onondaga version had male corn (Beauchamp 1922, 59–60), as does a more recently recorded Seneca corn song in which the man (corn) is sought by female beans growing on the same hill (Kurath 2000, 163). The format itself (posing the marriage question, then naming foods characteristic of different species) appeared in other riddlelike narratives having nothing to do with corn (Curtin 2001, 68–69; Parker 1989, 325).

The Iroquois had more than this one explanation for the origin of corn. In 1743, travelers approaching Onondaga were shown a hill on which a young woman from the sky had given a hunter corn, squash, and tobacco (Bartram, Evans, and Weiser 1973, 54). Alternatively, corn was something Sky Holder gave humankind after receiving it from his father, Turtle, in Dean's creation account of the late 1700s (see pp. 65–66). By at least the mid-nineteenth century, corn sprouted from the breasts of the twin's buried mother in a Seneca creation narrative (Morgan 1962, 199). Folklore at the turn of the twentieth century mentions, among other derivations, a corn maiden who brings maize from the South (Hewitt 1918, 636–53; Parker 1989, 205–7; Waugh n.d., A. Charles 202 f25).

In the Southeast, a considerable multiplicity of stories about the origin of corn testifies to the importance of corn there (Lankford 1987, 145). I wonder whether the same could be said of the Iroquois in whose folklore the subject seems relatively unimportant. None of the other Oneida stories deal with corn, although many speak of animals, hunting, the forests, and woods-related subjects. Allen's compendium is not unique in this respect. The same relative paucity of material focusing on domesticated crops characterizes every other collection of Iroquois folklore at the turn of the twentieth century. Did crops fail to inspire the same interest and wonder as woodland phenomena, or had a large corpus of corn-and-beans lore been forgotten by the late 1800s (see sidebar, chapter 4)?

Allen published only one other Oneida piece, "a tiny humorous Oneida fable from Mrs. Sarah Powlis Johns [1839–1918] . . . a respected elder" (1948a, H). It also appeared in the *Journal of American Folklore*.

A BOASTFUL LITTLE BIRD

The wren . . . must have been the tiny bird of which the following was told (as a tale to laugh over) to the present writer about 1916 by Mrs. Sarah Powlis, an Iroquois woman of the

Oneida tribe: "A very little bird sat on a twig and sang very hard, so that it shook the twig it was sitting on. Then it said, 'See what a great bird I am. I shake the world.' " (Allen 1935, 193)

John Swanton encountered much the same conceit attributed to (apparently) the same bird among the Kosati, Indians of the Southeast: "the Tciktcinigåsi (wren?) stood under a log close to the ground and said, 'Would not you say that I am very tall? When I rise on my toes I strike my head against the sky' " (1929, 202).

The Kosati word Swanton tentatively identified as "wren" *looks* as though it might be the chickadee instead. "Even though the names of the chickadee are obviously onomatopoeic in character," Claude Lévi-Strauss notes, "one cannot but be struck by the resemblance between them in widely different parts of North America and in communities speaking quite different languages" (1981, 486). The examples he cites include *tc-itc'ike* (Jicarilla Apache), *tcíski'kik* in Thompson, and *tsikilili* among the Iroquoian-speaking Cherokees. The Cherokees regard this bird and the closely related titmouse bird as the news bringers, the messengers par excellence of their narrative tradition (Mooney 1995, 285–86).

To this list could be added the Cayuga *(tsiks:ye:')* and Oneida *(tsikt-sile:l)* words for "chickadee" (Abbott 1996, 574; Mithun 1984, 268) with, apparently, associations similar to the ones of the Cherokees. In 1775, an Oneida sachem said they had heard the voice of this bird "called Tskleleli, a news carrier, that came among us" (Stone 1851, 1, appendix: viii). The news brought by this bird seems to have been considered gossip and rumor (see Hough 1861, 43).

Was this bird the same one whose excessive sense of self-worth was reported 150 years later to Hope Allen?

⟨⌂⟩

"Last Saturday, January 19, [1918] I went up to see Mrs. Powlis, the Indian woman and got the following notes. . . . She said that when she was young her first husband's mother used to tell her a great many stories in the evening when she and her husband used to bind the lady's baskets for the sake of her stories" (1948b, 1; see sidebar). One of those tales was the following:

THE MINISTER'S MIRACLE

It used to be the habit to bury people with what they liked best in life and these things were put with the coffin in the church for a day before the burial. Once a man died who was very fond of butternuts and they put a bag of butternuts with his body. A man went by one night and heard someone cracking nuts. The man went and told the minister who didn't believe it. This minister was a cripple and the man had to carry him on his back to the church to see. They came to the church and sure enough heard someone cracking nuts. When they came to the door a shadow was over the coffin (it was moonlight) and the shadow came towards them. The man carrying the minister was so terrified that he dropped him and ran but after a moment he was amazed to hear steps behind him and there was the minister running too. The minister's walking dates from that time. (1)

As with Mrs. Powlis's other narrative, "The Boastful Little Bird," a nearly identical example derives from the Southeast. In a Hitchiti story documented by John Swanton, a cripple is carried close to a walnut-cracking person believed to be a ghost. When a sudden movement frightens everyone, the cripple is dropped and suddenly finds himself capable of rapid locomotion. But whereas the Oneida story may imply hypochondria on the minister's part, the Hitchiti story aims toward a different moral: "The man who was crippled jumped up and ran. That man had nothing the matter with him any longer. He outran the others and reached his house and could walk ever after. Therefore, if a person has a sudden fright, sickness may disappear" (1929, 115–16).

Although the story "appears in nearly every medieval and Renaissance tale collection" (Thompson 1946, 213–14), it is probably best known through the Brothers Grimm. Both the Oneida and Hitchiti narratives are Old World in origin, and both may have been inspired by the Brothers Grimm. One Grimm fairy tale concludes with an incident in which a simpleton named Katy is grubbing for turnips in the parson's garden ("Freddy and Katy," story no. 59 of the 1857 edition). A passerby mistakes her for the devil and so informs the parson:

"Oh God!" exclaimed the parson, "I've got a lame foot and can't run out to expel him."

"I'll carry you on my back," said the man, and he carried him out to the field. When they got to the turnip patch, Katy straightened herself up.

"Oh, it's really the devil!" the parson cried out, and they both rushed off. Indeed, since his fright was so great, the parson was able to run faster with his lame foot than the man who had carried him with his two sound legs. (Zipes 2001, 443)

This story was told by Anna Johnson in early 1919:

THE GIFTED COMPANIONS

Once there was a man (perhaps he was a large man) who wanted to travel and he wanted to go in a different way from what other people went in and to go fast so he built an airship and set out.

After he [had] gone along awhile he thought he would look down and see what was happening on the earth. So he dropped a little and looked down and he saw a man with his ear to the ground. He wondered what this man would be doing so he alighted to find out and asked the man what he was about.

The man replied that he had planted some grain and now he was listening to it grow. The other asked him if he didn't want to get up and ride in the airship. He said yes and they set off together.

After awhile the man who owned the airship decided that he would like to see again how everything in the world was getting on so he dropped and looked. He saw a man with a bow and arrow looking up in the sky. He decided he would like to know what this meant so he stopped and asked.

This man said he had seen a butterfly flying up high above the clouds and was shooting at it. Just then the butterfly fell down with an arrow through its wing. The man with the airship asked this man to ride with him and they went off together.

After awhile the man again wanted to see what was going on

on the earth and he again came down. This time he saw a man running very, very fast and looking behind him all the time. He asked this man why he was doing this and the other told him he was chasing a rabbit. It was behind him now however because he was such a fast runner. He couldn't go slowly enough to catch it so he passed it by and could only look back at it. The man with the airship asked this man also to ride with him but logs had to be attached to his legs to keep him from running away.

After awhile they all alighted near a large city and camped. They were told there that there was a great witch who was a wonderfully swift runner and she challenged the man who was such a fleet runner to a race and the people bet three boxes on the race (in the old days Si said this was the way they counted; it means three thousands).

They took the logs off the man and the two set out to run, and went off at a great pace. After awhile the man with the airship asked the man who had such wonderful hearing that he could hear the grain grow, to listen and hear if they were still running. He listened and said that they were still running. Then the owner of the airship asked the man who had such sharp eyes that he could see a butterfly above the clouds, to look and see what they were doing.

He looked and said the man was ahead and then that he reached the goal and came back and met with the witch. When he met her she asked him to stop. She said there was no hurry, he might just as well rest awhile. "There is no rush—take your time."

Then she coaxed him to sit down and to let her comb his hair. When she had done this awhile he fell asleep and she went on to the goal. But before she had got back again to where he was, the man in the airship told the man who had such wonderful sight to shoot an arrow to wake the other man up.

So he shot an arrow that just missed the other's ear and as it just whistled by it waked him up and he got up and started again and got back to the starting place before the woman and so he won the three boxes.

Then the three passengers and the owner got into the airship and sailed off and he dropped each one of them at the place where he found them—the man who could run fast at the place where he was chasing the rabbit, and the man who could see a butterfly above the clouds at the place where he was shooting it, and the man who could hear grain grow at the place where he was listening to it. (Allen 1948b, 53–54)

Frederick Waugh recognized the European folklore theme of the gifted companions in similar stories at Six Nations Reserve (n.d., J. Echo 201 f 26, T. Smoke 202 f 23, and E. Cook 202 f 24). Indeed, the "Extraordinary Companions" is a story type (no. 513) centered in Europe (Thompson 1981, 181). The central incident of the Oneida version—the runner racing against a woman falls asleep and is awakened by the sharpshooter—was a fixture of the literary fairy tale tradition in Europe from at least Mme. d'Aulnoy ("Belle-Belle," published 1698) to the Brothers Grimm (no. 71 in the 1857 edition) (Thompson 1919, 345; Zipes 2001, 174–205).

The gifted companions, as incident or complete story, were adopted into native folklore even more enthusiastically than "The Little Red Ox" that inspired "The Magic Bull" and other tales (see pp. 141–42). Variants of the extraordinary companions are known literally from coast to coast and are, yet again, attributed to French Canadian sources (Thompson 1919, 335–47).

A probable native touch in the Oneida telling is the manner in which the woman bewitches the runner by combing his hair. Possibly the airship, or rather the idea of the flying platform, also derives chiefly from Iroquois lore. Stith Thompson defined a motif called "magic airships" on the basis of exclusively Iroquois examples, all of them flying canoes (1929, 275, motif D1118). Perhaps sending the Oneida companions abroad in an airship simply updated the traditional folkloric means of travel.

In January 1919, Doxtater told Allen about a contest between the spirit of cold and a human hunter armed with a blazing fire:

THE COLD WEATHER MAN

Lydia told me today that when your house cracked in cold weather it was because a little man with a wooden mallet under his arm came and knocked on the roof.

She said that once a man was out hunting and he met a man who told him he was going to visit him and spend the night. But when he came he said, "You must get plenty of wood or you will freeze."

The hunter began to think he was the "cold weather" man and he went home and told his wife and he said to her "I shall have to cut lots of wood and stack it all about the house or we will freeze for the cold weather man is coming to spend the night with us." So he worked very hard and cut lots of wood.

Then the night came the man had mentioned and sure enough he came but the others had a great fire blasting though it got cold as soon as he came into the house. The man kept piling on wood and the visitor when the fire blazed up shrank into the back of the room but he came to the fireplace when it was dying down.

Thus it went on all night and they kept the fire up and the house warm.

When morning came the visitor said, "You have beaten me. I haven't been able to freeze you out." Then they saw he was really the "cold weather" man. (1948b, 62)

This allegory was popular throughout Iroquoia. In a Seneca version, the hunter is challenged to a trial of strength between the blazing fire and ambient chill by Hótho or Cold, a naked man who has a hatchet in his hip (Curtin 2001, 257; Hewitt 1918, 356–57). According to Arthur Parker, it is the frost god, a fierce old man dressed in ice and wielding a maul with which he pounds the frozen lakes and rivers (1989, 14). At Six Nations Reserve, Frederick Waugh recorded four similar stories, all "concerned with Atu, who is Winter or Cold personified and usually described as a large man covered with ice. All four of these stories describe a contest between a mortal man and Atu, which illustrates how the theme of contest extends throughout Iroquois fictional thinking" (Randle 1953, 622). In New England and the Far Northeast, a trial in which the competitors endure cold as they pass the night around a fire seems a common form of the wizards' duel (Leland 1992, 76–77; Rand 1894, 70–73, 99–100).

⫛

"In Indian stories," Doxtater remarked to Allen in 1923, "the animals are always meeting in what we call a 'council,' but you would call it a 'convention' in English" (1948a, P).

THE CHIPMUNK'S STRIPES

At one of these councils of the beasts an Iroquois story says that all the animals debated whether there should be always day, or always night, or whether night and day should alternate. The Chipmunk led the party which chose the alternation, and of course they won; but the bear, who had led the party which preferred a continuous night, was so angry that he gave chase to the chipmunk, and, though he only managed to graze the back of the opponent, it is the mark of his claws which the chipmunk bears to this day. This is how the chipmunk got his stripes. (P)

Curiously, the same anecdote with the same point is found among widely separated peoples (Boas 1914, 393; Waterman 1914, 39). In a council of the animals in the Southeast (Yuchi), for example, Chipmunk proposes the diurnal alternation of light and dark and gets his pelt raked for the suggestion (Grantham 2002, 97–98). Along the Thompson River far to the northwest:

> The Black Bear and the Chipmunk once contended against each other, the former for darkness, the latter for light. . . . The Bear, finding that the Chipmunk was his equal in the possession of magic powers, finally became enraged, and would have killed his adversary; but the Chipmunk was too quick for him, and ran into his hole just as the Bear made a dash for him. The Bear scratched the Chipmunk when going into his hole. This is the origin of the present stripes on the chipmunk's back. If the Bear had managed to kill the Chipmunk, we should have had eternal darkness instead of day and night, as we have at present. (Waterman 1914, 1)

The regulation of day and night, John Bierhorst observes, is "one of the great themes in Indian mythology" (1985, 191). But why should the chipmunk, the chipmunk's stripes, and the bear be linked to such a theme in much the same fashion over vast distances? Was precisely the same scenario repeatedly invented at different locations? Is it a fable that happened to appeal to people living thousands of miles apart? Does it belong to a common stratum of belief dating back thousands of years? Interpreting similarities separated by distance, as Bierhorst also remarks, can be maddening (148).

⧽▲⧼

In the spring of 1918, Lydia Doxtater had birds and hungry children on her mind:

WHIPPOORWILL, MEADOWLARK, AND CUCKOO

Once there was a famine and a woman was cooking some hasty pudding and stirring it with a wooden stick (like a long wooden spoon). Her little granddaughter kept begging for some pudding and begging and begging and the [grand]mother kept threatening her "If you don't stop, I will hit you with the stick." Finally, all of a sudden the little girl turned into a bird and flew away repeating what her grandmother had said. Told also by Anna.

Some years later, Doxtater told Allen that "the song of the whippoorwill is in Indian 'Pudding stick hit you.' It doesn't make any difference whether the pudding stick comes first or last."

In a time of famine there was no food and a little girl was very hungry. Finally, her grandmother took a cobblestone and put it in a kettle to boil. The little girl kept asking "Is it done yet" and her grandmother would say "not yet." Finally she got desperate and then she flew away as a bird singing "It's done now" (a cry of the meadowlark).

Here is the origin of the cuckoo. Once there was a woman hoeing corn by a hedge and bushes and her little granddaughter was very lazy and would not help her, and she punished her severely and finally the little girl turned into a bird and flew away singing "enough"—cuckoo in Indian. Now cuckoos are very lazy birds and they make their nests very roughly of sticks without any lining. (Allen 1948b, 10)

Frederick Waugh encountered the idea that the cuckoo derives from a lazy child at the Grand River (n.d., J. Echo 201 f6). His tale, however, does not make explicit a major point of Doxtater's stories: the sound a bird makes (or, in the third instance, what the name of the bird sounds like) is explained by the child's transformation into a bird.

A contemporaneous Seneca piece gets at precisely that point. "An old woman had a hut in the woods, and a small grandchild," R. J. Weitlaner recounts.

> The grandchild was very hungry, and wanted something to eat; but she did not give him anything, and said to him, he should take his bow and go into the woods. He went out three times, and came back for the third time, and left again at once and could hardly walk. He came back and was a bird. He flew around the house, and said, "Axsoogi'otsai" ("Do you mean that breakfast is not ready?") and flew back into the woods. This bird sings at strawberry-time. His name is Da'tso. (1915, 310)

Oneida speakers I asked about these bird noises do not recognize the equivalences of sound and animal given by Doxtater. Clifford Abbott suspects the connection is not so much linguistic as rhythmic. In a Wisconsin Oneida version of the whippoorwill text, for example, *kwa'koli* (whippoorwill), *atkólyat* (the stick or stirring paddle), and *wa'uky'te* (the bird's cry: "she hit me") are not obviously similar phonetically. But when Abbott heard the story performed, the narrator "half-sang the words in a distinctive rhythm with an accent on the first and third syllables of each of the three words. I think that was the primary connection with the bird's call" (Abbott, personal communication).[2] The tale of a hungry child who be-

2. Clifford Abbott recorded the story of a hungry girl who changed into a bird as told in Oneida by elderly Melissa Cornelius in 1974. I am grateful to him for sharing that story and his linguistic opinions in this matter (letter of June 11, 2001).

In reference to Doxtater's second and third bird fables, Abbott observes: "I've not heard a word for cuckoo but one way to say 'enough' is *tho ni:ku* which has a distinctive

come a robin is widely known in the Great Lakes region (Barnouw 1977, 159; Michelson 1919, 307–9) where it dates to at least 1839 (Schoolcraft 1999, 103–6).

Ghosts, Devils, and Witches

"Indians liked spooky things," Allen concluded after documenting a fair number of examples (1948b, 74). Thus, Electa Johns (Anna Johnson's sister, 1889–1937) said the deteriorating house her parents once inhabited in the Windfall was haunted. "A stone rolls through it and then a ball of fire follows. Other places on West Road [no longer Oneida homes at the time of telling] have such tales connected with them" (18).

The same Mrs. Johns also said some Indians were picking beans by moonlight over on Marble Hill when a tall man suddenly appeared among them. When the bean pickers moved away, the newcomer followed:

GHOST STORY

They went down to the road till they came to Mr. Woods' farm house which was then empty. Luisa's [Luisa Day Johns's] grandfather led the way in here and as he went in he looked back and as the stranger was crossing the threshold he saw that he was a skeleton and he was saying: "Beans, beans."

When they got in the house Luisa's grandfather started down [to the] cellar and they shut the trap door on him and once down there he heard voices from a cupboard. They kept crying: "Beans, beans; bread, bread."

He went back up and said to the rest: "We must have a feast here to feed the dead" and they went down and found seven skeletons in the cupboard of men that had been murdered there. The next day they all came back with everything for a feast and again the second day. And thus they laid the ghosts. (22)

---

rhythm with the second syllable lengthened. There is a word for meadowlark—*otshulála*—and one way to say 'it's done' is *yo:lí* or 'it's done now' *o'n^yo:lí*. I don't know the actual calls of these birds, but I don't imagine it would be hard to adapt short Oneida words or phrases to imitate at least the rhythms of the calls."

William Rockwell wrote this note about an otherworldly presence.

THE MYSTERY MAN

He was a tall slender man. One of his feet was that of an unsplit hoof of an animal. He carried a satchel of a very old style. He wore a so-called stove pipe hat, making him look very tall. Two large animal ears. So, any person who without any reasonable excuse, makes it a habit of traveling around night after night, would sooner or later meet this mysterious man who walks without any noise. (n.d., bI c2 f3)

A man on Marble Hill did meet this fellow. The Oneida in question

> had a great deal of trouble finding his cows at night. Every night he had to search and search for them. Finally, one night he came up the hill and again they were lost and just as he started to go after them he met a stranger, a tall man with long hair. This man commenced to misuse him the moment they met and they got into a terrible fight at once. Finally the man managed to get his fingers into the stranger's hair and twist it around them well. But just then he fell asleep. When he woke up it was broad daylight and he had in his hand some of the coarse marsh grass the Indians call the "devil's hair." (Allen 1948b, 27)

Oneidas in New York as well as in Canada sometimes spoke of witches as people who caused sickness by magically inserting an object such as a hair in another's body (Allen 1948b, 5; Waugh n.d., Mrs. D. Williams and Mrs. M. Thomas 200 f 17). And, just as Oneidas of an earlier age believed they could assume the form of a personal guardian spirit or familiar, so the witches of Allen's time were capable of appearing in various guises, including animal forms.

KILLING A WITCH

Once there was someone sick over at Nick Hon Yost's house on the West Road. As they were watching with the sick person at night they used to hear something rubbing against the side of the house; once something peered in at the window and they saw it was a large black dog. This dog had been skulking around the house. Therefore, it was decided that this dog was a witch who was causing the sickness.

So the men got ten cent pieces or something like that—"we'll say ten cent pieces"—to make silver bullets for you can't kill a witch with lead, it's got to be silver. When night came they arranged themselves on each side of the West Road . . . with guns and silver bullets, all saying nothing in order to give no warning.

The dog came in sight but just then one man said, "There she goes." That gave the warning, and as they all started to fire, the dog leaped the fence and started towards the east into the fields in the darkness and they could not keep track of it though they felt sure it had been hit.

Now at this time there was an old woman living in the house on the Olmstead place . . . and at just this time she was taken sick. Her family however kept up the greatest secrecy about her condition and they didn't call the doctor or let anyone in to see her or say what was the matter. After a time she died, never having had a doctor. Some people forced their way in to help clean up and they found her bed soaked in blood. They were sure she was the witch. (Allen 1948b, 45)[3]

Quoting other examples of ghosts and witchcraft documented by Allen, Jack Campisi emphasized how the stories referenced "specific occurrences and people" (1974, 423). I find it striking how consistently they relate to space and local geography (Nabokov 2002, 130–31). Almost always, they are woven into the landscape, as in the instance given above that opens in the Windfall then proceeds toward Marble Hill.

⋈

On August 4, 1906, the *Oneida Post* announced: "The Indians will hold a picnic at Faulkners grove near Kenwood, August 18. An extensive program is being arranged and this is to be one of the old fashioned picnics where everybody can have a good time. At 10 a.m. the old timers of Ver-

---

3. Similar stories about shooting witches with silver bullets and witches transforming themselves into animals were documented among the Wisconsin Oneidas in about 1866 (Bloomfield 1907, 263, 271).

non will play a game of base ball with the Indians." We can still see the
Oneidas at that picnic as they gathered together in front of a camera so
long ago (ill. 21). Of the picnic itself, the newspaper reported: "Those
who attended the Indian picnic last Saturday were more than repaid. The
heat was very intense but for genuine enjoyment this picnic has them all
stopped. . . . In the morning Vernon played the Indians, winning 9 to 6.
It was an interesting game. The Indians can certainly give points on getting up a picnic" *(Oneida Post,* August 25, 1906).

The Oneidas were passionate though disadvantaged baseball players,
as William Rockwell recalled in the following reminiscence, possibly written in the 1940s:

"NINE AND ONLY NINE, THAT'S ALL"

About 45 years ago we Oneidas were so diminished in numbers
that we were just able to make up a nine for a baseball club from
two Oneida Indian settlements. The odds were so great against
us in playing ball with the white men, that the older Indians were
anxious to do something to help us. So one of the old-timers
told us what to do.

We were told to reach down into an old grave and pull up a
toe bone and a handful of the black dirt. And to bury the toe
bone in the pitcher's box. And each man to have a little of the
black dirt to rub in the palms of the hands. And we were all to
drink a small amount of liquor from one bottle. There was no
one in our crowd liked the idea; not because of the drink. It was
because of the specified small amount of only one bottle.

The toe bone buried in the pitcher's box, the heating
determination of the firewater in the heaving bosom of our hero,
and the black mystic powder on the hand that would deliver the
ball for the white man to hit, it would look to the white man as if
there were two balls coming instead of one.

Well, we played this one wonderful game with a team of
white men in Cazenovia. We were beaten 22–0.

I told this story to Jim Thorpe. And I asked him what he
thought was the cause of our getting beat with all of the hocus-
pocus backing us. He said the white man was able to hit both
balls. (n.d., bI c2 f 3)

21. *The Oneida picnic on August 18, 1906; courtesy of Oneida Community Mansion House, Oneida, N.Y. Depicted here are two informants mentioned in this chapter: Mrs. Sarah Powlis Johns (no. 10) and Mrs. Electa Doxtater Johns (no. 11). William Honyoust (no. 1) was already embroiled in legal difficulties having to do with the Honyoust place on the Windfall (see chapter 8).*

ONEIDA BASKET MAKING

The Oneidas regarded storytelling and basket making as closely related. The elderly Mrs. Sarah Powlis Johns, for example, recalled binding her mother-in-law's baskets in exchange for "a great many stories" (Allen 1948b, 1). Here, oral and material traditions were learned and practiced in the same setting.

Oneidas were making baskets from splints of black ash by the closing years of the 1700s. Although many forms of basketry and weaving certainly were autochthonous, the process of wood-splint construction may have originated in Europe. Whatever its derivation, Oneidas focused on this form of basketry out of economic necessity. With their land base diminished and the old ways of living dramatically disrupted, the Oneidas had to develop new ways to subsist, and basket making was, initially, one such industry of survival. When a new style coalesced locally out of diverse sources, however, basket making quickly became a distinctive Oneida art.

Oneidas probably learned wood-splint basketry from Algonquian-speaking guests after the Revolutionary War when two amalgamated groups of Christian Indians took refuge in Oneida country: the Brothertons from several communities in southern New England and the Stockbridges from western Massachusetts. Both groups had been selling baskets to whites for a long time (Brasser 1975, 20–26, 42).

Out of the mix of eastern basketry traditions came an original and strikingly colorful form of basketry characteristic of Oneida country after about 1830 (see ills. 22–23). The New Oneida style featured stamped or painted motifs comprising circular flowers, concentric rings, or asymmetric oval shapes—designs often outlined by dots and arranged in horizontal rows. Typically, these wide and boldly decorated rows alternated with narrower rows (wefts) of differing colors. The scheme favored bright colors, especially yellow, orange, green, and sometimes blue, and was often applied to the popular "fruit basket" shape (ill. 22) (McMullen and Handsman 1987, 116–19).

After the Civil War, numerous well-to-do tourists left the cities to spend their summers at resorts throughout the Northeast. Oneida families

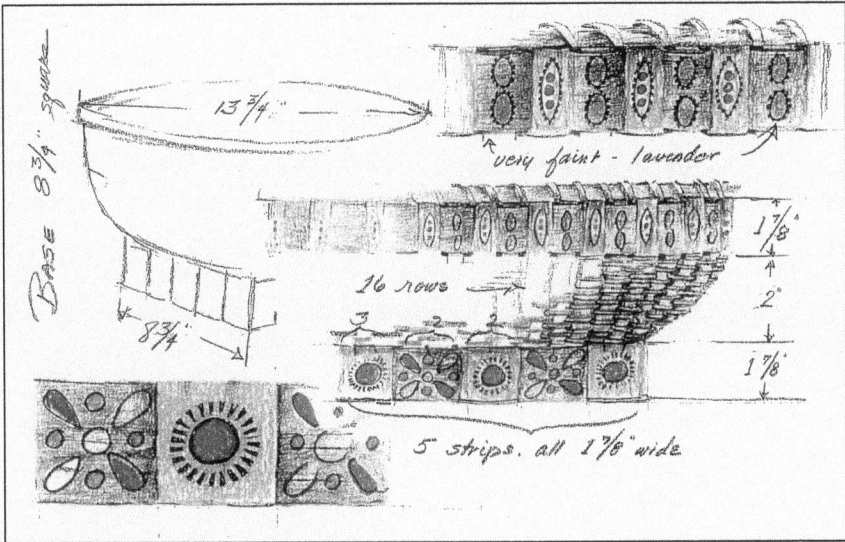

22. Oneida "fruit basket."

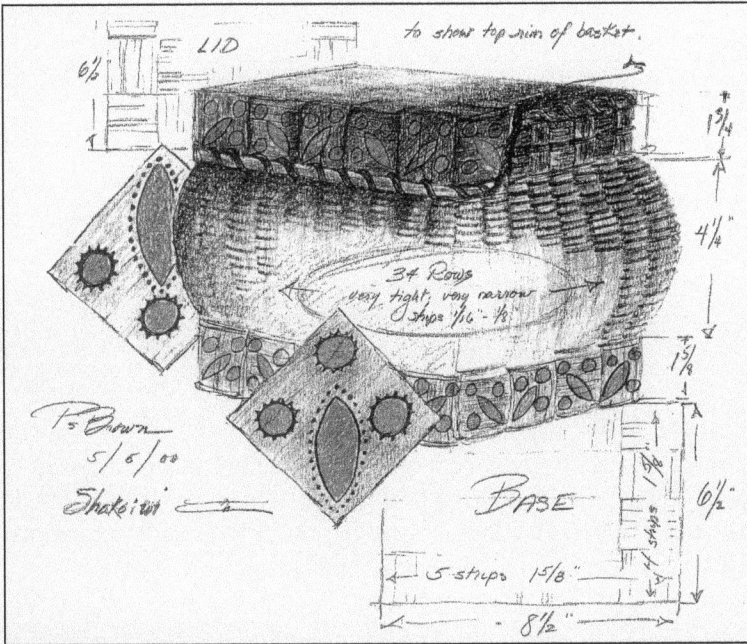

23. Oneida basket and lid.

followed them, drawn to the new seasonal circuit to offer craft work to an audience very different from the earlier rural clientele. Appraising the tastes of Victorian-era tourists, Oneidas and other Native Americans began to make "fancy baskets" after 1870. This style featured new shapes (smaller and more intricately worked), new materials (such as fragrant sweet grass), and new decorative techniques (including curlicue shavings protruding from the container's walls).

The grandmother in Lydia Doxtater's creation narrative (see p. 75) was a basket maker, and so was Doxtater herself. Much of her youth was spent making baskets for sale to nonnative customers at such summer resort towns as Saratoga Springs and Sylvan Beach on nearby Oneida Lake. In 1888, a legislative committee studying New York's "Indian problem" asked Lydia's father, William Doxtater (though the committee spelled it "Dockstater"), how he made a living:

> QUESTION: What do you raise on your land?
> DOCKSTATER: Potatoes and corn and garden stuff.
> QUESTION: Have you got a family?
> DOCKSTATER: Yes, sir . . . Six.
> QUESTION: You can not raise enough on your acre and a half to support them?
> DOCKSTATER: Well, it helps a good deal.
> QUESTION: What do you do besides get a living for them?
> DOCKSTATER: Well, we work Indian beads, canes and baskets.
> QUESTION: Where do you sell that stuff?
> DOCKSTATER: Saratoga Springs.
> QUESTION: How far are you from Saratoga?
> DOCKSTATER: One hundred and twenty-one miles.
> QUESTION: You can go down there and sell the goods you make?
> DOCKSTATER: All of us go down. (Whipple et al. 1889, 2:508)

Anna Johnson's mother had welcomed Hope Allen into the world with the gift of a basket (Allen 1948a, G), and Allen's earliest memories of Lydia Doxtater centered on basket making and tourist crafts.

> [Lydia] with her mother, sister Electa, and cousins Stella and Josephine, perhaps not all at once, used to make baskets, bows and arrows, etc.

which her parents with one or two girls would take to Sylvan Beach for sale in the season. In my childhood, summers they could be seen coming down the hill on their way to the 9:00 o'clock train going north laden with their wares. (1948b, 11)

8

⋈

A People Resurgent

This chapter reenters historic time to take up the history of the Oneida Nation during the twentieth century and to search for reflections of social reality in oral narrative. Toward the end of the century, the Oneidas became an American success story of epic proportions. However, the foundation for their meteoric rise had been laid in two sets of legal proceedings: the *Boylan* cases during the first quarter of the century and the land claim cases of the last quarter. Due to the nature of these underpinnings, recent history takes on a strongly legalistic flavor.

At the dawn of the twentieth century, some Oneida families managed to retain a little land in the eastern community. The larger western community, however, suffered more severely from land loss, and, in 1909, its last residents on communally owned land were thrown into the road as the result of a mortgage foreclosure. Outlined here are the complex legal proceedings known as *Boylan v. George et al.* (1905–1909) that culminated in the eviction mentioned in chapter 2. This story is worth recounting for its historical lessons because it demonstrates that Oneidas were regarded as an acculturated underclass lacking distinctive traditions and a sense of community. Although that interpretation helps to explain why the Oneidas were so victimized, it also illustrates how dispossession continued to be the central experience of Oneida life.

The tale of the Honyoust place did not, however, end with the forcible ejection. Loss of the thirty-two acres was contested at every level of the federal judicial system (in *United States v. Boylan et al.* [1916–1919] and *Boylan et al. v. United States* [1920–1922]) until—amazingly—the property was returned to the Oneidas, along with federal recognition of the Oneida Nation. The *Boylan* cases kept alive an Oneida dream for justice and land return for nearly half a century.

Yet the meaning of the victory remained elusive because the case had not been won for Oneida reasons or expressed in Oneida terms. It was in this context that an older tradition of the Revolutionary War became salient. The legend of Polly Cooper spoke of an Oneida woman whose gift of corn helped the American army to survive the terrible winter at Valley Forge. Retelling and projecting this story into the public domain, Oneidas made sense of *Boylan* with reference to ancient tradition. In effect, *Boylan* reinvigorated Oneida oral narrative and regained something of what seemed lost with the Oneida Stone: the idiom of their own national expression.

And, as exegesis for U.S. support of the Oneida Nation, Polly Cooper has continued to make sense throughout a new round of litigation begun in 1970. The current Oneida land claims maintain that New York's acquisitions within the 1788 reservation were illegal without federal approval. They also provide the cloth from which Oneidas weave themselves a new and prosperous future.

After 1850: Allotment on the Windfall

I noted (see pp. 23–24) how New York State's 1842 treaty with the western Oneida group acknowledged that the remaining lands belonged to the remaining Oneidas in common. However, a schedule appended to the treaty designated certain Oneida families (each family member named) as owners in severalty of specific lots (Treaties 1842). This mode of private ownership apparently became permissible under state law the following year in a legislative act that, without federal sanction, authorized Oneidas to hold land in severalty (Laws of New York 1843, chap. 185, article 1). Subsequently, Oneidas lost nearly all of what little land remained to them through the workings of private-ownership transactions.

A similar policy was visited on Indians beyond the state of New York by the federal government in its General Allotment or Dawes Act of 1887. The result of this act nationwide, as explained on pp. 49–50, was that Indian lands melted away to non-Indians in legal transactions. Allotment legislation did not itself mandate this loss. Indeed, the Dawes Act and its subsequent modifications contained provisions supposed to safeguard the Indians in the possession of private property. Such measures, however, tended to be inadequately administered and enforced. In general, federal allotment laws failed to defend Indians from English speakers more knowledgeable in nonnative law and property relations.

New York's legislation of 1843 similarly seemed to restrict the alienation of Oneida land. It stated that such conveyances required the consent of two non-Indian officials—the state Indian superintendent and the first judge of the county—and the majority of Indian leaders (Laws of New York 1843, chap. 185, articles 3, 5). But these provisions likewise proved ineffective as protections of Indian interests. How allotment actually worked locally to the detriment of Indian property retention is illustrated by legal proceedings concerned with the last remaining parcel of the Oneida western, or Windfall, community.

Shortly after 1843, the Oneidas were treated by the people around them as New York citizens, subject to the same standing in the court system as the nonnative (actual) citizens, Such treatment developed out of (and, in turn, justified) the erroneous assumption that the Oneidas were no longer Indians constituting a distinct community. Nevertheless, it was a common belief, especially among nonnative officials. For example, a state fact-finding commission visiting Oneida in 1888 concluded:

> The land formerly the Oneida reservation and now commonly known as such, by an act of Legislature was long since divided among the Indians there in severalty, and they now own it in fee. . . . [These Indians] have observed the habits and practices of the white farmers among them, and have so profited by their examples that the committee in going over the territory was unable to distinguish, in point of cultivation, the Indian farms from those of the whites. . . . Those [Oneidas] remaining in this State are nearly all well-to-do farmers, comparing very favorably, from a material standpoint, with their white neighbors. (Whipple et al. 1889, 1:46, 76)

These comments registered the diminishment of the Oneida land base, not the absence of Oneida Indians. As nonnatives acquired more and more Oneida land, the community of Indians in the same place became harder and harder for them to see. At the same time, nonnatives became increasingly disposed to see no Indian-ness at all. Generally, Oneidas were not invited to contribute much to deliberations resulting in such conclusions. Often they were not consulted at all. As one Oneida observed of the commission quoted above:

> In the past the Commissions sent would make a flying trip, stop on the outside of the reservation and ask some Irishman about the Indians and then report on what the Irishman said. . . . [In 1888] they came through in hacks. . . . I suppose the next Commission will come in aeroplanes. Well, they came in hacks, we saw them go by but did not know until two or three days after who they were. . . . They said when they visited Oneida that they found such improvements among the Indians that had been given the allotted land. That we [were] such big farmers they could not distinguish the difference between them and the white farmers of Oneida. I beg to differ for not much farming could be done on four and a half acres of land and not only that but the lands were disposed of by loans. That is if a white man got possession which is nine points of the law that is all he was looking for that gave him the right. There were actually only one or two places where they had more than 25 acres, one was this Honyoust place recently referred to as the case in Court having about 32 acres. (Testimony of Joseph Johnson, Everett 1922, 111–12, 407–8)

This Honyoust (also Hanyost, Honyost, and other spellings) place was the last piece of land in the southeast corner of the 1842 tract still in common ownership. The Honyousts were descendants of the Charles family, one of four families assigned in the 1842 treaty to this section (lots 17 and 19). At about the time the New York commission visited Oneida, the Honyousts consisted of Margaret Charles Honyoust, an individual named in the schedule attached to the 1842 treaty; her children, including Mary Honyoust Skenandoah (eldest surviving child, later called Mary George), Margaret, Isaac, and William; and various grandchildren, including Chapman and Albert Shenandoah, sons of Mary and William Honyoust Rockwell, son of Margaret. Structured around a matriarchal core, this family was an extended matrilineage, the traditional Oneida unit of residence for centuries (see p. 8). It seems likely the women were reasserting traditional roles as overseers or supervisors of the land on behalf of all, regardless of who was said to own the land in nonnative terms. Late in the nineteenth century, female control over Oneida land reemerged as a means of maintaining Oneida ownership.

One provision of the 1843 legislative act authorizing Oneidas to hold land in severalty stated, "A deed of an Indian shall be valid to convey the title of himself, his wife and minor children" (Laws of New York 1843, chap. 185, article 3). Privileging the man over the rest of the household in a way foreign to Oneida tradition, this clause permitted men to circumvent rights of ownership exercised by women on behalf of all. This provision may have undermined the Oneidas' capacity to retain land nearly as much as the foreign-imposed mode of private ownership because it struck at the heart of the customary social fabric. By the mid-1880s, at any rate, most land the Oneidas were able to keep was in the hands of women (Whipple et al. 1889, 2:506–8).

The Honyoust family, however, was one matriarchy that apparently failed to hold land against the flood of nonnative acquisitiveness. The twentieth century opened to a set of legal proceedings focused on ownership of these thirty-two acres. In one way or another, this case would be argued in the nonnative court systems for seventeen years, and, in some sense, it continues to play out a century later.

Julia Boylan Acquires and Quiets a Title

In March 1905, nonnative lawyer Joseph Beal instituted a statutory foreclosure on a mortgage belonging to the Honyoust acreage by posting a public announcement in downtown Oneida. Though legal if measured solely by state law, the action was, at the least, an inconvenient one for Oneida residents of the property who were virtually uneducated and illiterate, ill at ease in English, and living four walking miles away. The mortgage and associated proceedings had come about in this fashion.

Among documents registering landownership in Madison County in 1885 was a deed to the thirty-two acres in the name of Isaac Honyoust, a tract Isaac was said to have bought from his mother, Margaret, and sister Mary for $3,000 (Madison County Deeds, Liber 160, p. 429). This transaction was witnessed by nonnative neighbor George Lawrence and notarized by one J. D. Kilbourne. Soon after, another nonnative neighbor named Philander Spaulding gave Isaac Honyoust a mortgage on the property for $1,250. This conveyance was also witnessed by Lawrence and notarized by Kilbourne (Madison County Mortgages, Liber 97, p. 488).[1] In 1888, Spaulding signed his mortgage on the Honyoust place over to farmer Patrick Boylan who, at his death in 1897, willed it to his widow, Julia.

Lawyer Beal was the executor of Patrick Boylan's estate. Foreclosing the mortgage was an action to recover a debt on the part of the Indians said to have reached $1,650—that is, the principal amount plus $400 in interest. As a result of the foreclosure proceeding in 1905, the property was auctioned off for $1,250 to the highest bidder. Probably acting on Julia Boylan's behalf, that individual then transferred his title back to Boylan. Thus, by the late summer of 1905, Mrs. Boylan seemed to be the legal owner of the Honyoust place.

The Indians had never seen such fabulous sums of money as were mentioned in these documents, and they declared that all the deeds and mortgages were the work of acquisitive white neighbors (Decker n.d., Document 48, p. 7, Oneida Memorial to the State Legislature, May 15, 1910). More specifically, William Rockwell attributed the Honyoust deed to the efforts of

> George Lawrence, the man that my uncle [Isaac Honyoust] worked for. He wanted to get a hold on this place. He lived down the road here about 1/3 of a mile. Then there was another man in Oneida, by the

1. William Rockwell attributed Isaac Honyoust's lease to Maggie Honyoust, meaning perhaps his mother or, more likely, his grandmother Margaret Charles Honyoust. This lady, he explained, "mortgaged the whole place to Philander Spaulding for a sum of $600.00 and a shave of $10.00 on each $100.00, making a total of $660.00. Said Maggie Honyoust had not at that time nor any other time ever owned any particular part of this reservation or any stated amount of the property of which she mortgaged as if it were all her own. Two old horses and some farming implements that were no longer serviceable, and some old clothes and shoes; no one seems to know just what was received by the Indian woman to make the mortgage run up to $1,250.00" (Decker n.d., Document 41, Rockwell to Governor Hughes, October 14, 1907).

"There was a threat there to put us out of here on a foreclosure of a mortgage," he later wrote, "if they did not pay up the interest more on time. The Indians only got $637 in cash or credit to the funeral directors. People died off here, and that's what the money was used for. They charged the Indian up $1250—they were charging him 6% interest on that amount that never existed and never was received by the Indians" (Rockwell n.d., bI cl f3, p. 5, untitled typescript).

name of Kilbourn [*sic*], another "skinner" for the poor people, and two
or three others. It was all through a conspiracy, so that they would get a
title of this land in existence. And the Indians did not know enough to
defend themselves. (n.d., bI c1 f3, p. 5, untitled typescript)

Rockwell's charge was echoed in the 1916 testimony of Mary Honyoust Skenandoah, one of the supposed sellers of the Honyoust place back
in 1885:

THE COURT: This purports to be a warranty deed executed by Margaret
Honyost and Mary Honyost and purports to be witnessed and acknowl-
edged by the grantors before A.D. Killim [*sic*], Notary Public. . . .
QUESTION: Are you the Mary Honyost that signed that paper?
ANSWER: She claims [speaking through an interpreter] that
[George] Lawrence and Isaac [Honyoust] came to her mother with the
deed before she died and lifted her hand to make this cross and she claims
she did not sign.
QUESTION: The witness herself claims she did not sign?
ANSWER: No, she wouldn't sign. (*United States v. Boylan et al.*
1916, p. 9, Stenographer's Minutes)

No one inquired further into these circumstances, and they did not figure
importantly in the subsequent history of the case.[2]
Although widow Boylan's title to the Honyoust place seemed to vest
her with exclusive ownership, there were, in fact, other recorded deeds
overlapping her claim. Her title problems derived from the same source as
her title: Philander Spaulding's seemingly tireless efforts to acquire liens on

---

2. Those individuals the Oneidas believed were defrauding them were prosperous and
probably prominent local businesspeople. George Lawrence owned a substantial hop farm
across the road from the Windfall (see map 4). He was, according to an admiring biographical notice of 1880, "one of the stable, enterprising men who do much in any community to
give it character and progress" (J. Smith 1880, 737). Philander Spaulding, "one of the
largest land-owners of the county," was a farmer who also served as the local constable,
deputy sheriff, and assistant revenue collector (Biographical Review 1894, 113). In addition, he was a founder and owner of the "Central Bank of Oneida," a business in which one
of his partners was James K. Kilborn, presumably the "J. D. Kilbourne" who notarized the
Isaac Honyoust deed. The location of Spaulding's main residence is shown just north of the
Windfall on map 4.

Oneida land ("Non-suit in the Case of Phoebe Cornelius Against John Morris and Philander Spaulding," *Oneida Democratic Union,* July 14, 1886). In 1882, for example, Spaulding had obtained deed to about fifteen acres of the Honyoust property in separate transactions with James and Henry George, sons of the deceased Lucy Honyoust George (daughter of Margaret Charles Honyoust and sister of Mary Honyoust Skenandoah). In both cases, the documents vaguely define the fifteen acres as being in the middle of a thirty-two-acre tract attributed to uncounted and unnamed Indian owners (Madison County Deeds, Liber 152, pp. 446, 472).

Consequently, Julia Boylan's problem was complex. There apparently existed various deeds describing an area infringing on hers. Because she could scarcely question their validity without casting doubt on her own, she would have to acknowledge the rival deeds while minimizing whatever area they entitled. Not wishing to share property with other titleholders, she would want to avoid having the tract subdivided as she pursued complete ownership. Further, if Spaulding could get the George brothers to do it, other Indians might claim ownership to the thirty-two acres anytime. Resolution from Boylan's point of view would have to include limiting the extent to which Oneidas could advance similar claims in the future.

Boylan went to work to quiet her title. In July 1906, she commenced an action in state court (called the state supreme court in New York) to have the property partitioned or, if that were impractical, to have it sold. Because the proceeding required that those individuals with interests at stake be named as defendants, several Oneidas of the Honyoust place—including Mary (Honyoust Skenandoah) George, William Honyoust, Isaac Honyoust, and apparently William Honyoust Rockwell—were so named. They were represented by Syracuse attorney W. J. McClusky who agreed to submit the issues to arbitration. The referee, Charles Coville, was to evaluate the ownership claims and determine whether the property could be partitioned *(Boylan v. Mary George et al.,* 1906, Decree of Judge Lyon, October 15).

Coville discovered yet another deed to the Honyoust place. In 1898, Isaac Honyoust had signed over the premises to his nephew, Chapman Shenandoah, who, in assuming the $1,250 mortgage, hoped to save the property for the Oneidas (Rockwell n.d., bI c1 f3, p. 6, untitled typescript). In January 1907, Coville brought Shenandoah into the proceedings as another defendant and, in July, he issued his findings:

1. The Oneidas had given up all Indian ways. They maintained no tribal relations and supported no tribal government.

2. Some forty years before (then the customary term for a title search), four women (Katie Charles; her daughter, Margaret Honyoust; and Margaret's daughters, Mary Honyoust and Lucy [Honyoust] George) were the exclusive owners of the property. The implication was that, after the death of Katie Charles and at the time of the deeds in question, all title in fee would devolve proportionately from Margaret (about 50 percent), Mary (25 percent), and Lucy (25 percent) to their descendants. Coville determined total ownership to be divided among forty shares, about three-quarters of which were owned by Julia Boylan (actually $^{31}/_{40}$) and the remainder assigned to several Oneidas.

3. The tract, worth about $1,200, could not be partitioned without prejudice to the property's value. These findings derived from the bald testimony of a local farmer who said the property might be worth about that. When asked if he thought the parcel could be subdivided, he said no.

Accepting the referee's report, the court directed the property to be sold (again) at public auction, the money received to be distributed among the owners in proportion to their shares. Coville, now serving as auctioneer, promptly sold the Honyoust place to the highest bidder— Julia Boylan for $725 *(Boylan v. George et al.,* 1907, Application for Final Judgment by William Coville, September 21).

Thus, the plaintiff, Boylan, prevailed in every respect. Her own chain of title validated, competing claims of the same sort were acknowledged but limited to less than one-quarter interest in the property. The door to future claims was slammed shut by declaring all property right to derive from a woman and her two daughters. Boylan and Oneida shares alike were liquidated through sale resulting in new ownership and, as they thought, clear title. And, just as in the earlier auction, the new owner happened to be Julia Boylan.

The Oneidas Win a Round

Having apparently lost the property, William Honyoust Rockwell tried a last-minute appeal to the governor. His letter to that official stated that, having been dispossessed by the local courts, the Oneidas expected to be "thrown off the place bodily" within days. "We, therefore, beg of you to investigate our mislead [*sic*] conditions and rectify it to the extent of our Indian rights" (Decker n.d., Document 41, Rockwell to Governor Hughes, October 14, 1907).

Chief Rockwell and two other Oneidas took the train to Albany and somehow managed to obtain an interview with the Honorable Charles E. Hughes, governor of the state of New York. The highest state official was deeply moved as he accepted the Oneidas' letter. "You ought to see that old man Hughes cry," Rockwell remembered. "[H]e says to me, 'Chief, I'm going to take this matter up. . . . I'll have my legal adviser make a study of this, and in two weeks I shall let you know whether I can take the case or not' " (n.d., bI cl f3, p. 8, untitled manuscript). The governor was as good as his word and soon received a substantial legal analysis from the attorney general's office. Incredibly, the report concluded the case against the Oneidas was unjust.

Attorney General William Schuyler Jackson's statement sharply refuted the assumption that Oneidas were no longer Indians but state citizens and private landowners. According to Jackson, the problematic treaty phrase "in severalty" had fostered a popular misconception that the Oneida tribe was extinct and their reservation long since defunct (ibid., Jackson to Governor Hughes, October 28, 1907).

The attorney general's analysis touched on two points that would become central to the subsequent federal case. First, by continuing to fulfill terms of the 1794 Canandaigua treaty with the Oneidas and other Iroquois, the United States still recognized the Oneida nation as in existence. However, the implication of federal recognition and the supremacy of federal over state law were topics not explored. Second, even if it was possible to obtain ownership of Indian land, Julia Boylan's chain of title had not been approved by all the parties required in the 1843 (and other) legislation. The procedure by which she pretended to such ownership, therefore, violated state law.

But it was not possible for Boylan to have obtained ownership. The thrust of Jackson's opinion was that allotment to individuals subject to New York property laws had never occurred. The Oneidas on the property were an Indian collectivity who, owning and using the land in accordance with native custom, had never divided it up among themselves. Because it had never passed out of Indian ownership, the parcel was not subject to state ownership laws, practices, and taxes, and Boylan's claim to it was invalid. "In my opinion," the attorney general concluded, "if the band is dispossessed under a sale in the pending suit, that act would constitute a violation of Indian rights" (ibid., bI cl fl, p. 16, Jackson to Governor Hughes, October 28, 1907). Having delayed confirmation of the Boylan settlement to learn the attorney general's findings, Justice Lyon of the state supreme court ruled that Boylan had neither valid title nor right to partition the property.

Rockwell learned of these developments from George Decker, the deputy attorney general, in a letter revealing that much of the work behind the finding had been Decker's. "I took great interest in looking into this matter and I think I went to the bottom of it and it was with no little satisfaction to me personally that I found facts which require the conclusions which were reached" (ibid., bI cl fl, Decker to Rockwell, October 29, 1907). Soon after, the Oneidas expressed their gratitude to Governor Hughes, whose timely aid, they said, taught them a lesson about fair treatment that reached deeply into their lives (Boylan Letters 1907–1910, Oneidas to Governor Hughes, January 24, 1908).

The Honyoust Place Lost

But the auction had taken place, and, as purchaser of the property, Boylan appealed the denial of final judgment to the state appellate court. That body reversed Lyon's decision, insisting that if Coville's sale was fairly conducted, state law required its confirmation. Not granting final judgment was tantamount to reversing the interlocutory judgment—an action beyond the power of the court (Opinion 1909). Based solely on procedure and not on substance, this ruling effectively annulled Judge Lyon's finding that the sale of the Honyoust place was illegal.

The case was remitted to the state supreme court, which confirmed Coville's actions, ordered a deed to be made out to Boylan, and directed the money taken at auction to be distributed. After various costs were deducted, Boylan received $307.07 as former owner of $^{31}/_{40}$ shares. In effect, therefore, the amount of Boylan's purchase ($725) was discounted more than 40 percent from what was already a bargain price for a property supposedly worth $1,200. The Oneida defendants were awarded $89.15 for their ⁹⁄₄₀s share. However, because they were charged $95.20 to reimburse the cost of Boylan's appeal, they ended up $6.05 in debt to the party who had taken their land *(Boylan v. George et al.,* 1909, Final judgment, August 3).

The Oneidas' lawyer apparently resigned from the case in a letter informing his clients they would have to appeal within thirty days or become liable to eviction. When Rockwell sent that note on to the governor, he received only perfunctory acknowledgement that this fact was so and the month had expired (Boylan Letters 1907–1910, Governor's Office to Rockwell, September 24, 1909). Clearly, the air in Albany had turned distinctly chilly toward the Oneidas.

In October, Oneida chiefs Day, Elm, and Rockwell wrote a note to the governor summarizing their case but bleakly recognizing dispossession as imminent (Decker n.d., Document 46, Oneidas to Governor Hughes, October 15, 1909). This letter was forwarded to the new state attorney general, Edward O'Malley.

Like Jackson before him, O'Malley responded quickly, although the quality of his work was distinctly inferior to his predecessor's. The key question, as O'Malley saw it, was whether the land belonged communally to the Oneida Nation as a tribe. O'Malley's answer was no because "the purpose of this treaty [presumably 1842] was to give the individual Indians the same kind of ownership of land as is enjoyed by citizens." Wasting no time analyzing legal precedents, he merely alluded to the findings of the 1888 state commission (quoted at the beginning of this chapter) as proving him correct ("The Oneida Indian Case . . . Attorney General's Opinion in Full," *Oneida Dispatch,* December 3, 1909).

Ordered by the court to put Julia Boylan into possession of her property, the Madison County sheriff ejected the Windfall Oneidas from their home on November 30 (as described on p. 50) (ill. 24). The sheriff's posse "forcibly dragged" the residents from their home "and expelled them from the land and carried the furniture from the houses and the chattels and other movable property from the land, locking the doors and forbidding said occupants to re-enter the land, and left them helpless on the roadside with their belongings" (Decker n.d., Document 48, Memorial of a Band of Oneida Indians, State Assembly Document 70, May 18, 1910).

WILLIAM HONYOST AND SISTER DISPOSSESSED

Oneida Indian Carried Out of His Home by Force and His Effects Placed in the Street by Madison County Deputy Sheriff and a Posse.

POST-STANDARD BRANCH OFFICE,
ROOM NO. 8,
NO 71 MADISON ST.
TELEPHONE NO. 816-1.

ONEIDA, Nov. 30.—A posse headed by Under-Sheriff Michael Mooney of Morrisville and consisting of Deputy Sheriffs Comstock of Oneida, Gibbs of Canastota, Crouse of Morristown, Officer Ross Beckwith of this city and several other officers met in Oneida this morning and proceeded to the farm occupied by an Indian named William Honyost, situated in the First ward of the city of Oneida, and proceeded to dispossess the occupants.

The case is the outcome of a mortgage foreclosure proceedings commenced in 1906 by Julia Boylan. William G. Santry of this city was attorney for the plaintiff and W. J. & S. E. McClusky of Syracuse for the defendants. The case was last tried in the Appellate Division of the Supreme Court and an order to dispossess was granted. The order was resisted on the ground that it was Indian reservation territory.

The case has a long and interesting his-tory and closed to-day with an exciting experience. The officers reached the premises, which consist of thirty-two acres and two houses, just before noon. The occupants refused to move out and the posse commenced at once to put the things into the road.

All went well until the Indian and his sister, Mrs. Schanandoah, were asked to vacate. They refused to obey. Deputy Sheriff Gibbs picked the woman up in his arms and carried her out of the house The brother was also taken out by force. After the house had been emptied the front door was securely fastened with a padlock.

The Indian declared that the government would have to pay him for his property. Among the articles removed was twenty-five bushels of potatoes. The furniture was the accumulation of many years. Honyost is an old man and he was born on the premises. There were many articles of value among the effects. A neighbor living across the road opened his house to the dispossessed Indians.

24. *Newspaper account of the Oneida eviction, 1909;* The Syracuse Post-Standard, *December 1, 1909.*

United States v. Boylan

The quotation above is from the Oneidas' petition to the state government requesting the legislature's protection and an indemnity "for the property lost as well as the indignity suffered." Its author was George Decker who, back in private practice, had now taken up the Oneidas' case at Rockwell's request (Rockwell n.d., bI cl fl, Decker to Rockwell, December 13, 1909). When the legislature dismissed the memorial, Decker began to redefine the Oneida situation with respect to the federal government. "The position of this band is that they are politically independent of the state," Decker wrote in his last letter to the governor, "and that no action by any state department is legally conclusive upon their rights" (Boylan Letters 1907–1910, June 14, 1910).

Finally, in 1912, he was able to draw on a significant court ruling bolstering his argument for federal intervention on behalf of the Oneidas. When Decker asked the U.S. attorney general to consider the Oneidas' plight, he cited *Heckman et al. v. United States,* a Supreme Court decision in which allotments to individual Cherokees without U.S. consent were found to be void:

> The court in that case distinctly holds that tribal Indians are under the protection of the United States government and are entitled to the active intervention of the federal government. . . . In the case of these Oneidas we consider that inasmuch as they have been evicted from tribal lands under process of state courts, it is the state which must answer. (Decker n.d., Decker to U.S. attorney general, July 3, 1912)

Less than a year later, Chief Rockwell received sensational news testifying to the effectiveness of Decker's lobbying efforts in Washington: "I am pleased to inform you that I have at last gotten the federal government to say they will take action in your behalf" (Rockwell n.d., bI cl fl, Decker to Rockwell, May 13, 1913).

The Boylan matter entering U.S. District Court (Northern District, New York) became *United States v. Julia Boylan and Anna Siver Moyer,* the latter a nonnative woman who had purchased the Honyoust place through a mortgage agreement with Boylan. The government's case, as it was finally laid out two years later, emphasized that the property was situated within the lands recognized as Oneida by the United States in the 1794 Canandaigua Treaty. The United States acknowledged that obligations incurred in that treaty to protect Oneida land were still in effect. More specifically, the Honyoust place was on land assigned by the state in 1842 to an Oneida band, and that band had remained in common and continuous possession of it since. Because the land was inalienable by individuals, the ejection based on individual title was unlawful, and the band was entitled to U.S. protection. Therefore, on behalf of the Oneidas, the United States brought suit seeking recovery of the property *(United States v. Boylan et al.,* 1916, Plaintiff's Complaint, September 28).

Replying in early November, the defendants claimed there was no Oneida Reservation because nearly all of it had been disposed of in legally binding sales to the state. The thirty-two-acre tract was traceable to the 1842 treaty that assigned the land to Oneidas in severalty, a condition of private ownership characteristic of New York citizens. As individual landowners, Oneidas were subject to the same courts and laws as other citizens. The defendants strongly asserted a principle thousands of New Yorkers (including Oneidas) had fought against in the Civil War: the supremacy of state over federal law. New York's laws were alleged to be "binding and conclusive" not only upon the Oneidas but on the United States of America as well *(United States v. Boylan et al.,* 1915, Defendants' Answer, November 10).

Testimony was taken next summer in Syracuse, both parties having agreed to waive trial by jury. Most was given by four Oneidas—the elderly siblings Mary Honyoust Skenandoah (George) and William Honyoust, who had been evicted seven years before (Isaac Honyoust having died in the interim), and the younger cousins William Rockwell and Chapman Shenandoah (ill. 25).

Questions focused on who the Oneidas were (especially their genealogical connections to senior generations listed in the 1842 treaty), who was living on the Honyoust place, and whether the land had ever been taxed (apparently not). Inquiring into Oneida tribal organization, the defense sought to show no meaningful group existed, whereas the prosecution established there were chiefs, group meetings, and distributions of annuity cloth from the U.S. government. The defense pressed particularly hard on the issue of Indian appearance. How could the Oneidas be regarded as Indians, Rockwell was asked, if he worked like any white citizen, wore the same clothes as white men, and did not "live in the style of Indians pursuing the chase, hunting and fishing?" *(United States v. Boylan et al.,* 1916, Stenographer's Minutes, pp. 45–47, July 26).

Pondered for more than two and a half years, Judge George W. Ray's decision sidestepped the issue of federal-versus-state supremacy. Ray found that the United States continued to recognize treaty obligations to the Oneidas extending back to 1794, a relationship he understood as one

Front row, left to right—William Honyost, William Rockwell, Mrs. Mary Shenandoah, Albert Shenandoah. Back row—Webster Thomas, Alex Verning, Nicholas Honyost, Chapman Shenandoah. This photograph was taken yesterday at the Court House.

INDIANS PLEAD FOR THEIR LAND

Seven Oneidas and Two Onondagas Testify at Federal Trial.

400 ACRES ARE IN DISPUTE

W. H. Rockwell of Rochester Declares the Oneidas Were Loyal to Colonists and Yet Were Victims of Encroachment.

With the completion of the Indian land case yesterday afternoon, Judge George W. Ray adjourned Federal Court until 10 o'clock this morning. Frank J. Cregg, assistant Federal attorney, representing the government, and Joseph Beal for the defendants submitted all evidence and later will file briefs. Judge Ray will not render a decision until sometime in the fall.

"The descendants of twenty-three Oneida Indians are affected by the loss of the land in question, consisting of thirty-two acres with two buildings. In addition to the land, the government stipulated that damages amounting to $25 a year for five years should also be allowed. If the suit was decided in favor of the government and against the defendants, Julia Hoylan and Anna Silver Mover.

W. H. Rockwell of Rochester, member of the Oneida tribe, and the man who instigated the government action, said there were about 400 acres of land worth at least $100 an acre that should never have been taken from the Oneidas. All this land is located near the city of Oneida.

Old Deeds as Exhibits.

Mr. Beal submitted other exhibits, a number of old deeds showing that the tribesmen made transfers among themselves, assuming that the land was theirs to dispose of as they desired. Mr. Rockwell was the last witness examined and he testified that he had exercised the privilege of a citizen and voter on a number of occasions.

"The Oneidas are the only Indians," said Mr. Rockwell, "who never fought against the United States. Instead, they were allies of the colonist during the Revolution. They were a peaceful, thrifty tribe. At various times white neighbors encroached upon their land, but always assuring them that if they wanted the land they could have it. One reason why so many of the Oneidas moved away from the reservation was because they were continually annoyed by the white men's encroachments.

"If an Indian had horses or cattle a white neighbor would want to buy from him, and if the Indian did not want to sell at the white man's price, hard feelings developed. The Indian is naturally of a roving disposition, and if his surroundings became disagreeable he moved elsewhere. In that way the tribe became scattered."

Several Indians on Stand.

One of the contentions that came up in the case was to the effect that by their act of breaking tribal relations and removing to other parts of the country the Oneida Indians relinquished all allegiance to tribal control and became citizens of the state. Mr. Cregg held that they could not become citizens without a special act of Congress, and that the state of New York had no jurisdiction over them.

The Oneida Indians called as witnesses were as follows: William Honyost, Nicholas Honyost, Chapman Shenandoah, Albert Shenandoah, William Rockwell, Mrs. Mary Shenandoah and Alex Verning, former Oneida chief. The Onondaga tribesmen who testified were Webster Thomas and Mrs. Chapman Shenandoah.

Federal Court will be adjourned to-day and reopen September 18 with the case of the Edwin J. Knapp Candle Company against the Will & Baumer Company, an action to recover damages for infringement on a patent.

25. Newspaper coverage of *United States v. Boylan et al.*, 1916; The Syracuse Post-Standard, *July 28, 1916.*

of guardian to ward. The Oneidas retained aboriginal title to the soil of the thirty-two acres and "had not abandoned their tribal relations." How they dressed or made a living was immaterial (Opinion 1919, 486).

Possibly, Ray mused, New York had the right to enter into the 1842 treaty and to enact the 1843 law with its conditions on alienating land being binding. But even if that were so, the 1843 statute had not been complied with because the proper officials never approved the transactions resulting in Boylan's title. If, on the other hand, authority in the matter resided solely with the federal government, Congress had never terminated the Oneidas' tribal relations, nor had it ever authorized the Oneidas to hold land in severalty. Therefore, New York had no power or authority to do these things. Either way, Boylan's title was invalid. It was not in compliance with New York law or it was taken in violation of federal law or both.

The defendants appealed and received the decision of the circuit court of appeals one year to the day after Judge Ray's decision. Circuit judge Martin T. Manton agreed that Boylan's title was invalid because it did not comply with state law. However, that line of reasoning was peripheral to the primary analysis that unambiguously championed the supremacy of federal over state law. The Oneidas, Judge Manton declared, "constitute a distinct tribe or nation, and exclusive jurisdiction over them is vested in the federal government which may maintain actions in this behalf." No conveyance of Indian land is valid without federal approval, and, "in the absence of federal legislation authorizing it, a mortgage executed by a member of the Oneida Tribe of Indians in New York on his interest in the tribal lands [is] held invalid, and a decree of a state court foreclosing it and making partition of the lands [is] held null and void" (Opinion 1920, 165). Affirming and clarifying the decision of the district court, this judgment directed the Indians to be restored to possession of their land.

Playing out one last hand, the defendants managed to reach the United States Supreme Court. In the end, however, the matter was resolved on a technicality. The U.S. solicitor general asked the court to set aside the Boylan proceeding because it had not been filed within three months of the circuit court decision, the time limit required by the law. The Supreme Court agreed and, in late 1921, dismissed the case for want of jurisdiction. In refusing to review the matter, the Supreme Court let stand the decision of the circuit court of appeals *(Boylan et al. v. United States* 1921, Motion to Dismiss, October, and Order of Dismissal, November 7).

Early the following year, the U.S. attorney for the Northern District of New York directed Chief Rockwell to take possession of the land on behalf of the Oneidas (Rockwell n.d., bI c1 f1, Hiram C. Todd to Rockwell, March 27, 1922).

A Federal Covenant and Polly Cooper

The return of Indian land was a stunning development with significant implications for the future in its affirmation of the continued federally recognized status of the Oneida Nation, and in its assertion of federal supremacy over state law in matters of Indian land. But the victory was a curiously non-Indian affair won largely in the absence of Indian people. The Oneidas had been asked to contribute little to the government's case, and, indeed, their presence was scarcely required. Oneidas tended to be invoked as abstract, distant, and passive wards of the United States, deserving of federal help in the way children need a parent's supervision. The fact that the Oneidas had been cruelly defrauded by their neighbors was never central to the case. Nor was the Oneidas' view of why the United States was helping them taken into account—with one strange exception.

Although it is not clear from *Boylan* case records how Oneidas saw things, their view was recorded in testimony given to the Everett Commission, a legislative fact-finding board formed in response to questions of New York Indian title raised by the *Boylan* decisions (Upton 1980, 77, 138). Two Oneidas, one of them Chapman Shenandoah, spoke to these state officials while *Boylan* was still pending in the Supreme Court. Both stressed how the Oneidas had fought for the United States, and both implied that George Washington had caused treaty cloth to be distributed annually to them in gratitude for their aid in the Revolution (Everett 1922, 108–13). Oneidas expressed much the same opinion throughout the 1800s on the few occasions anyone bothered to ask them.

Possibly the only nonnative people involved in the *Boylan* case who understood this point were local city of Oneida lawyers such as Joseph Beal who, on behalf of Julia Boylan, tried to use it *against* the Oneidas. In the course of testimony taken in 1916, the defense asserted that if the Oneidas received an annuity from the federal government, it was not because they were wards of the government but in recognition of what they had done during the Revolution *(United States v. Boylan et al.,* 1916, Stenographer's Minutes, pp. 16–17). Apparently, the defense was trying to employ the Oneida interpretation to argue that if the government's annuity payment resulted from a specific historical circumstance, then it could not be evidence that the government continued to recognize treaty obligations toward the Oneidas. Consequently, the Oneida Nation would not be regarded as federally recognized.

Judge Ray was puzzled by the claim and devoted a considerable passage to refuting it (Opinion 1919, 488–90). The annuity from the federal government, he found, resulted from the 1794 Treaty of Canandaigua and had "nothing whatever to do with compensation for loyalty or services or losses during the Revolutionary War." Thus, the Oneida view of why the United States was helping them was not only irrelevant to the government's case, but actually denied by the government.

Highly specialized in language and rationale, the *Boylan* cases were argued in arcane courtroom terms that could not have been satisfying to the Oneidas and, in all probability, were not particularly informative for them. But neither, on the other hand, did the contemporaneous newspaper coverage explain why land was returned to the Indians for the first time in anyone's memory and what that reversal might portend for the future. There was, in fact, a void of explanation from the perspective of virtually everyone around.

Into that void flowed an Oneida explanation and justification. It was articulated in characteristically Oneida fashion—the mythopoeic language of storytellers uncomfortable in formal English expression and ill-at-ease in an alien and often hostile courtroom setting. What happened, I believe, was that Oneidas, in or formerly of the Windfall, dusted off a tradition and offered it to the world. In the context of the concern created by *Boylan,* the old legend of Polly Cooper became salient.

In undated papers written on the Windfall, Chief Rockwell often mentioned his great-great-grandmother Polly Cooper, whose historic shawl was still Oneida owned. Although he knew of a tradition concerning Skenandoa taking corn to Valley Forge, he never elaborated on this aspect of the story. Instead, Rockwell invariably highlighted Polly Cooper, praising her selflessness and bravery, and admiring how she personified the matriarchal wisdom of his people:

POLLY COOPER

George Washington is called the father of this country. An Indian woman of the Oneida Nation should be called the mother of this country. Her name was Polly Cooper. She cooked for Geo. Washington and his staff of officers when they were located [in] Philadelphia. Polly Cooper would not accept cash payment for her part in the Revolutionary War. Isn't that just like a mother in doing for her children?. . . . So the wives of the officers invited Polly Cooper to take a walk downtown. As they were looking in the store windows, Polly saw a black shawl on display that she thought was the best article in the window. When the women returned to their homes, they told their husbands what Polly saw that she liked so well. Money was appropriated (by Congress) for the purpose of the shawl. And it was given to Polly Cooper for her services as a cook for the officers of the 13 colonies' army. When I was a boy, I often heard people speak of Polly Cooper. (n.d. bI c2 f4)

The earliest public notice of this tradition may have been the announcement that visitors to the 1928 New York State Fair (held in Syracuse) could view a shawl given to an Oneida woman by Mrs. Benjamin Franklin ("Indians Show Heirlooms at Fair Grounds," *Syracuse Post-Standard*, August 24). The object was owned by the family of Chapman Shenandoah, then living on the Onondaga Reservation in Syracuse. Shenandoah, like Rockwell, was an alumnus of the *Boylan* case and a great-great-grandchild of Polly Cooper. Presumably, Shenandoah was the source of the Polly Cooper story as it appeared to the newspaper-reading public in 1935:

Polly Cooper lived near Rome at that time, and when Skenandoa went to Valley Forge she went with him. The relationship of Polly Cooper and Chief Skenandoa is given by descendants today as that of sister-in-law and brother-in-law, indicating she married his brother, tho both Polly Cooper and the chief are claimed as ancestors by the Shanandoahs [*sic*] of today.

As the story is told now, Polly and Skenandoa took 100 bushels of corn, and, riding horses, went to Valley Forge. Probably other Oneidas went with them.

Polly Cooper cooked in the camp of Washington that winter, making the corn into dishes which saved the famished army until more provisions arrived, and then she mounted her horse and rode back to her home among the Oneidas.

She would take no pay for what she did. She had given all that an Indian woman could give to the American cause, helping feed the army at Valley Forge when the army faced starvation, and when pay was proffered she said she wanted nothing for what she had done. It had not been done for pay.

She was asked what she would like to have, but to that question she did not reply. However, before she returned home she visited Philadelphia, Pa., and while there admired a silk shawl and a hat she saw in a store. If there was one thing an Indian woman of that day, and even a much later day, wanted more than anything else it was a beautiful shawl. But Polly Cooper only admired. She felt a shawl like that was not for an Oneida woman, and she rode her horse back to Rome.

It was springtime then, the spring of 1778, and violets were blooming in the valley of the Mohawk.

Polly Cooper went back to her cabin, to the prosaic life of an Indian woman, caring for her home, tilling her field and doing the work required.

One day two soldiers on horseback rode into Rome, and asked the way to the home of the Skenandoas and Polly Cooper. They found it, and they stopped in front of the door. They dismounted. Polly saw them coming. She was frightened. She did not know what it meant. She did not know what was about to happen.

But her alarm was soon dispelled. The soldiers had come with a present. They had come with the hat and the shawl she had seen in the Philadelphia shop, sent by Washington himself in appreciation of what she had done. They put the shawl about her shoulders and the hat upon her head, and rode away. Whatever became of that hat is not known now, but there is a tradition that it was wonderful with flowers and feathers.

Polly Cooper kept the hat and shawl as long as she lived, her most treasured possessions. How the hat disappeared is not known, but the shawl was handed down from generation to generation, carefully guarded, and so it came into possession of

the parents of Albert Schanandoah [*sic*] [Chapman
Shenandoah's recently deceased brother] many years ago.
("Descendant Has Shawl Given Polly Cooper by Washington for
Her Aid at Valley Forge," *Syracuse Post-Standard,* March 17,
1935)

Although the "documentary record is silent concerning these events,"
Karim Tiro observes, the story "conveys certain undeniable truths"
(1999, 99). Clearly, the Oneidas made a substantial contribution to the
outcome of the war and aided Washington's army at Valley Forge (see pp.
19–20). Just as clearly, the tradition of Polly Cooper also expresses an
Oneida view of what happened in *Boylan:* the federal government helped
because of its unique relationship with the Oneida Nation. Because the
Oneidas rendered crucial aid to the Americans during the Revolutionary
War, it was simple justice that the United States should acknowledge its
gratitude and recognize continuing obligations to its allies.

The Oneida perspective was expressed in Oneida terms resonant with
the connotations of traditional associations. Tiro suggests, for example,
that the Oneidas' gift of corn was symbolically meaningful, inasmuch as
corn "was imbued with sacred power" symbolic of life (100). The shawl itself bears witness, in customary Iroquois fashion, to its own story. Recall
that, in the past, any agreement of the Iroquois was accompanied and sol-
emnized by a gift. Frequently, it was wampum, but it might be an animal
skin or textile also. Tied to the words of the message, the gift underlined
the truth and importance of accompanying words. In much the same fashion, Oneidas considered the shawl as tangible American acknowledgement of Oneida help and sacrifice, testament to a wartime pact between
two nations.

I pointed out (see pp. 30–31) that the wellsprings of Oneida mythic
expression—at least as concerned the Oneida Stone—seem to have run
dry. In fact, Oneida oral narrative, as an idiom of figurative and metaphorical language explaining a present with reference to a past, seems to have
been alive and well during the early twentieth century. In the eastern community, Hope Allen was learning folklore from the Orchard-Marble Hill
Oneidas, including at least one tale, "Where the Earth Opens," speaking
to the contemporary situation in an ancient tongue. Further, as a sort of
community-relations bulletin inserted into the public domain, the Polly

Cooper legend offered a credible justification of complicated legal events from an Oneida point of view.

The Land Claims and Rise of the Oneida Nation

Chief Rockwell remained the sole inhabitant of the old Honyoust place for more than thirty-five years, the former residents and their descendants having been dispersed around the environs of Oneida, to the Onondaga Reservation near Syracuse, and to other places. Only after Rockwell's death in 1960 did a number of Oneidas begin moving back to the old Honyoust place, mostly from the Onondaga Reservation. Fearing the property might pass out of Oneida hands again as the inheritance of Rockwell's nonnative widow, they initially came to occupy the land in order to secure its continued Oneida ownership. They also came back, of course, because they had never ceased to regard this area as their home and hearth, even while living (sometimes for generations) as guests of other Iroquois nations. This reason remains operative, and the process of moving back continues to this day. In common cause with Oneidas who had never left the area (including those inhabitants of Marble Hill), this gathering resulted in the revitalization of the Oneida Indian Nation.

On the eve of their return, several Oneidas living in Onondaga, in cooperation with Oneidas from Canada and Wisconsin, embarked on a new land-claim initiative. Such action required federal intervention on their behalf as in *Boylan* or a way would have to be found around a major legal dilemma: New York could not be sued in its own courts without its consent, yet it seemed unlikely New York could be sued in federal court, either.

In 1970, the Oneidas instituted a test case naming the counties (rather than state) as defendants and requesting a little money as trespass damage for the rental value of part of the land for two years. The case targeted a single New York-Oneida treaty, the one of 1795. This land grab was New York's first and largest taking of land within the 1788 reservation guaranteed to the Oneidas by the federal government at Canandaigua in 1794.

This Oneida case also focused on one legislative act. When the constitution became effective in 1789 (the point at which the present federal government came into being), Indian relations were supposed to become the exclusive province of the United States and not any individual state. As one of its first acts, the new government operationalized this principle of federal supremacy into law.

The Trade and Intercourse Act of 1790 essentially codified into U.S. law an Old World idea. Most European jurists conceded to indigenous people a limited condition of ownership to the soil on which they lived before Europeans arrived. That so-called Indian title, however, was nothing more than the right to continued residence at that location. Actual ownership was vested in a European sovereign, by virtue of conquest or discovery ultimately authorized, as the Europeans saw it, by divine agency. When the sovereign accepted the transfer of indigenes' limited title, the condition of the sovereign's full fee ownership became activated. In theory, only the sovereign could "extinguish Indian title," and only the sovereign could then sell the land to another party. The Trade and Intercourse (or Nonintercourse) Act, therefore, explicitly vested these ownership rights in the new U.S. government. Thereafter, any conveyance of Indian land without the consent of the central government was a breach of federal law. This legislation was reenacted on a number of occasions and remains a fixture of federal Indian law today.

The assertion at the heart of the main Oneida land claim case is that New York's land acquisitions within the 1788 Oneida Reservation were illegal if executed without federal consent. Like *Boylan*, the argument is not really concerned with morality. Rather, it poses a legal question to which the answer is yes or no as determined, presumably, by historical findings. Was a federal representative present at the treaty, and, if so, was the agreement duly ratified by the United States?

Because the federal government repeatedly refused to intervene on the Oneidas' behalf (Shattuck 1991, 27–29), the initial issue was whether the federal court system would acknowledge jurisdiction in the case. The district court and the circuit court of appeals said no on the grounds "that the claim made was one under state law for ejectment, not one arising under federal law" (Locklear 1988b, 144). The Supreme Court, however, accepted the case and found the decisive consideration to be the obligations incurred by the U.S. government under the Canandaigua and earlier federal treaties to secure the Oneidas' land to the Oneidas. In January 1974, the United States Supreme Court ruled that the Oneidas had the right to a federal hearing rooted in federal treaty and, further, that "Indian title is a matter of federal law and can be extinguished only with federal consent" (opinion quoted in Shattuck 1991, 159).

This historic decision transformed American Indian law as the first to establish definitively that claims for Indian land fall within federal jurisdiction. Further, it was now clear that such a claim could be advanced by the tribe itself and did not have to be filed by the United States on the tribe's behalf (Locklear 1988b, 150; Shattuck 1991, 37).

The substance of the case was remanded to the U.S. District Court, Northern District of New York. Reminiscent of *Boylan,* a trial without jury was conducted quietly in late 1975, and, again, a decision required more than two years of judicial reflection. In the summer of 1977, Judge Edmund Port agreed with the historical facts of the matter: no U.S. commissioner had been present at the 1795 treaty, and no subsequent federal ratification of the treaty had occurred (Campisi 1976; Hauptman 1999, 58–81).

Consequently, Judge Port ruled, New York's purchase of 1795 violated the Nonintercourse Act and was thus void. A conveyance of land that is void under federal law cannot be made legal by subsequent state law. The Oneidas never acquiesced in the land transfer and never ceased to protest its injustice. In any event, no state or federal statute of limitations barred the Oneidas' claim nearly two centuries after the fact. On appeal, this ruling wound its way, yet again, through the court system. Port's finding was upheld by the second circuit court, then confirmed by the Supreme Court of the United States.[3]

The subject of this, the principal land claim, is the taking of Oneida land not by individuals such as Julia Boylan but by the state of New York. Nevertheless, one would assume some of the ground covered in the 1970s–1980s crosses territory traversed during the 1910s–1920s: the federally recognized status of the Oneida Nation and the supremacy of federal law, for example. Strangely, from a nonlegal perspective, *Boylan* received scarcely a mention in these proceedings.

Continuity between *Boylan* and recent land claims certainly exists, however, from the Oneidas' point of view. On one level, the Oneidas never forgot *Boylan,* and the case continued to inspire the pursuit of jus-

3. These two federal decisions (434 F. Supp., 527 [July 12, 1977] and 470 U.S. 226, 84 L. Ed. 2d 169 [March 4, 1985]) are reprinted in Shattuck 1991, 175–96, 209–36.

tice that came to fruition in the land claims. On another, and just as in *Boylan*, no Oneida perspective and no Oneida sense of morality find voice in the legal premises of the land-claim argument. It should not be surprising to find, therefore, that the legend of Polly Cooper continues to inspire and offer justification for esoteric legal victories:

> We Oneidas are very proud of our alliance, believing that we stood on the side of the freedom and liberty that had always been practiced in our society. We fought in critical battles alongside the colonists, delivered food to the starving troops at Valley Forge and in the end were victorious in that struggle. As a result of our alliance, the Oneida Nation entered into treaties with the United States that gave special protection to our lands, superior to that accorded to the land of the other Six Nations. Today the Oneidas continue to hold to the promises made to them in their treaties with the federal government. In addition, the guarantees given to us as victorious allies to protect our lands form the basis of our two victories in the Supreme Court in our claims for the return of our homeland. (Halbritter and McSloy 1994, 546–49)

Sadly, no settlement resulted from the Oneidas' unambiguous and spectacular victories in court.[4] While they waited, their economic situation continued to deteriorate, and, as recently as 1991, the prospects seemed

---

4. Land-claim issues remain unresolved at the start of the twenty-first century. Frustrated by the lack of progress in resolving the case, the Oneidas and the U.S. Department of Justice asked permission, in December 1998, to name landowners within the claims area as defendants. In September 2000, the U.S. District Court (Syracuse) determined that landowners cannot be sued but that the state should be added as a defendant party in the proceedings. If the parties fail to negotiate a settlement, the case presumably will return to court where each of the Oneida-New York treaties will be scrutinized, one by one, for federal representation and ratification.

In a related development, the city of Sherrill foreclosed on Oneida Nation properties for failure to pay property taxes in 1999. The Oneidas filed suit to block the proceedings. Sherrill, joined by Madison County and supported by Oneida County, argued that a federal treaty of 1838 had dissolved the Oneida Reservation, rendering the land non-Indian and therefore taxable. The U.S. District Court (Utica) ruled in June 2001 that the Oneida Indian Nation prevailed on every point: the land in question was within the Oneida Reservation guaranteed to the Oneidas by the United States, the United States never disestablished that reservation, and, as Indian land, it is nontaxable. Sherrill is appealing the decision at this writing.

bleak. The Oneida rate of unemployment was 44 percent, two-thirds of the households earned less than fifteen thousand dollars per annum, and no more than a dozen people had enrolled in college-level courses of any kind. On the territory (the old thirty-two-acre Honyoust place), the Oneida community consisted of secondhand mobile homes clustered along a path of mud with no running water or street lighting.

Impoverishment compounded by hope proved a combustible mixture in which the direction of land claims and economic development were contested internally. Reemerging out of a tumultuous decade of divisiveness was a traditional government, rooted in clan representation and led by a Harvard-educated lawyer, Ray Halbritter. Regarding economic power as necessary to national sovereignty and cultural renewal, this leadership committed itself to reversing the cycle of poverty they saw cursing the Oneida people.

By the late 1970s, the Oneidas went into business on the territory as hosts of a bingo game and subsequently of a high-stakes bingo operation and a smoke shop. In 1993, they constructed a casino. The Oneidas were one of the first Indian nations to take advantage of federal precepts that place such enterprises beyond state jurisdiction:

> The big issue for the Oneida as a people was, of course, whether selling cigarettes or gaming was an "Indian" thing to do. Was it a sell-out, a sacrifice of what we believed as traditional Haudenosaunee people? In answer, we felt that the way we were forced to live, on the small, thirty-two acre piece of land, had put our backs to the wall, and no one seemed to offer any alternative solutions. Our elders were passing on every year, and our language, culture, and ceremonies were being forever lost with them, never to be retrieved. The federal and state governments were in no rush to settle our land claims, even with two Supreme Court victories behind us. . . . Our only option was to exercise our sovereignty and simultaneously to exploit the long-standing principle of United States law that barred New York State statutes and taxation from reaching our activities. At least until the federal government closes the window, we are free to conduct business on our land without state regulation and tax, and given that the window might be a narrow one, we felt that gaming was the quickest way to build an economic base. Since we have never believed that as Indians we could have an opportunity for too long before the white man coveted it, we have never believed that the federal govern-

ment would let us get away with making money for too long. We have, therefore, never viewed the casino as anything but a temporary measure. The casino is not a statement of who we are, but only a means to get us where we want to be. We had tried poverty for 200 years, so we decided to try something else. (Halbritter 1994, 566–68)

In fewer than ten years, the casino grew into the Turning Stone Resort complex composed of a hotel with restaurants, a conference center and showroom, and several golf courses. The Oneidas also diversified their enterprises beyond gaming through such businesses as textile printing, a recreational vehicle park, a boat marina, and a chain of gas stations and convenience stores. In 1991, the Oneida Nation employed six people; in 2001, that figure was nearly three thousand. The past decade of the Oneida Indian Nation is one of the most astonishing success stories of our time.

At the opening of the twenty-first century, these initiatives resulted in renewed pride among Oneida people now enjoying a higher standard of living than seemed possible even ten years before. Services funded for nation members by enterprise income include several options for affordable housing and expanded educational opportunities (nearly sixty Oneidas were enrolled in college degree programs in 2000). The old Honyoust place now has sidewalks along a paved road and water, sewer, and electric services; youth and recreational facilities; a health center providing medical and dental services; an educational resource center with a library and a language program teaching the Oneida tongue; a council house with an adjacent cookhouse; and a cultural center and museum. Nearby is a social services office, a center for elders and children, and a housing development office. In effect, the old Windfall community is being rebuilt.

Economic success has permitted the Oneidas to reclaim their rich heritage in other ways. The Oneidas were the first of New York's native people to get land returned to them in *Boylan*. More recently, they became the first to rebuild a real land base, reacquiring some fifteen thousand acres of ancestral homeland purchased at fair market value from willing sellers. The new acreage includes a number of the Oneidas' old village locations. In becoming owners of their own archaeological record, the Oneidas are probably the first native people in the United States to take possession of their past solely through their own efforts.

They may also be the first Indian nation to regain their national symbol. In 1974, at about the time the Oneidas obtained their initial Supreme Court decision, the Forest Hill Cemetery in Utica returned the Oneida Stone to its rightful owners. It was done quietly, without fanfare—such being the way, perhaps, of symbolic closure. Today, the Oneida Stone sits beside the Oneida Nation's council house on the old thirty-two-acre Honyoust tract. Home again, the ancient emblem resumes its place in the Oneidas' national epic of survival, resilience, and creative change.

EPILOGUE

Studying Iroquois Folklore

This material then, is the sum of what Hope Allen and others recorded of Oneida oral narrative early in the twentieth century, material adding to our knowledge of Iroquois oral narrative as a whole. What does it add up to? What are its most essential features?

One must first acknowledge that a number of the stories Iroquois people told around 1900 were European in derivation. Far from negligible, the Old World content included the most popular Iroquois tale of the twentieth century—the fox and the bear—in addition to the magic bull, the naughty girl, the gifted companions, and, probably, the preacher's miracle (see chapters 7–8). I noted how much the same European repertoire was widely adopted throughout native America, and, at least as regards the Oneida examples, the stories seem to have derived from exclusively French Canadian sources. When Oneidas told these foreign wonder tales, they customized them to an Iroquois setting. Thus, in the case of "The Magic Bull," the wicked stepmother dreams the boy's death, the bull is lashed with red-willow whips, a pursuit becomes an Iroquois obstacle chase, and the boy's wife must be rescued from a giant water snake.

Yet the basic European story line remains intact. Victor Barnouw remarked on the same phenomenon elsewhere in native North America: "It is striking that, despite their alien content, these stories closely resemble the tales told in Europe. They have been faithfully transmitted in the Indian setting, although some Indian patterns do intrude. The narrators of these stories seem to have wished to get the details right" (1977, 181). There is much to wonder at here and much more to learn about this process of faithful cultural transmission from essentially one foreign source.

The other side of the coin is that European elements have not greatly

221

changed what appears to be the indigenous bedrock of the oral literature. When a fairy godmother shows up in Lydia Doxtater's creation story, for example, she does not alter the ancient plot. This European character merely fills in for a traditional Iroquois figure Doxtater had forgotten. "Iroquois mythology," as William Fenton put it, "is little affected by European contact; what has been adapted constitutes an added literature" (1947, 393).

What is the indigenous character of this oral narrative? The earliest description of Iroquois oral narrative is that of Lewis Henry Morgan, quoted extensively at the opening of chapter 4. Stith Thompson offered a very different assessment: "No other tribes show such thorough independence in their tales and detachment from other sections as do the Iroquois. Though their origin myth has much in common with that of the Central Woodland, the rest of their tales show little outside influence. The reader is impressed with a great monotony of motivation and treatment" (1929, xxii). Thompson's characterization intrigues but puzzles me. Whether the material is monotonous is surely a matter of taste, and, as for the relationship of Iroquois lore to others' oral literature, "no study has been made of the areal affiliations of Iroquois tales to determine whether they really are unique" (Fenton 1947, 394).

Fenton also observed that a recurring theme in Iroquois folklore is "They went to the woods to hunt for meat" (1978, 298). This summation succinctly states what seems to me the essence of the matter. Oneida and other Iroquois oral narrative at the turn of the twentieth century was dominated by a focus on the forest. These stories are of the woods. Often they take place there; usually, they seem interested in little that is not at home in the forest. Over and over again, the concern manifested in plot, character, and setting is with hunting and forest animals. Such essential creatures of Iroquois folklore as Flying Heads, Stone Giants, and Little People are denizens of the woods and, more often than not, are closely associated with game animals.

Stated differently, there is a general lack of themes making reference to the clearing and to agriculture. As indicated in chapter 7, the riddlelike piece "Who Will Marry Me?" makes one of the few allusions to corn and domesticated crops in the Oneida corpus. One might suppose Thunders are essentially agricultural gods, but they are not, or at least they should not be equated with Old World agricultural deities. Iroquois statements on the subject repeatedly stress that Thunders bring water to cleanse the earth—not necessarily to grow maize. Was there more at one time? Perhaps. Formerly, the creation myth was more clearly an allegory of subsistence in which Sky Holder signified the dominance of horticulture over hunting. A greater concern with domesticated crops in the past may also be indicated in the ceramic effigies interpreted as alluding to maize (see sidebar, chapter 4).

To point out that Oneida and other Iroquois folklore at the turn of the twentieth century was dominated by the hunt and by the woods is to imply a strong male orientation. Most of the protagonists are males, and, indeed, the majority of all characters are male. Sometimes it seems downright misogynist as, for example, when the older creation story specifies the evil one as female and details three generations in which women suffer unpleasant fates for having been magically impregnated.

A strong male bias in such material has been noticed elsewhere in the Americas (Taggart 1983, 7; Urton 1985, 9–10) and seems to be rather common throughout the Eastern Woodlands. Victor Barnouw noted that Chippewa oral narrative, dominated by the hunt and animals, was very much a man's world (1977, 48, 51, 92). Likewise, John Bierhorst remarked that Delaware lore is markedly male in cast and plot (1995, 14–15). Indeed, it is so strongly male in posture that both researchers wondered whether we are not getting just half of it. Could there have been a women's oral literature? Barnouw thought Chippewa women told stories about women more frequently, but there is no Iroquois evidence for such a thing (1977, 93). In this Oneida material, it is women speaking to women on the subject.

Two themes recur. First, the oral narratives Hope Allen heard frequently offer comments on family values and especially emphasize lessons about marriage and sexual behavior. The most important stricture is: Bad things happen if you do not marry when you should. Don't be promiscuous, and don't be too picky when the time comes for matrimony. Thus, Lydia Doxtater's flirty women get abandoned on islands or—and this fate is the most common for haughty young Iroquois women everywhere—they end up with serpents as mates. Women, however, are often reprieved from their fates; men are not. William Beauchamp's young man, for example, got stuck with a snakish spouse and was then destroyed. Similarly, the young hunter who slept with a Stone Giant woman lost his wife and family and then was spurned by all the women in the village.

The second great theme of these oral narratives is: A supernatural needs human help to overcome an enemy. The domesticated Stone Giant cannot dispatch his or her savage mate without help from the human hosts. Magic bulls and horned serpents need a person to revive them as they tire in the face of great danger. Over and over again, Thunders cannot prevail over the monsters unless some person helps to find or slay the evil brutes. As a point of view affirming humans as necessary to the scheme of things, this perspective is reminiscent of the sentiment expressed in the Iroquois Thanksgiving Address—an all-purpose and probably ancient ritual speech (Chafe 1961; Shimony 1994, 140). Humans announce, in this oration, that they are still performing their ordained duty: to acknowledge and give thanks for the cosmos. By fulfilling these specifically human obligations, people make a crucial contribution toward the maintenance of the universal order and are, therefore, very important (Hamell 1987, 77).

One of the most striking features of worldview shining through the oral narratives considered here is that Oneidas felt an easy congeniality for Thunders, beings they regarded as laboring on their behalf to keep evil monsters—horned water serpents are most frequently mentioned—confined beneath us. These sentiments seem to have been common to Iroquois everywhere as a kind of underlying folk belief that was neither Christian nor enthusiastically endorsed by the Handsome Lake religion. Iroquois Thunders battling snakes must be the local variant of what Michael Foster called "one of the most widely diffused themes in North America and northeastern Asia, that of the Thunder Bird and the serpent" (1974, 69). On the basis of limited comparisons, I suggest the mythological trail of birds dueling underwater animals leads directly toward Algonquian speakers of the Great Lakes region and farther west.

An easier topic to investigate historically is the great Iroquoian myth of beginnings. I believe the first reasonably complete picture of the myth as known to Oneidas and other Iroquois dates to the late 1700s. However, there is good reason to suppose it is the same narrative as that documented among the Iroquoian-speaking Hurons of the early 1600s and that the Iroquois details are of comparable age. In fact, this myth can safely be projected into pre-European times because it was documented among the Hurons prior to major Christian influence.

The old creation myth tells of a woman who fell into our world from one above. She came to rest on land brought up from the ocean bottom and placed on Turtle's back. She had a daughter who bore twin sons. One brother released game animals impounded underground and killed the other whose name was Flint. The surviving brother, along with the woman from the sky, were of opposite disposition, and were regarded as major gods actively intervening in human affairs. As the malicious grandmother and kindly disposed grandson, these two deities were documented from the opening of the seventeenth century among the Hurons to the close of the eighteenth century among the Oneidas.

Major parts of the Iroquoian creation myth were distributed throughout the Northeast. The earth-diver episode was known virtually everywhere. The incidents folklorists call the-woman-who-fell-from-the-sky and earth-from-Turtle's-back were also told by the Algonquian-speaking Delawares, Shawnees, and Mahicans south of the Iroquois. Undoubtedly, the Delaware cosmogony was most closely related because it included rival twin brothers. However, the motif of the dueling siblings occurs sporadically in Algonquian mythology over a vast area (including the Great Lakes and New England). Presumably, the widespread distribution of mythic elements referable to the Iroquois creation myth implies a fair amount of in-place antiquity, particularly for the contiguity of the Iroquois and Delaware people.

The old gods—the nasty grandmother and the beneficent grandson-twin named Sky Holder—testify to some kind of good-versus-evil religious dichotomy dating to pre-European times. Giver of corn to humankind, Sky Holder was the major culture hero, the principal deity of all the Iroquois nations, and probably the war god as well. I cited evidence in this study indicating that Sky Holder may also have been a thunder god or, at least, had thunder attributes. Linking thunder to the Iroquois twins and cosmogony suggests a mythological connection to the Cherokee twins of the Southeast who free the game and become the Thunders.

Being able to document the old look of things allows one to discern the character of change occurring in the early nineteenth century. The origin myth was reconfigured to emphasize the brothers, and their competition assumed greater importance redefined as a struggle over creation. Flint came to be regarded as the Evil Spirit, occasionally identified as the devil. Sky Holder, usually recast as the Good Spirit, offered moral guidance and rendered postmortal judgment in heaven. At the same time, Thunder became separate from and subservient to Sky Holder. These changes in oral narrative reflected alterations in religion. During these years, the Christian-influenced creed of Handsome Lake became established, a faith imbuing its participants with "ideas of special salvation as long as they adhere to [it], and of damnation as soon as they deviate from the rules of conduct prescribed by Handsome Lake and endorsed by the Great Creator" (Shimony 1994, 203). The conservative tenor of this religion may have contributed to toning down the more colorful and emotional aspects of belief. Thus, it seems to me that Thunder's combat waged against fearsome monsters is not a concept showcased in the recorded events of formal speech, and the violent war dance may have been domesticated through association with the relatively tame Thunder.

The study most nearly comparable to this one is William Simmons's work on the Indian folklore of southern New England spanning, like the Iroquois material, nearly four centuries of written documentation. He justly claimed his subject was "one of the oldest continually recorded bodies of Indian folklore known in North America," and his book may be "the longest-term historical study on oral narratives" in the anthropological, historical, or folklore literature (1986, 8). Simmons demonstrated that folklore is ethnically salient for the New England Indians; it sets them apart from others and testifies to their native spirit. His book, however, is mostly made up of late-nineteenth- and twentieth-century folktales including little if any subject matter demonstrably surviving from the seventeenth century.

I claim, in contrast, that a significant portion of Iroquois oral narrative—much of the great myth of beginning and something of Thunders—has been verified as being four or more centuries old. Being able to date some aspects of the lore through documentary means establishes the fact of substantial continuity while alerting us to some of the specific content of a truly autochthonous core of oral narrative.

But beyond this fact, the documents, speaking to only a limited range of subjects, fail us. To go further requires inferential means of other sorts. An obvious first step is suggested by astonishing similarities in the oral narratives of the Wyandots, mostly recorded around 1900 some one thousand miles from Iroquois country. The Wyandots share much of the creation myth. They have the same attitudes toward and name for Thunders, and their Thunder stories replicate the same motifs and themes. The Wyandots know the story of the pet snake who becomes a monstrous man-eater, and they know that it is the foxes who fool the person awaiting the return of another. They speak of almost identical races of forest beings in almost precisely the same stories. Wyandots, for example, are familiar with a giant buffalo killed by the Little People at salt licks in Kentucky. Wyandots tell of a giant made of stone who flees from the ax he unwittingly sharpened and loses his human-finger game pointer to a person bearing the same name in Wyandot and Iroquois languages.

Similarities so close and consistent, so detailed and numerous, must be cognates derived from a common ancestral source. The historically plausible scenario is that Wyandot-Iroquois resemblances result from a culture shared by the seventeenth-century ancestors of Wyandots and Iroquois. The motifs and stories known to both, therefore, date to the period of the earlier shared condition. This supposition is far from original—some have long regarded the folklore and mythology of these peoples to be identical. My only contribution is to make the terms of the comparison more explicit and to highlight the implications for dating. The first appearance of Iroquois Stone Giants I can document, for example, occurs about 1827. Now, knowing that similar plots about giants are known to Oklahoma Wyandots, the dating can plausibly be extended about two centuries back in time.

More original but problematic is my advocacy of age-area thinking, a dated—perhaps even retrogressive—realm of interpretation. I found no alternative, however, to going back to the old literature to relearn the issues as they must have seemed to researchers early in the twentieth century. Let me try to illustrate.

I summarized (see p. 145) the story of the young Iroquois woman marooned on an island and carried back to the mainland by a horned serpent. She kept the serpent going, it will be recalled, by lashing him with osiers. In similar stories told by the Delawares and Ojibwas, the rescued person must interact with the animal in some fashion to keep it moving (the Delaware passenger is supposed to warn the snake of danger; the Ojibwa passenger has to hit the snake's horn with a stone).

Much the same incident occurs even further afield. In a Wyandot story, a boy rescued by a horned serpent must tap the beast with a stone to make it go faster (Barbeau 1915, 102–3). When a woman stranded on an island in a Passamaquoddy tale is rescued by a horned creature, she makes the being go by tapping on its horns (Fewkes 1890, 269–70). In other words, a remarkably similar event (I would say it is the same motif)[1] was widely—though sporadically—distributed across the northeastern United States. The phenomenon demands explanation. The notion that this story was independently thought up five times or that it came about through sheer chance seems wildly unlikely. The same story is found in more than one locale because people in one place told it to people in another— it diffused.

A very similar ministory occurs even more frequently in oral narratives of the Southeast. In that region, the horned snake again carries a person across water, while the passenger, again, must make the snake go—typically by throwing food in front of the animal. At least a half-dozen incidents of this sort are documented among the Alabama, Caddo, Creeks, Kosati, and Natchez (Grantham 2002, 183–84; Lankford 1987, 205–6; Swanton 1929, 126–28, 172–75, 234–39). One has to conclude, I think, that these southern examples say the same thing as the northern examples. They are variants of the same motif. Does it mean anything that the motif seems more densely and frequently represented in Southeast? Again, it looks like something demanding explanation, and, of course, several explanations are possible. The one I find simultaneously most satisfying and promising for future research is that the motif is probably oldest in the Southeast and spread outward from there.

That theory essentially is the age-area principle. Analysis proceeds mostly as a series of comparisons resulting in judgments often richly connotative of ancient and distant connections. To be sure, the method has serious limitations. It offers plausible conclusions, not certain ones. One researcher may not replicate the comparisons of another. It cannot estab-

---

1. The common thread distinguishing these stories is that a human, crossing a body of water on the head of a horned creature, has to induce the beast to continue in its efforts. Possibly this incident is a subset of a more widely distributed motif Thompson called "Whale-boat" (R245): "A man is carried across the water on a whale (or fish). In most cases he deceives the whale as to the nearness to the shore or as to hearing thunder" (1929, 327).

lish whether specific events took place. On the other hand, Franz Boas was right—the method does focus on subject matter defined by the story-tellers. I think it has a certain integrity in compelling us to pay attention to what that evidence is—not what we might like it to be. Above all, it invites us to imagine the evidence *does* exist. Some of ancient America survives in this form and is, in fact, under our noses if we would see it.

REFERENCES

INDEX

References

Certain references given in the text are stand-alone citations not repeated here, notably newspaper articles, laws of New York, and county deeds and mortgages.

Aarne, Antti. 1930. *Die magische Flucht: Eine Märchenstudie.* Folklore Fellows Communications 92. Helsinki: Academia Scientiarum Fennica.

Abbott, Clifford, ed. 1996. *An Oneida Dictionary with Amos Christjohn and Maria Hinton.* Oneida, Wisc.: [privately published].

Abel, Timothy James. 2001. "Clayton Cluster: Cultural Dynamics of a Late Prehistoric Village Sequence in the Upper St. Lawrence Valley." Ph.D. diss., State Univ. of New York at Albany.

Abler, Thomas S. 1987. "Dendrogram and Celestial Tree: Numerical Taxonomy and Variants of the Iroquoian Creation Myth." *Canadian Journal of Native Studies* 7: 195–221.

Allen, Hope Emily. 1935. "Little King, Sow, Lady-Cow." *Journal of American Folklore* 48: 191–93.

———. 1944. "An Oneida Tale." *Journal of American Folklore* 57: 280–81.

———. 1948a. Hope Allen Papers. Oneida Community Records, Box 40, File D. Special Collections Research Center, Syracuse Univ. Library, Syracuse, N.Y.

———. 1948b. HEA Indian Notebook. Special Collections, Hamilton College Library, Clinton, N.Y.

Andrews, William. 1714. Letter from the Lower Mohawk Castle to the Secretary of the Society, May 25. Records of the Society for the Propagation of the Gospel, Letter Books Series A, vol. 9, 123–25. London.

Aquila, Richard. 1997. *The Iroquois Restoration: Diplomacy on the Colonial Frontier, 1701–1754.* 1983. Reprint. Lincoln: Univ. of Nebraska Press.

Axtell, James. 1985. *The Invasion Within: The Contest of Cultures in Colonial North America.* New York: Oxford Univ. Press.

Barbeau, C. Marius. 1914. "Supernatural Beings of the Huron and Wyandot." *American Anthropologist* 16: 288–313.

————. 1915. *Huron and Wyandot Mythology*. Canada Department of Mines, Geological Survey, Memoir 80, Anthropological Series 11. Ottawa: Government Printing Bureau.

————. 1916. "Contes populaires canadiens." *Journal of American Folklore* 29: 1–136.

Barnouw, Victor. 1977. *Wisconsin Chippewa Myths and Tales and Their Relation to Chippewa Life*. Madison: Univ. of Wisconsin Press.

Bartram, John, Lewis Evans, and Conrad Weiser. 1973. *A Journey from Pennsylvania to Onondaga in 1743*. Barre, Mass.: Imprint Society.

Bascom, William R. 1965. "Four Functions of Folklore." In *The Study of Folklore*, edited by Alan Dundes, 279–98. Englewood Cliffs, N.J.: Prentice-Hall.

Beauchamp, William M. n.d. *Antiquities of Onondaga*. 10 vols. Manuscript, New York State Library, Albany.

————. 1888a. "Onondaga Customs." *Journal of American Folklore* 1: 195–203.

————. 1888b. "Onondaga Tales." *Journal of American Folklore* 1: 44–48.

————. 1892. *The Iroquois Trail; or, Foot-Prints of the Six Nations*. Fayetteville, N.Y.: H. C. Beauchamp.

————. 1922. *Iroquois Folklore, Gathered from the Six Nations of New York*. Syracuse: Onondaga Historical Association.

Beers, D. G., surveyor. 1875. *Atlas of Madison County, New York*. Philadelphia: Pomeroy, Whitman.

Belknap, Jeremy. 1882. *Journal of a Tour from Boston to Oneida, June, 1796*. Cambridge, Mass.: John Wilson and Son.

Belknap, Jeremy, and Jedidiah Morse. 1955. "Report on the Oneida, Stockbridge, and Brotherton Indians." *Indian Notes and Monographs* (Museum of the American Indian, Heye Foundation, New York) 54: 5–39.

Bennett, Monte R. 1979. "The Blowers Site, Ond 1–4: An Early Historic Oneida Settlement." *Chenango Chapter Bulletin* (New York State Archaeological Association, Norwich) 8, no. 2.

————. 1981. "A Longhouse Pattern on the Cameron Site (Ond 8–4)." *Chenango Chapter Bulletin* (New York State Archaeological Association, Norwich) 19, no. 2.

————. 1983. "Glass Trade Beads from Central New York." In *Proceedings of the 1982 Glass Trade Bead Conference*, edited by Charles F. Hayes III, 51–58. Research Record 16. Rochester: Rochester Museum and Science Center.

————. 1988. "The Primes Hill Site, Msv. 5–2: An Eighteenth Century Oneida Station." *Chenango Chapter Bulletin* (New York State Archaeological Association, Norwich) 22, no. 4.

————. 1991. "Onneyuttehage, Thurston, Msv. 1: A Story of a Screened Sidehill

Midden." *Chenango Chapter Bulletin* (New York State Archaeological Association, Norwich) 24, no. 3.

———. 1999. "A Longhouse Pattern on the Thurston Site (Msv 1–2)." *Chenango Chapter Bulletin* (New York State Archaeological Association, Norwich) 27, no. 1: 9–41.

Bennett, Monte R., and Henry Hatton. 1988. "The Cameron Site (Ond 8–4) Revisited." *Chenango Chapter Bulletin* (New York State Archaeological Association, Norwich) 23, no. 1.

Berkhofer, Robert F., Jr. 1978. *The White Man's Indian: Images of the American Indian from Columbus to the Present.* New York: Alfred A. Knopf.

Bierhorst, John. 1985. *The Mythology of North America.* New York: William Morrow.

———. 1995. *Mythology of the Lenape: Guide and Texts.* Tucson: Univ. of Arizona Press.

Billington, Ray A. 1944. "The Fort Stanwix Treaty of 1768." *New York History* 25: 182–94.

Biographical Review. 1894. *The Leading Citizens of Madison County, New York.* Boston: Biographical Review.

Bloomfield, J. K. 1907. *The Oneidas.* New York: Alden Brothers.

Boas, Franz. 1909. "Notes on the Iroquois Language." In *Putnam Anniversary Volume: Anthropological Essays,* edited by Franz Boas, 425–60. New York: Stechert.

———. 1914. "Mythology and Folk-Tales of the North American Indians." *Journal of American Folklore* 27: 374–410.

———. 1916. "Tsimshian Mythology." In *Thirty-first Annual Report of the Bureau of American Ethnology to the Secretary of the Smithsonian Institution, 1909–1910,* 27–1037. Washington, D.C.: Government Printing Office.

———. 1940. *Race, Language, and Culture.* New York: Macmillan.

Boyce, Douglas W. 1973. "A Glimpse of Iroquois Culture History Through the Eyes of Joseph Brant and John Norton." *Proceedings of the American Philosophical Society* 117, no. 4: 286–94.

Boylan et al. v. United States. 1920–1921. Supreme Court of the United States, October term 1920, No. 458, and October term 1921, No. 111. Washington, D.C.

Boylan Letters. 1907–1910. Boylan Case correspondence. AO531 (investigative case files of charges and complaints against public officials and agencies, 1857–1919), New York State Library, Albany.

Boylan v. George et al. 1906–1909. State of New York Supreme Court, Madison County Clerk, Wampsville.

Bragdon, Kathleen J. 1996. *Native People of Southern New England, 1500–1650.* Norman: Univ. of Oklahoma Press.

Brandão, José António. 1997. *"Your Fyre Shall Burn No More": Iroquois Policy Toward New France and Its Native Allies to 1701.* Lincoln: Univ. of Nebraska Press.

Brasser, Ted J. 1975. *A Basketful of Indian Culture Change.* Canadian Ethnology Service, Mercury Series Paper 22. Ottawa: National Museum of Man.

———. 1980. "Self-directed Pipe Effigies." *Man in the Northeast* 19: 95–104.

Bricker, Victoria Reifler. 1981. *The Indian Christ, the Indian King: The Historical Substrate of Maya Myth and Ritual.* Austin: Univ. of Texas Press.

Bruyas, Jacques. 1863. *Radical Words of the Mohawk Language with Their Derivatives.* Sixteenth Annual Report of the Regents of the University of the State of New-York, Senate Document 115. Albany: Comstock and Cassidy.

Bryden, Sherry. 1995. "Ingenuity in Art: The Early 19th Century Works of David and Dennis Cusick." *American Indian Art Magazine* 20, no. 2: 60–69, 85.

Campisi, Jack. 1974. "Ethnic Identity and Boundary Maintenance in Three Oneida Communities." Ph.D. diss., State Univ. of New York at Albany.

———. 1976. "New York-Oneida Treaty of 1795: A Finding of Fact." *American Indian Law Review* 4, no. 1: 71–82.

———. 1988. "The Oneida Treaty Period, 1783–1838." In *The Oneida Indian Experience: Two Perspectives,* edited by Jack Campisi and Laurence M. Hauptman, 48–64. Syracuse: Syracuse Univ. Press.

Canfield, William W. 1902. *The Legends of the Iroquois, Told by "The Cornplanter."* New York: A. Wessels.

Carrington, Henry B. 1892. "Condition of the Six Nations of New York." *In Extra Census Bulletin: The Six Nations of New York,* by Thomas Donaldson, 19–82. Washington, D.C.: United States Census Printing Office.

Caswell, Harriett S. 1892. *Our Life among the Iroquois Indians.* Boston: Congregational Sunday-School and Publishing Society.

Cave, Alfred A. 1999. "The Delaware Prophet Neolin: A Reappraisal." *Ethnohistory* 46: 265–90.

Century. 1907. *New Century Atlas: Oneida County, New York.* Philadelphia: Century Map.

Cervone, Gian Carlo. 1991. "Native Ceramic Vessels." In *Tram and Cameron: Two Early Contact Era Seneca Sites,* edited by Charles F. Hayes III, 84–103, 258–92. Research Record 21. Rochester: Rochester Museum and Science Center.

Chafe, Wallace L. 1961. *Seneca Thanksgiving Rituals.* Bureau of American Ethnology Bulletin 183. Washington, D.C.: Smithsonian Institution.

———. 1963. *Handbook of the Seneca Language.* New York State Museum and Science Service, Bulletin 388. Albany: State Univ. of New York.

Chamberlain, A. F. 1890. "The Thunder-Bird Amongst the Algonkins." *American Anthropologist* (old series) 3: 51–54.

———. 1891. "Nanibozha Amongst the Otchipwe, Mississagas, and Other Algonkian Tribes." *Journal of American Folklore* 4: 193–213.

Clermont, Norman. 1996. "The Origin of the Iroquoians." *Review of Archaeology* 17: 59–62.

Colby, B. N. 1973. "A Partial Grammar of Eskimo Folktales." *American Anthropologist* 75: 645–62.

Colden, Cadwallader. 1964. *The History of the Five Nations Depending on the Province of New-York in America.* 1727 and 1747. Reprint. Ithaca, N.Y.: Cornell Univ. Press.

Connelley, William E. 1899. "Notes on the Folk-Lore of the Wyandots." *Journal of American Folklore* 12: 116–25.

Converse, Harriet Maxwell. 1908. *Myths and Legends of the New York Iroquois.* Edited by Arthur Caswell Parker. New York State Museum, Bulletin 125. Albany: State Univ. of New York.

Cornplanter, Jesse J. 1986. *Legends of the Longhouse.* 1938. Reprint. Ohsweken, Ontario: Irocrafts.

Count, Earl W. 1952. "The Earth-Diver and the Rival Twins: A Clue to Time Correlation in North-Eurasiatic and North American Mythology." In *Indian Tribes of Aboriginal America: Selected Papers of the XXIXth International Congress of Americanists,* edited by Sol Tax, 55–62. Chicago: Univ. of Chicago Press.

Cruikshank, Julie. 1994. "Oral Tradition and Oral History: Reviewing Some Issues." *Canadian Historical Review* 75: 403–18.

———. 1998. *The Social Life of Stories: Narrative and Knowledge in the Yukon Territory.* Lincoln: Univ. of Nebraska Press.

Curtin, Jeremiah. 2001. *Seneca Indian Myths.* 1922. Reprint. Mineola, N.Y.: Dover.

Day, Gordon M. 1998. "The Western Abenaki Transformer." In *In Search of New England's Past: Selected Essays by Gordon M. Day,* edited by Michael K. Foster and William Cowan, 183–94. Amherst: Univ. of Massachusetts Press.

Dean, James. 1915. "Mythology of the Iroquois; or, Six Nations of Indians." Typescript prepared by Katharine P. Judson. Document 13805. New York State Library, Albany.

Decker, George. n.d. Papers. Special Collections, Lavery Library, St. Johns Fisher College, Rochester, N.Y.

Dégh, Linda. 1972. "Folk Narrative." In *Folklore and Folklife: An Introduction,* edited by Richard M. Dorson, 53–83. Chicago: Univ. of Chicago Press.

Dennis, Matthew. 1993. *Cultivating a Landscape of Peace: Iroquois-European Encounters in Seventeenth-Century America.* Ithaca: Cornell Univ. Press.

Dirr, Michael A. 1990. *Manual of Woody Landscape Plants: Their Identification, Ornamental Characteristics, Culture, Propagation, and Uses.* 3d ed. Champaign, Ill.: Stipes Publishing.

Dixon, Roland B. 1909. "The Mythology of the Central and Eastern Algonkins." *Journal of American Folklore* 22: 1–9.

Doxtater, Lydia Beechtree. 1926. Probate of the Last Will and Testament of Lydia Beechtree Doxtater. Surrogate's Court, no. 25605. Oneida County Courthouse, Utica, N.Y.

Draper, Lyman C. n.d. Manuscripts, Series U (Frontier War Papers), vol. 11. Wisconsin Historical Society, Archives Division, Madison.

Drummond, Lee. 1981. "The Serpent's Children: Semiotics of Cultural Genesis in Arawak and Trobriand Myth." *American Ethnologist* 8: 633–60.

Dundes, Alan. 1962. "Earth-Diver: Creation of the Mythopoeic Male." *American Anthropologist* 64: 1032–51.

———. 1964. *The Morphology of American Indian Folktales.* Folklore Fellows Communications 195. Helsinki: Academia Scientiarum Fennica.

———. 1967. "North American Indian Folklore Studies." *Journal de la Société des Américanistes* 56, no. 1: 53–79.

———. 1980. "Projection in Folklore: A Plea for Psychoanalytic Semiotics." In *Interpreting Folklore,* edited by Alan Dundes, 33–61. Bloomington: Indiana Univ. Press.

———. 1999. *International Folkloristics: Classic Contributions by the Founders of Folklore.* Lanham, Md.: Rowman and Littlefield.

Dwight, Timothy. 1822. *Travels in New-England and New-York.* Vol. 4. New Haven: Timothy Dwight.

Edmonson, Munro S. 1971. *Lore: An Introduction to the Science of Folklore and Literature.* New York: Holt, Rinehart, and Winston.

Ekirch, Arthur Alphonse, Jr. 1951. *The Idea of Progress in America, 1815–1860.* 1944. Reprint. New York: Peter Smith.

Engelbrecht, William. 1995. "The Case of the Disappearing Iroquoians: Early Contact Period Superpower Politics." *Northeast Anthropology* 50: 35–59.

Erickson, Kirstin C. 2003. "'They Will Come from the Other Side of the Sea': Prophecy, Ethnogenesis, and Agency in Yaqui Narrative." *Journal of American Folklore* 116: 465–82.

Everett, E. A. 1922. "Report of the New York State Indian Commission." Typescript, U.S. Department of Justice, New York.

Fenton, William N. 1942. "Contacts Between Iroquois Herbalism and Colonial Medicine." In *Annual Report of the Board of Regents of the Smithsonian Institution, 1941,* 503–26. Smithsonian Publication 3651. Washington, D.C.: Government Printing Office.

———. 1947. "Iroquois Indian Folklore." *Journal of American Folklore* 60: 383–97.

———. 1948. "Letters to an Ethnologist's Children." *New York Folklore Quarterly* 4: 109–20.

———. 1962. "This Island, the World on Turtle's Back." *Journal of American Folklore* 75: 283–300.

———. 1978. "Northern Iroquoian Culture Patterns." In *Handbook of North American Indians.* Vol. 15, *Northeast,* edited by Bruce G. Trigger, 296–321. Washington, D.C.: Smithsonian Institution.

———. 1985. "Structure, Continuity, and Change in the Process of Iroquois Treaty Making." In *The History and Culture of Iroquois Diplomacy: An Interdisciplinary Guide to the Treaties of the Six Nations and Their League,* edited by Francis Jennings et al., 3–36. Syracuse: Syracuse Univ. Press.

———. 1987. *The False Faces of the Iroquois.* Norman: Univ. of Oklahoma Press.

———. 1991. *The Iroquois Eagle Dance: An Offshoot of the Calumet Dance.* 1953. Reprint. Syracuse: Syracuse Univ. Press.

———. 1998. *The Great Law and the Longhouse: A Political History of the Iroquois Confederacy.* Norman: Univ. of Oklahoma Press.

Fenton, William N., and Elizabeth L. Moore, eds. and trans. 1974. *Customs of the American Indians Compared with the Customs of Primitive Times by Father Joseph François Lafitau.* Vol. 1. Toronto: Champlain Society.

———. 1977. *Customs of the American Indians Compared with the Customs of Primitive Times by Father Joseph François Lafitau.* Vol. 2. Toronto: Champlain Society.

Fewkes, J. Walter. 1890. "A Contribution to Passamaquoddy Folk-Lore." *Journal of American Folklore* 11: 256–80.

Fiedel, Stuart J. 1991. "Correlating Archaeology and Linguistics: The Algonquian Case." *Man in the Northeast* 41: 9–32.

Fischer, J. L. 1963. "The Sociopsychological Analysis of Folktales." *Current Anthropology* 4, no. 3: 235–95.

Fisher, Margaret W. 1946. "The Mythology of the Northern and Northeastern Algonkians in Reference to Algonkian Mythology as a Whole." In *Man in Northeastern North America,* edited by Frederick Johnson, 226–62. Papers of the Robert S. Peabody Foundation for Archaeology, vol. 3. Andover, Mass.: Phillips Academy.

Flannery, Regina. 1939. *An Analysis of Coastal Algonquian Culture.* Washington, D.C.: Catholic Univ. of America Press.

Flint, Harrison L. 1983. *Landscape Plants for Eastern North America.* New York: John Wiley and Sons.

Fogelson, Ray D. 1980. "Windigo Goes South: Stoneclad among the Cherokees." In *Manlike Monsters on Trial: Early Records and Modern Evidence,* edited by Marjorie M. Halpin and Michael M. Ames, 132–51. Vancouver: Univ. of British Columbia Press.

Forest Hill. 1872. *Forest Hill Cemetery: Rules and Regulations and Catalogue of Lot Holders.* Utica: Curtiss and Childs.

Foster, Michael K. 1974. *From the Earth to Beyond the Sky: An Ethnographic Approach to Four Longhouse Iroquois Speech Events.* Canadian Ethnology Service, Mercury Series Paper 20. Ottawa: National Museum of Man.

Gehring, Charles T., and William A. Starna, eds. and trans. 1988. *A Journey into Mohawk and Oneida Country, 1634–1635: The Journal of Harmen Meyndertsz van den Bogaert.* Syracuse: Syracuse Univ. Press.

Geier, Philip Otto, III. 1980. "A Peculiar Status: A History of Oneida Indian Treaties and Claims: Jurisdictional Conflict within the American Government, 1775–1920." Ph.D. diss., Syracuse Univ.

George-Kanentiio, Doug. 2000. *Iroquois Culture and Commentary.* Santa Fe, N.M.: Clear Light.

Glassie, Henry. 1988. "Meaningful Things and Appropriate Myths: The Artifact's Place in American Studies." In *Material Life in America, 1600–1800,* edited by Robert Blair St. George, 63–92. Boston: Northeastern Univ. Press.

Goldenweiser, Alexander A. 1914. "On Iroquois Work, 1913–1914." In *Summary Report of the Geological Survey Branch of the Canadian Department of Mines for the Calendar Year 1913,* 365–72. Ottawa: Canadian Department of Mines.

———. 1933. *History, Psychology, and Culture.* New York: Alfred A. Knopf.

Goldschmidt, Walter. 2000. "A Perspective on Anthropology." *American Anthropologist* 102: 789–807.

Granger, Joseph E. 1978. "Cache Blades, Chert, and Communication: A Reappraisal of Certain Aspects of Meadowood Phase and the Concept of a Burial Cult in the Northeast." In *Essays in Northeastern Anthropology in Memory of Marian E. White,* edited by William E. Engelbrecht and Donald K. Grayson, 96–122. Occasional Publications in Northeastern Anthropology 5. Rindge, N.H.: Department of Anthropology, Franklin Pierce College.

Grantham, Bill. 2002. *Creation Myths and Legends of the Creek Indians.* Gainesville: Univ. Press of Florida.

Graymont, Barbara. 1976. "New York Indian Policy after the Revolution." *New York History* 57: 438–74.

Grimm, Jacob, and Wilhelm Grimm. 1944. *Grimms' Fairy Tales: Complete Edition*. Translated by Margaret Hunt and James Stern. New York: Pantheon Books.

Guzzardo, John C. 1976. "The Superintendent and the Ministers: The Battle for Oneida Allegiances, 1761–75." *New York History* 57: 254–83.

Halbritter, Ray, with Steven Paul McSloy. 1994. "Empowerment or Dependence? The Practical Value and Meaning of Native American Sovereignty." *New York University Journal of International Law and Politics* 26, no. 3: 531–72.

Hale, Horatio. 1888. "Huron Folk-Lore." *Journal of American Folklore* 1: 177–83.

———. 1889. "Huron Folk-Lore." *Journal of American Folklore* 2: 249–54.

———. 1891. "Huron Folk-Lore." *Journal of American Folklore* 4: 289–94.

———. 1969. *The Iroquois Book of Rites*. 1883. Reprint. New York: AMS Press.

Hall, Robert L. 1977. "An Anthropocentric Perspective for Eastern United States Prehistory." *American Antiquity* 42: 499–518.

———. 1983. "The Evolution of the Calumet-Pipe." In *Prairie Archaeology: Papers in Honor of David A. Baerreis*, edited by Guy E. Gibbon, 37–52. Publications in Anthropology 3. Minneapolis: Univ. of Minnesota.

———. 1989. "The Cultural Background of Mississippian Symbolism." In *The Southeastern Ceremonial Complex: Artifacts and Analysis—the Cottonlandia Conference*, edited by Patricia Galloway, 239–78. Lincoln: Univ. of Nebraska Press.

———. 1997. *An Archaeology of the Soul: North American Indian Belief and Ritual*. Urbana: Univ. of Illinois Press.

Hallowell, A. Irving. 1976. "Ojibwa Ontology, Behavior, and World View." In *Contributions to Anthropology: Selected Papers of A. Irving Hallowell*, edited by Raymond D. Fogelson et al., 357–90. Chicago: Univ. of Chicago Press.

Hamell, George R. 1979. "Of Hockers, Diamonds, and Hourglasses: Some Interpretations of Seneca Archaeological Art." Paper delivered at the Annual Conference on Iroquois Research, Albany.

———. 1987. "Strawberries, Floating Islands, and Rabbit Captains: Mythical Realities and European Contact in the Northeast During the Sixteenth and Seventeenth Centuries." *Journal of Canadian Studies* 21, no. 4: 72–94.

———. 1998. "Long-Tail: The Panther in Huron-Wyandot and Seneca Myth, Ritual, and Material Culture." In *Icons of Power: Feline Symbolism in the Americas*, edited by Nicholas J. Saunders, 258–91. London: Routledge.

Hammond, L. M. 1872. *History of Madison County.* Syracuse: Truair, Smith.

Harrington, M. R. 1906. "Da-ra-sá-kwa: A Caughnawaga Legend." *Journal of American Folklore* 19: 127–29.

———. 1907. Field Notes: June-Oct. 1907. Papers of Mark Raymond Harrington, OC 151, Archives of the Museum of the American Indian, Suitland, Md.

———. 1908. "Some Seneca Corn-Foods and Their Preparation." *American Anthropologist* 10: 575–90.

———. 1909. "Some Unusual Iroquois Specimens." *American Anthropologist* 11: 85–91.

———. 1921. *Religious Ceremonies of the Lenape.* Indian Notes and Monographs 19. New York: Museum of the American Indian, Heye Foundation.

Hauptman, Laurence M. 1999. *Conspiracy of Interests: Iroquois Dispossession and the Rise of New York State.* Syracuse: Syracuse Univ. Press.

Herrick, James W. 1995. *Iroquois Medical Botany.* Edited by Dean R. Snow. Syracuse: Syracuse Univ. Press.

Hewitt, J. N. B. 1892. "Legend of the Founding of the Iroquois League." *American Anthropologist* 5, no. 2: 131–48.

———. 1918. "Seneca Fiction, Legends, and Myths: Collected by Jeremiah Curtin and J. N. B. Hewitt." In *Thirty-second Annual Report of the Bureau of American Ethnology to the Secretary of the Smithsonian Institution, 1910–1911,* 37–819. Washington, D.C.: Government Printing Office.

———. 1974. *Iroquoian Cosmology, Parts I and II.* 1903 and 1928. Reprint. New York: AMS Press.

Hightshoe, Gary L. 1988. *Native Trees, Shrubs, and Vines for Urban and Rural America: A Planting Design Manual for Environmental Designers.* New York: Van Nostrand Reinhold.

Hill, Jonathan D. 1988. "Introduction: Myth and History." In *Rethinking History and Myth: Indigenous South American Perspectives on the Past,* edited by Jonathan D. Hill, 1–17. Urbana: Univ. of Illinois Press.

Hinton, Maria, ed. and trans. ca. 1997. *A Collection of Oneida Stories.* Oneida, Wisc.: privately published.

Hirsh, John C. 1988. *Hope Emily Allen: Medieval Scholarship and Feminism.* Norman, Okla.: Pilgrim Books.

———. 1989. "Past and Present in Hope Emily Allen's Essay 'Relics.' " *Syracuse University Library Associates Courier* 24, no. 1: 49–61.

Horsman, Reginald. 1981. *Race and Manifest Destiny: The Origins of American Racial Anglo-Saxonism.* Cambridge: Harvard Univ. Press.

———. 1999. "The Origins of Oneida Removal to Wisconsin, 1815–1822." In *The Oneida Indian Journey: From New York to Wisconsin, 1784–1860,* edited by Laurence M. Hauptman and L. Gordon McLester III, 53–69. Madison: Univ. of Wisconsin Press.

Hosbach, Richard E., and Stanford Gibson. 1980. "The Wilson Site (Ond 9–4): A Protohistoric Oneida Village." *Chenango Chapter Bulletin* (New York State Archaeological Association, Norwich) 18, no. 4A.

Hough, Franklin B., ed. 1861. *Proceedings of the Commissioners of Indian Affairs, Appointed by Law for the Extinguishment of Indian Titles in the State of New York*. Albany: Munsell.

Hudson, Charles M. 1976. *The Southeastern Indians*. Knoxville: Univ. of Tennessee Press.

Hueguenin, Charles A. 1956. "The Sacred Stone of the Oneidas." *New York Folklore Quarterly* 13, no. 1: 16–22.

Hultkrantz, Åke. 1981. *Belief and Worship in Native North America*. Edited by Christopher Vecsey. Syracuse: Syracuse Univ. Press.

Ireland, Emilienne. 1988. "Cerebral Savage: The Whiteman as Symbol of Cleverness and Savagery in Waurá Myth." In *Rethinking History and Myth: Indigenous South American Perspectives on the Past*, edited by Jonathan D. Hill, 157–73. Urbana: Univ. of Illinois Press.

Jameson, J. Franklin, ed. 1909. *Narratives of New Netherland, 1609–1664*. New York: Charles Scribner's Sons.

Jennings, Francis. 1984. *The Ambiguous Iroquois Empire: The Covenant Chain Confederation of Indian Tribes with English Colonies from Its Beginnings to the Lancaster Treaty of 1744*. New York: W. W. Norton.

Johnson, Elias. 1881. *Legends, Traditions, and Laws of the Iroquois; or, Six Nations and History of the Tuscarora Indians*. Lockport, N.Y.: Union Printing and Publishing.

Jones, Dorothy V. 1982. *License for Empire: Colonialism by Treaty*. Chicago: Univ. of Chicago Press.

Jones, Pomroy. 1851. *Annals and Recollections of Oneida County*. Rome, N.Y.: Pomroy Jones.

Judkins, Russell A. 1987. "David Cusick's *Ancient History of the Six Nations:* A Neglected Classic." In *Iroquois Studies: A Guide to Documentary and Ethnographic Resources from Western New York and the Genesee Valley*, edited by Russell A. Judkins, 26–40. Geneseo: Department of Anthropology, State Univ. of New York.

Kammen, Michael. 1991. *Mystic Chords of Memory: The Transformation of Tradition in American Culture*. New York: Alfred A. Knopf.

Kent, Barry C. 1984. *Susquehanna's Indians*. Anthropological Series 6. Harrisburg: Pennsylvania Historical and Museum Commission.

Klaw, Spencer. 1993. *Without Sin: The Life and Death of the Oneida Community.* New York: Penguin.

Klinck, Carl F., and James J. Talman, eds. 1970. *The Journal of Major John Norton, 1816.* Toronto: Champlain Society.

Köngäs, Elli Kaija. 1960. "The Earth-Diver (Th. A812)." *Ethnohistory* 7: 151–80.

Krohn, Kaarle. 1971. *Folklore Methodology: Formulated by Julius Krohn and Expanded by Nordic Researchers.* Translated by Roger L. Welsch. 1926. Reprint. Austin: Univ. of Texas Press.

Kuhn, Robert D., and Martha L. Sempowski. 2001. "A New Approach to Dating the League of the Iroquois." *American Antiquity* 66: 301–14.

Kurath, Gertrude Prokosch. 1968. *Dance and Song Rituals of Six Nations Reserve, Ontario.* National Museum of Canada, Bulletin 220, Folklore Series 4. Ottawa: Queen's Printer.

———. 2000. *Iroquois Music and Dance: Ceremonial Arts of Two Seneca Longhouses.* 1964. Reprint. Mineola, N.Y.: Dover.

Lankford, George E. 1987. *Native American Legends, Southeastern Legends: Tales from the Natchez, Caddo, Biloxi, Chickasaw, and Other Nations.* Little Rock: August House.

Lehman, J. David. 1990. "The End of the Iroquois Mystique: The Oneida Land Cession Treaties of the 1780s." *William and Mary Quarterly* 47: 523–47.

Leland, Charles G. 1992. *Algonquin Legends.* 1884. Reprint. Mineola, N.Y.: Dover.

Lévi-Strauss, Claude. 1981. *The Naked Man: Mythologiques.* Vol. 4. Translated by John and Doreen Weightman. Chicago: Univ. of Chicago Press.

———. 1987. *Anthropology and Myth: Lectures, 1951–1982.* Translated by Roy Willis. New York: Basil Blackwell.

———. 1988. *The Jealous Potter.* Translated by Bénédicte Chorier. Chicago: Univ. of Chicago Press.

Locklear, Arlinda F. 1988a. "The Allotment of the Oneida Reservation and Its Legal Ramifications." In *The Oneida Indian Experience: Two Perspectives,* edited by Jack Campisi and Laurence M. Hauptman, 83–93. Syracuse: Syracuse Univ. Press.

———. 1988b. "The Oneida Land Claims: A Legal Overview." In *Iroquois Land Claims,* edited by Christopher Vecsey and William A. Starna, 141–53. Syracuse: Syracuse Univ. Press.

Long, Charles H. 1963. *Alpha: The Myths of Creation.* New York: George Braziller.

Lounsbury, Floyd G. 1978. "Iroquoian Languages." In *Handbook of North American Indians.* Vol. 15, *Northeast,* edited by Bruce G. Trigger, 334–43. Washington, D.C.: Smithsonian Institution.

Lounsbury, Floyd G., and Bryan Gick, trans. and eds. 2000. *The Oneida Creation Story: Demus Elm and Harvey Antone.* Columbia S.C.: Yorkshire Press.

Lowie, Robert H. 1908. "The Test-Theme in North American Mythology." *Journal of American Folklore* 21: 97–148.

Malinowski, Bronislaw. 1984. "The Role of Myth in Life." In *Sacred Narrative: Readings in the Theory of Myth,* edited by Allen Dundes, 193–206. Berkeley and Los Angeles: Univ. of California Press.

Margry, Pierre, ed. 1876. *Découvertes et établissements des Français dans l'ouest et dans le sud de l'Amérique septentrionale, 1614–1754: Mémoires et documents originaux.* Vol. 1. Paris: Jouast.

McMullen, Ann, and Russell G. Handsman, eds. 1987. *A Key into the Language of Woodsplint Baskets.* Washington, Conn.: American Indian Archaeological Institute.

Mechling, W. H. 1913. "Maliseet Tales." *Journal of American Folklore* 26: 219–58.

Merrell, James H. 1987. "'Their Very Bones Shall Fight': The Catawba-Iroquois Wars." In *Beyond the Covenant Chain: The Iroquois and Their Neighbors in Indian North America, 1600–1800,* edited by Daniel K. Richter and James H. Merrell, 115–33. Syracuse: Syracuse Univ. Press.

Michelson, Karin, ed., and Georgina Nicholas, storyteller and trans. 1981. *Three Stories in Oneida.* Canadian Ethnology Service Paper 73, Mercury Series. Ottawa: National Museum of Man.

Michelson, Truman, ed. 1917. *Ojibwa Texts, Collected by William Jones.* Publications of the American Ethnological Society, vol. 7, pt. 1. Leyden: E. J. Brill.

———. 1919. *Ojibwa Texts, Collected by William Jones.* Publications of the American Ethnological Society, vol. 7, pt. 2. New York: G. E. Stechert.

Mithun, Marianne. 1984. "The Proto-Iroquoians: Cultural Reconstruction from Lexical Materials." In *Extending the Rafters: Interdisciplinary Approaches to Iroquoian Studies,* edited by Michael K. Foster, Jack Campisi, and Marianne Mithun, 259–81. Albany: State Univ. of New York Press.

Moerman, Daniel E. 1998. *Native American Ethnobotany.* Portland, Oreg.: Timber Press.

Mooney, James. 1995. *Myths of the Cherokee.* 1900. Reprint. Mineola, N.Y.: Dover.

Morgan, Lewis Henry. 1962. *League of the Iroquois.* 1851. Reprint. Secaucus, N.J.: Citadel Press.

Morrison, Kenneth M. 1979. "Towards a History of Intimate Encounters: Algonkian Folklore, Jesuit Missionaries, and Kiwakwe, the Cannibal Giant." *American Indian Culture and Research Journal* 3, no. 4: 51–80.

Moulton, Anne L., and Thomas S. Abler. 1991. "Lithic Beings and Lithic Technology: References from Northern Iroquoian Mythology." *Man in the Northeast* 42: 1–7.

Myrtle, Minnie. 1855. *The Iroquois; or, The Bright Side of Indian Character.* New York: D. Appleton.

Nabokov, Peter. 2002. *A Forest of Time: American Indian Ways of History.* New York: Cambridge Univ. Press.

O'Callaghan, E. B., ed. 1849–1851. *The Documentary History of the State of New-York.* 4 vols. Albany: Weed, Parsons.

———. 1853–1887. *Documents Relative to the Colonial History of the State of New York, Procured in Holland, England, and France, by John R. Brodhead.* 15 vols. Albany: Weed, Parsons.

Opinion. 1909. *Boylan v. George et al.* State of New York Supreme Court. Appellate Division, Third Department, June 24. 133 App. Div. 514, 117 N.Y. Supp. 573.

Opinion. 1919. *United States v. Boylan et al.* No. 319, United States District Court for the Northern District of New York. March 3. 256F 468.

Opinion. 1920. *United States v. Boylan et al.* No. 67, United States Circuit Court of Appeals, 2d Circuit, March 3. 265F 165.

Oring, Elliott. 1986. *Folk Groups and Folklore Genres: An Introduction.* Logan: Utah State Univ. Press.

Overholt, Thomas W., and J. Baird Callicott. 1982. *Clothed-in-Fur and Other Tales: An Introduction to an Ojibwa World View.* Washington, D.C.: Univ. Press of America.

Paper, Jordan. 1983. "The Post-contact Origin of an American Indian High God: The Suppression of Feminine Spirituality." *American Indian Quarterly* 7, no. 4: 1–24.

Parker, Arthur C. 1913. *The Code of Handsome Lake, the Seneca Prophet.* New York State Museum, Bulletin 163. Albany: State Univ. of New York.

———. 1916. *The Constitution of the Five Nations.* New York State Museum, Bulletin 184. Albany: State Univ. of New York.

———. 1989. *Seneca Myths and Folk Tales.* 1923. Reprint. Lincoln: Univ. of Nebraska Press.

———. 1994. *Skunny Wundy: Seneca Indian Tales.* 1926. Reprint. Syracuse: Syracuse Univ. Press.

Parsons, Elsie Clews. 1925. "Micmac Folklore." *Journal of American Folklore* 38: 55–133.

Pearce, Roy Harvey. 1965. *The Savages of America: A Study of the Indian and the Idea of Civilization.* Rev. ed. Baltimore: Johns Hopkins Univ. Press.

Pearson, Bruce L., ed. and trans. 2001. *Huron-Wyandotte Traditional Narra-*

tives: Told by Catherine Johnson, Smith Nichols, John Kayrahoo, Star Young, Mary McKee, Collected by Marius Barbeau. Columbia, S.C.: Yorkshire Press.

Pendergast, James F. 1991. "The St. Lawrence Iroquoians: Their Past, Present, and Immediate Future." *Bulletin: Journal of the New York State Archaeological Association* 102: 47–74.

Penrose, Maryly B., ed. 1981. *Indian Affairs Papers: American Revolution.* Franklin Park, N.J.: Liberty Bell.

Petrides, George A. 1972. *A Field Guide to Trees and Shrubs.* 2d ed. Boston: Houghton Mifflin.

Pickering, Timothy. n.d. Papers, 1758–1829. Letters and Papers of Pickering's Missions to the Indians, 1792–1797. Vols. 60 and 62. Massachusetts Historical Society, Boston.

Pilkington, Walter, ed. 1980. *The Journals of Samuel Kirkland: 18th-Century Missionary to the Iroquois, Government Agent, Father of Hamilton College.* Clinton, N.Y.: Hamilton College.

Powers, Mabel. 1923. *Around an Iroquois Story Fire.* New York: Frederick A. Stokes.

Pratt, Peter Paul. 1976. *Archaeology of the Oneida Iroquois.* Vol. 1. Occasional Publications in Northeastern Anthropology 1. George's Mills, N.H.: Man in the Northeast.

Preston, Richard A., trans. 1958. *Royal Fort Frontenac.* Edited by Leopold Lamontagne. Toronto: Champlain Society and Univ. of Toronto Press.

Propp, V. 1968. *Morphology of the Folktale.* Translated by Laurence Scott. 2d English ed. Austin: Univ. of Texas Press.

Prucha, Francis Paul. 1984. *The Great Father: The United States Government and the American Indians.* Vol. 2. Lincoln: Univ. of Nebraska Press.

———. 1990. *Documents of United States Indian Policy.* 2d ed. Lincoln: Univ. of Nebraska Press.

Radin, Paul. 1926. "Literary Aspects of Winnebago Mythology." *Journal of American Folklore* 39: 18–52.

———. 1948. *Winnebago Hero Cycles: A Study in Aboriginal Literature.* Indiana Univ. Publications in Anthropology and Linguistics, International Journal of American Linguistics Memoir 1. Baltimore: Waverly Press.

Rafferty, Sean M. 2001. "'They Pass Their Lives in Smoke, and at Death, Fall into the Fire': Smoking Pipes and Mortuary Ritual During the Early Woodland Period." Ph.D. diss., State Univ. of New York at Binghamton.

Rand, Silas Tertius. 1894. *Legends of the Micmacs.* New York: Longmans Green.

Randle, Martha Champion. 1952. "Psychological Types from Iroquois Folktales." *Journal of American Folklore* 65: 13–21.

———. 1953. "The Waugh Collection of Iroquois Folktales." *Proceedings of the American Philosophical Society* 97: 611–33.

Reichard, Gladys A. 1921. "Literary Types and Dissemination of Myths." *Journal of American Folklore* 34: 269–307.

Richter, Daniel K. 1992. *The Ordeal of the Longhouse: The Peoples of the Iroquois League in the Era of European Colonization*. Chapel Hill: Univ. of North Carolina Press.

Ritchie, William A. 1968. *Recent Discoveries Suggesting an Early Woodland Burial Cult in the Northeast*. New York State Museum and Science Service, Circular 40. 1955. Reprint. Albany: State Univ. of New York.

Robertson, Constance Noyes. 1970. *Oneida Community: An Autobiography, 1851–1876*. Kenwood, N.Y.: Oneida Community Mansion House, in association with Syracuse Univ. Press.

Robinson, Brian S. 1996. "Archaic Period Burial Patterning in Northeastern North America." *Review of Archaeology* 17, no. 1: 33–34.

Rockwell, William Honyoust. n.d. Papers, 1870–1960. History Archives Collections, Oneida Indian Nation. Oneida, N.Y.

Rooth, Ann Birgitta. 1957. "The Creation Myths of North America." *Anthropos* 52: 497–508.

Rustige, Rona. 1988. *Tyendinaga Tales*. Kingston: McGill-Queen's Univ. Press.

Sanborn, John Wentworth. 1888. "Folk-Lore of the Seneca Indians of North America." *Folk-Lore Journal* (Folk-Lore Society, London) 6: 196–99.

Sapir, Edward. 1994. "Time Perspective in Aboriginal American Culture: A Study in Method" (originally published 1916). In *The Collected Works of Edward Sapir*. Vol. 4, *Ethnology*, edited by Regna Darnell and Judith Irvine, 31–120. Berlin: Mouton de Gruyter.

Schoolcraft, Henry Rowe. 1851–1857. *Historical and Statistical Information Respecting the History, Conditions, and Prospects of the Indian Tribes of the United States, Parts 1–6*. Philadelphia: Lippincott, Grambo.

———. 1975. *Notes on the Iroquois; or, Contributions to the Statistics, Aboriginal History, Antiquities, and General Ethnology of Western New-York*. 1846. Reprint. Millwood, N.Y.: Krauss Reprint.

———. 1999. *Algic Researches: North American Indian Folktales and Legends*. 1839. Reprint. Mineola, N.Y.: Dover.

Schwartz, Helen S. 1999. Interview with Irma Altman. January 12. Elders Oral History Project. History Archives Collections, Oneida Indian Nation, Oneida, N.Y.

Scott, Duncan C. 1912. "The Traditional History of the Confederacy of the Six Nations, Prepared by a Council of Chiefs." *Transactions of the Royal Society of Canada*, 3d ser., 5, no. 2: 195–246.

Seaver, James E. 1990. *A Narrative of the Life of Mrs. Mary Jemison . . . Carefully Taken from Her Own Words,* Nov. 29th, 1823. Syracuse: Syracuse Univ. Press.

Shattuck, George C. 1991. *The Oneida Land Claims: A Legal History.* Syracuse: Syracuse Univ. Press.

Shimony, Annemarie Anrod. 1994. *Conservatism among the Iroquois at the Six Nations Reserve.* Syracuse: Syracuse Univ. Press.

Simmons, William S. 1986. *Spirit of the New England Tribes: Indian History and Folklore, 1620–1984.* Hanover, N.H.: Univ. Press of New England.

Skinner, Alanson. 1911. "The Menomini Game of Lacrosse." *American Museum Journal* (New York) 11: 138–41.

———. 1919. "Plains Ojibwa Tales." *Journal of American Folklore* 32: 280–305.

———. 1921. *Notes on Iroquois Archeology.* Museum of the American Indian, Heye Foundation, Indian Notes and Monographs.

———. 1924–1927. "The Mascoutens or Prairie Potawatomie Indians, Parts I–III." *Bulletin of the Public Museum of the City of Milwaukee* 6: 1–411.

Smith, Erminnie A. 1983. *Myths of the Iroquois.* 1883. Reprint. Ohsweken, Ontario: Irocrafts.

Smith, James H. 1880. *History of Chenango and Madison Counties, New York.* Syracuse: D. Mason.

Smith, Richard. 1989. *A Tour of the Hudson, the Mohawk, the Susquehanna, and the Delaware in 1769.* Edited by Francis W. Halsey. 1906. Reprint. Fleischmanns, N.Y.: Purple Mountain Press.

Snow, Dean R. 1980. *The Archaeology of New England.* New York: Academic Press.

———. 1995a. "Migration in Prehistory: The Northern Iroquoian Case." *American Antiquity* 60: 59–79.

———. 1995b. *Mohawk Valley Archaeology: The Sites.* Albany: Institute for Archaeological Studies, State Univ. of New York.

———. 1996. "More on Migration in Prehistory: Accommodating New Evidence in the Northern Iroquoian Case." *American Antiquity* 61: 791–96.

———. 1997. "The Architecture of Iroquois Longhouses." *Northeast Anthropology* 53: 61–84.

Soper, James H., and Margaret L. Heimburger. 1982. *Shrubs of Ontario.* Toronto: Royal Ontario Museum.

Speck, Frank G. 1917. "Malecite Tales." *Journal of American Folklore* 30: 479–85.

———. 1925. "Montagnais and Naskapi Tales from the Labrador Peninsula." *Journal of American Folklore* 38: 1–32.

———. 1937. *Oklahoma Delaware Ceremonies, Feasts, and Dances.* Memoirs no. 7. Philadelphia: American Philosophical Society.

———. 1995. *Midwinter Rites of the Cayuga Long House.* 1949. Reprint. Lincoln: Univ. of Nebraska Press.

Springer, James Warren. 1981. "An Ethnohistoric Study of the Smoking Complex in Eastern North America." *Ethnohistory* 28: 217–35.

Starna, William A. 1988. "The Oneida Homeland in the Seventeenth Century." In *The Oneida Indian Experience: Two Perspectives,* edited by Jack Campisi and Laurence M. Hauptman, 9–22. Syracuse: Syracuse Univ. Press.

Sternberg, Guy, and Jim Wilson. 1995. *Landscaping with Native Trees: The Northeast, Midwest, Midsouth, and Southeast Edition.* Shelburne, Vt.: Chapters Publishing.

Stone, William L. 1851. *Life of Joseph Brant—Thayendanegea: Including the Border Wars of the American Revolution.* 4th ed. 2 vols. Buffalo: Phinney.

Strong, Nathaniel T. 1857. "Indian Reservations in New York, 1855." In *Census of the State of New-York,* edited by Franklin B. Hough, 500–507. Albany: Charles van Benthuysen.

Swanton, John R. 1929. *Myths and Tales of the Southeastern Indians.* Bureau of American Ethnology Bulletin 88. Washington, D.C.: Government Printing Office.

Taggart, James M. 1983. *Nahuat Myth and Social Structure.* Austin: Univ. of Texas Press.

Thompson, Stith. 1919. *European Tales among the North American Indians: A Study in the Migration of Folk-Tales.* Publication 34. Colorado Springs: Colorado College.

———. 1929. *Tales of the North American Indians.* Cambridge: Harvard Univ. Press.

———. 1946. *The Folktale.* New York: Holt, Rinehart, and Winston.

———. 1955–1958. *Motif-Index of Folk-Literature: A Classification of Narrative Elements in Folktales, Ballads, Myths, Fables, Mediaeval Romances, Exempla, Fabliaux, Jest-Books, and Local Legends.* 6 vols. Bloomington: Indiana Univ. Press.

———. 1965. "Myth and Folktales." In *Myth: A Symposium,* edited by Thomas A. Sebeok, 169–80. 1955. Reprint. Bloomington: Indiana Univ. Press.

———. 1981. *The Types of the Folktale: A Classification and Bibliography: Antti Aarne's Verzeichnis der Märchentypen.* 2d ed. Folklore Fellows Communications 184. Helsinki: Academia Scientiarum Fennica.

Thwaites, Reuben Gold, ed. 1896–1901. *The Jesuit Relations and Allied Documents.* 73 vols. Cleveland: Burrows Bros.

———. 1903. *A New Discovery of a Vast Country in America by Father Louis Hennepin.* Vol. 2. Chicago: A. C. McClurg.

Tiro, Karim Michel. 1999. "The People of the Standing Stone: The Oneida Indian Nation from Revolution Through Removal, 1765–1840." Ph.D. diss. Univ. of Pennsylvania.

Tooker, Elisabeth. 1970. *The Iroquois Ceremonial of Midwinter.* Syracuse: Syracuse Univ. Press.

———. 1978a. "The League of the Iroquois: Its History, Politics, and Ritual." In *Handbook of North American Indians.* Vol. 15, *Northeast,* edited by Bruce G. Trigger, 418–41. Washington, D.C.: Smithsonian Institution.

———. 1978b. "Wyandot." In *Handbook of North American Indians.* Vol. 15, *Northeast,* edited by Bruce G. Trigger, 398–406. Washington, D.C.: Smithsonian Institution.

———. 1991. *An Ethnography of the Huron Indians, 1615–1649.* 1964. Reprint. Syracuse: Syracuse Univ. Press.

Tracy, William. 1872. "The Oneida Stone." In *Forest Hill Cemetery: Rules and Regulations and Catalogue of Lot Holders,* 37–39. Utica: Curtiss and Childs.

Treaties. 1842. Treaties Between the People of the State of New York and the First and Second Christian Parties of the Oneida Indians, May 23, and the Orchard Party of the Oneida Indians, June 25. Original Treaties and Other Indian Papers, bk. 1, pp. 209, 231. Albany: New York State Library.

Trigger, Bruce G. 1969. *The Huron: Farmers of the North.* New York: Holt, Rinehart, and Winston.

Tuck, James A. 1978. "Regional Cultural Development, 3000 to 300 B.C." In *Handbook of North American Indians.* Vol. 15, *Northeast,* edited by Bruce G. Trigger, 28–43. Washington, D.C.: Smithsonian Institution.

Turner, Glen D., and Harold Hickerson. 1952. Field Report (Sept.-Oct., 1950). Thirty-five-page typescript composing pp. 7–41 (handwritten pagination) of the manuscript accompanying "Testing Procedures for Estimating Transfer of Information among Iroquois Dialects and Languages," Freeman Guide no. 1835. Philadelphia: American Philosophical Society.

United States v. Boylan et al. 1915–1919. United States District Court for the Northern District of New York, No. 319. Utica: Office of the Court Clerk.

Upton, Helen M. 1980. *The Everett Report in Historical Perspective: The Indians of New York.* Albany: New York State American Revolution Bicentennial Commission.

Urton, Gary. 1985. Introduction to *Animal Myths and Metaphors in South America,* edited by Gary Urton, 3–10. Salt Lake City: Univ. of Utah Press.

———. 1990. *The History of a Myth: Pacariqtambo and the Origin of the Inkas.* Austin: Univ. of Texas Press.

Vecsey, Christopher. 1988. *Imagine Ourselves Richly: Mythic Narratives of North American Indians.* New York: Crossroad.

Voegelin, Erminnie W. 1984. "Lodge-Boy and Thrown-Away." In *Funk & Wag-*

nalls Standard Dictionary of Folklore, Mythology, and Legend, edited by Maria Leach, 642. 1949. Reprint. San Francisco: Harper and Row.

Wallace, Anthony F. C. 1972. *The Death and Rebirth of the Seneca.* New York: Vintage Books.

Wasson, George, and Barre Toelken. 2001. "Coyote and the Strawberries: Cultural Drama and Cultural Collaboration." In *Native American Oral Traditions: Collaboration and Interpretation,* edited by Larry Evers and Barre Toelken, 176–99. Logan: Utah State Univ. Press.

Waterman, T. T. 1914. "The Explanatory Element in the Folk-Tales of the North-American Indians." *Journal of American Folklore* 27: 1–54.

Wauchope, Robert. 1962. *Lost Tribes and Sunken Continents: Myth and Method in the Study of American Indians.* Chicago: Univ. of Chicago Press.

Waugh, Frederick W. n.d. Iroquois Folklore Papers. Canadian Museum of Civilization, Library, Archives, and Documentation. Hull, Quebec.

Weitlaner, R. J. 1915. "Seneca Tales and Beliefs." *Journal of American Folklore* 28: 309–10.

Whipple, J. S., et al. 1889. *Report of Special Committee to Investigate the Indian Problem of the State of New York, Appointed by the Assembly of 1888.* 2 vols. Assembly Document 51. Albany: Troy Press.

Whitcomb, Carl E. 1983. *Know It and Grow It, "II": A Guide to the Identification and Use of Landscape Plants.* Stillwater, Okla.: Lacebark.

Whitney, Theodore. 1964. "Thurston, Onneyuttehage, Msv 1." *Chenango Chapter Bulletin* (New York Archaeological Association, Norwich) 6, no. 1.

———. 1970. "The Buyea Site, Ond 13–3." *Bulletin: Journal of the New York State Archaeological Association* 50: 1–14.

———. 1971. "The Olcott Site, Msv–3." *Chenango Chapter Bulletin* (New York State Archaeological Association, Norwich) 12, no. 3.

Williams, Mentor L., ed. 1956. *Schoolcraft's Indian Legends.* East Lansing: Michigan State Univ. Press.

Wintemberg, W. J. 1936. *Roebuck Prehistoric Village Site, Grenville County, Ontario.* Canada Department of Mines, National Museum of Canada, Bulletin 83, Anthropological Series 19. Ottawa: J. O. Patenaude.

Wissler, Clark. 1938. *The American Indian: An Introduction to the Anthropology of the New World.* 3d ed. 1917. Reprint. New York: Oxford Univ. Press.

Witthoft, John, and Wendell S. Hadlock. 1946. "Cherokee-Iroquois Little People." *Journal of American Folklore* 59: 413–22.

Wolf, Eric. 1982. *Europe and the People Without History.* Berkeley and Los Angeles: Univ. of California Press.

Wonderley, Anthony. 1998. "An Oneida Community in 1780: Study of an Inventory of Iroquois Losses During the Revolutionary War." *Northeast Anthropology* 56: 19–41.

———. 2000a. "Brothertown, New York, 1785–1796." *New York History* 81: 457–92.

———. 2000b. "The Elm-Antone Creation Story in Comparative and Historical Context." In *The Oneida Creation Story: Demus Elm and Harvey Antone,* edited by Floyd G. Lounsbury and Bryan Gick, 155–62. Columbia, S.C.: Yorkshire Press.

———. 2001. "The Iroquois Creation Story over Time." *Northeast Anthropology* 62: 1–16.

———. 2002. "Oneida Ceramic Effigies: A Question of Meaning." *Northeast Anthropology* 63: 23–48.

Woodbury, Hanni, Reg Henry, and Harry Webster, trans. and eds. 1992. *The Iroquois League Tradition as Dictated in Onondaga by John Arthur Gibson.* Memoir 9. Winnipeg, Manitoba: Algonquian and Iroquoian Linguistics.

Wray, Charles F., et al. 1987. *The Adams and Culbertson Sites.* Edited by Charles F. Hayes III. Research Record 19. Rochester: Rochester Museum and Science Center.

Wright, J. V. 1994. "The Prehistoric Transportation of Goods in the St. Lawrence River Basin." In *Prehistoric Exchange Systems in North America,* edited by Timothy G. Baugh and Jonathon E. Ericson, 47–71. New York: Plenum Press.

Wrong, George M., ed. 1939. *The Long Journey to the Country of the Hurons by Father Gabriel Sagard.* Translated by H. H. Langton. Toronto: Champlain Society.

Yarnell, Richard Asa. 1964. *Aboriginal Relationships Between Culture and Plant Life in the Upper Great Lakes Region.* Anthropological Papers 23, Museum of Anthropology. Ann Arbor: Univ. of Michigan.

Zipes, Jack, ed. and trans. 2001. *The Great Fairy Tale Tradition: From Straparola and Basile to the Brothers Grimm.* New York: W. W. Norton.

———. 2002. *Breaking the Magic Spell: Radical Theories of Folk and Fairy Tales.* Rev. ed. Lexington: Univ. Press of Kentucky.

Index

Italic page number denotes illustration or map.

255

9 780815 606949